# inside
# MONACO

## Second Edition

### By
### SIRI CAMPBELL

POST OAK PRESS

© 2000

# CONTENTS

# ACKNOWLEDGEMENTS

This guidebook is the cumulative effort of many to which I am ever grateful for their, knowledge, support and advice. A special thanks to Mr. Règis Lecuyer, Conservator of the Palace Archives, for setting the history record straight.

When Siri Campbell asked me to write the foreword to her new guide about the Principality, I was surprised to discover an *"Inside Monaco"* I did not know.

Reading this book will open your eyes to a world of unforgettable beauty, fun, culture, places where you can meet interesting people from around the world, and most of all experience my well-known city with a different eye, the one of a foreign resident well integrated into the life of Monte-Carlo. She cares about this country, its people and it shows.

After you have taken home this guide and wandered through it, you will agree Monaco is a multifaceted place with year-round events, activities, and an international financial center. That is why this book is so welcomed and needed. Everyone from individuals to businessmen, as well as the travel industry should have a copy of this definitive guide of the Principality, a look from the "Inside".

**His Serene Highness
Prince Albert of Monaco**

# INTRODUCTION

*"I am on a rock. I neither sow nor harvest;
however, I want to live."*

*- Old Monégasque saying*

Indeed, I live on this very rock that has made Monaco so famous. I can hardly believe it, but I am in an apartment that has been in the same Monégasque family for the past 500 years. If only these walls could talk what tales they could tell.

As an American expatriate, the tales I could tell are numerous and I can share them with you. Since I first moved here in 1989 my life has been quite different from my life back in the United States. For one thing, I live in a virtual paradise. The weather, even in winter, almost never gets below freezing (snow is very rare except in the mountains where it is great for skiing). It is tropical in summer without being too sticky . . .yet warm enough in the winter to sit outside in a café in the sun. Oh yes, the sun shines virtually all the time (bring sunscreen).

The flora is non-stop – bright yellows, purples, rose flowers, palm trees, cacti and gnarled plane trees with thick green and brown camouflage trunks. All year round. The air always smells sweet to me. No pollution from industry; instead only the perfume of growing things.

The Principality of Monaco is small and contained. Because there is little landmass it was necessary to build up. Some people like the hi-rises, some do not; but no one can dispute that it allows comfortable accommodations for many people and lends certain exhilaration. And, of course, combined with the new, Monaco is studded with the old villas, apartment houses, hotels, palaces and casinos.

To walk through Casino Square is to understand the character of Monaco: a stunning garden filled with modern sculpture, cascading fountains; the turn-of-the-century Hotel de Paris and Salle Garnier, the outdoor Café de Paris crowded with people from all over the world; the high-priced cars ringing the circle that encompasses it all.

Is it any wonder that after a short visit here I elected to stay, live and work? And I have really come to love it. In the years I have lived here, I have developed the unique perspective of both an insider and an outsider, someone who can appreciate, yet evaluate, what is around me. I have found a Hidden Monaco.

As your guide, I believe this special vantage point will be very helpful when you plan your vacation, business meeting or extended stay in Monaco. I can offer practical advice, inside tips on what and where and an entryway to genuine Monégasque fun. As the they say: "I want to live." And. . . so do you.

**Siri Campbell**
**Monaco-Ville, Monaco**

# HOW TO USE THIS GUIDE

This guide is designed for both visitors and residents. It answers the questions that every guest wants to know and what every resident should know about the Principality. There are many myths about Monaco, such as: everything is so expensive that you have to be a millionaire to have any life there... Monte Carlo is only for gamblers. . . there is nothing for families and children to do... people only speak French... the police are unfriendly... the list of misconceptions goes on. This guide sets the record straight by providing current, accurate and often overlooked information that dispels the myths.

*"Inside Monaco"* will show you why this is a great place to visit or live. There are many cultural activities and special events besides gambling. Many of them are free. There are things to do with your children. Monaco has some of the best sports facilities in the world and they are only moments away from your hotel. The Shopping section is broken down by quarters and streets as well as by product. Bet you didn't know there is discount shopping in Monaco!

The Entertainment, Big Event, Restaurant and Shoestring sections will tell you where you can go to mix with the locals, where to find the rich and famous, the "in" spots, the restaurants for splurging, the restaurants you can afford, the hottest cabaret floor shows and the liveliest discos. Always wanted to see the Grand Prix? The Big Event Calendar tells you how to get tickets for the best spots to view the race, even if you're on a budget. To find out what's happening throughout the calendar year at the world famous Monte Carlo symphony, ballet and opera and where to get tickets.

Les Basics A-Z chapter furnishes you with priceless practical information, how to figure out currency exchange rates and the new Euro currency, like where to get a baby-sitter or kosher butcher; where to find the lowest-price film developing; the best or cheapest dry cleaners, luggage or computer repair shops. Where to find the best deals on rental cars, and how to find English-speaking doctors and dentists. What to do and where to go when you have a car accident or you've been towed. How to understand French driving quirks. Where to find a handy parking garage. Even where to rent snow tires or chains for a day trip to local ski areas.

The chapter called " Savoir Faire" gives you tips on greeting customs, (kiss, kiss) local holidays and traditions. Hey, want to go truffle hunting? The Regional Food and Wine section will tell you how to do it.

Thinking of a move to Monaco? "The Living and Working" section tells you where you can find affordable temporary housing while you look for an apartment to rent or buy. How to bargain with the agency or owner and how much it will cost you. You don't have to become a registered resident if you're not planning to spend more than three months at a time. But if you want to take advantage of the no-personal income tax, then we'll tell you how to apply for your *carte de séjour*, which is the equivalent to a resident alien. This chapter will also give pointers on how to set up a business in Monaco and notes what businesses qualify. Other authors have charged as much as $200 for the same information. One of the more frequently asked questions is "How can I become a Monégasque citizen?" This chapter will explain.

Monaco is conveniently located in Europe within France and near the Italian border, and it's an ideal base from which to explore the surrounding areas. The "Day Trips" section sets down some personal favorites. To correct the myth that only millionaires can afford Monaco, take a look at "Monaco on a Shoestring". This section offers a wide variety of accommodations, restaurants and activities that are guaranteed to keep you within your budget.

## A LITTLE ORIENTATION

Monaco is divided into five official areas. Knowing them is the easiest way to find your way around the places of interest, restaurants, hotels and shopping. The first developed area is MONACO-VILLE, which is referred to as The Rock, Le Rocher, or Old Town. This area can be reached by taking the Rampe Major, located at the bottom of the hill at Place d'Armes that brings you to the Palace Square. Or take Bus marked 1 or 2 destination Monaco-Ville that will take you there and drop you off in front of the Lycée (public school) in the Place de la Visitation.

LA CONDAMINE is the second-oldest area in Monaco. It is a combination of old and the very new, extending from the Monaco-Ville to Monte-Carlo. FONTVIEILLE is an environmentally planned community on the southwest side of Monaco-Ville. All the land was reclaimed from the sea and was the major building project from the 60's through the 80's. It is where you will find the heliport and the new commercial center. On the northeastern border of Monaco you will find the Jardin Exotique, the Museum of Anthropology and the Princesse Grace Hospital.

    **MONTE CARLO** is the area surrounding the Casino and the Opera. It is a residential and commercial district that was build up during the reign of Prince Charles III. To locals, **LARVOTTO BEACH**, which runs along and in back of Avenue Princesse Grace extending to the border with France and the Monte Carlo Beach Hotel, is unofficially considered another area. You'll find a pullout map with street guide, parking garages, elevators and places of interest clearly marked in the back of this guide.

**BIENVENUE!**

# 1
# GETTING THERE,
# GETTING AROUND

If location is everything, then few countries are as ideally located as Monaco. Nestled between France and Italy – Monaco is only 6 miles (10km) from the Italian border - it is easy to get to from all major cities in Europe via **Nice Côte d'Azur Airport**. This chapter will tell you everything you need to know in order to get to and around Monaco, whether by helicopter, boat, train, bus, elevator, chauffeur-driven limousine or rental car. Yes, you too can drive like a local (more later) by leasing a brand-new car from a discount car rental agency. Or, if you prefer to do the Riviera by sea, by renting a boat.

## GETTING THERE
## BY AIR

**THE AIRPORT**

Two terminals comprise **Nice Côte d'Azur International Airport. Terminal One** handles international flights and is serviced by most major European airlines. Terminal Two handles all domestic flights within France. If your international destination is via Paris, your flight leaves from **Terminal Two.** Shuttle service runs between both terminals. There is an information service provided on television monitors for incoming and outgoing flights and a tourist information desk where you can alert friends if there are any difficulties. The phone number to leave messages in English is 33 (0) 4 9321-3012. The general number for the airport is 33 (0) 4 9321-3030. Nice Airport is equipped to handle disabled passengers. For information, call 33 (0) 4 9321-3030, extension 2424. Internet site www.nice.aeroport.fr

## BY HELICOPTER

The fastest and most fun way to reach Monaco is by helicopter. The flight takes just seven minutes and leaves about every 15 minutes. A bus shuttle service picks you up and drops you off door to door. You can also arrange charter flights and aerial tours. Service is also available to Cannes, St. Tropez and to ski areas in the winter. Prices to the airport are 375FF (57€) one way, except during the Grand Prix. The helipad is located in Fontvieille.

**Heli-Air Monaco**                              **9205-0050**
                                            *Fax: 9205-7617*

Connects to all towns along the coast, Italy, golf clubs, ski areas and panoramic flights. Service begins at 7:00 AM so don't book those early flights or you'll have to take a taxi.

Web site www.heliair-monaco.com   E-mail: heliair@monaco.net

**Heli Inter Riviera**                           **9777-8484**
**Monacair**                                     **9205-6070**

## BY CHARTERED JET

Aviasud                                    33 (0) 4 9321-3450
                                    *Fax: 33 (0) 4 9321-3447*
For a list of International airline telephone numbers, see page 170

## BY BUS VIA AUTOROUTE TO MONACO

Rapides Côte d'Azur                        33 (0) 4 9321-3083
( RCA ) provides direct service by freeway from the airport to
Monaco and Menton for the reasonable price of 80FF (12€) one
way or round trip for 140FF (21€). They also offer 6 trip cards for
390FF (60€). Departure areas are just outside the arrival baggage
areas of Nice Côte d'Azur airport terminals 1 and 2. Tickets can
be bought at the transportation desks or on the busses. RCA
Web site: www.rca.tm.fr

## DEPARTURES - FROM MONACO TO THE AIRPORT

Stops at the Monte Carlo Beach Hotel, Le Meridien Beach Plaza
Hotel (Larvotto stop), Mirabeau Hotel, Monte Carlo Grand
Hotel (Les Spélugues stop), Park Palace Galerie (Les Allées
Lumières-stop), the Hotel Hermitage-Casino stop, Place
St.Dévote stop (near the port and new train station) Place
d'Armes stop (next to Monte Carlo Brasserie). Then into
Fontvieille next to the Marriott-Stadium Louis II (Le Port stop),
the Hotel Abela (La Roseraie stop) and the last place the bus stops
is Port Fontvieille (or near the Commercial Center). The trip to
the airport takes 45 minutes.

## MONACO TO AIRPORT

Starting at the Park Palace Galerie (Les Allées Lumières) at the
top of the Casino gardens pick up times run: 06:05* 06:55; 07:55,
08:55, 09:55, 10:55, 11:55, 12:55, 13:55, 14:55, 15:55, 16:55,
17:55, 18:55, 19:55.
* This bus runs M-F except on public holidays.
All bus stops have signs indicating **"Airport Direct"** service, so
don't confuse them with other bus service to Nice city.

## AIRPORT TO MONACO

Departures from the airport to Monaco and Menton
09:00, 10:00, 11:00, 12:00, 13:00, 14:00, 15:00, 16:00, 17:00,
18:00, 19:00, 20:00 and the last bus from the airport is at 21:00.
They drop off at the points above, including the Tourist Office.

## BY TAXI

No doubt one of the most expensive airport cab rides in the world,
around 420FF (64€) Monte Carlo city, 450FF (69€) MC Beach
one-way without tip. These prices are based on using *"Cheque*

*Taxis"* to be purchased in advance at the transportation counter in the airport. It's about a 35-minute ride through the tunnel connecting Monaco to the A8 autoroute. The cab driver should give you your choice of the autoroute or Moyenne corniche, those being the two fastest routes. The coast road, Basse corniche, is pleasant if you have the time.

## BY TRAIN

From the airport there is either public Nice bus service to the Nice train station (Nice-Ville) or a specially marked airport bus direct to the train station. Look for the large departure sign, direction Monaco. It's a 20-minute ride, and the commuter trains run every half-hour during peak commuter times, or every hour at other times.

You can purchase your ticket from a dispensing machine or at the ticket counter. Be sure you **time-stamp** it at the orange posts before getting on the train. Alas, heavy penalties and ejection from the train may result if you are caught without a time stamp. There is a new *Carte Isabelle* that gives you unlimited train travel on the same day in either 1st or 2nd class on all trains for 60FF (9€) except the TGV. Carte Isabelle tickets can be purchased at all SNCF train stations.

## BY LOCAL BUS

The fastest way is a special RCA bus, which goes directly to Monaco by the autoroute, but you can also take a special bus from the airport to the train station and transfer to a public bus, which takes you to the public bus terminal. Then you transfer to the local RCA or Broch bus that takes the local coast (Basse Corniche) route to Monaco. This procedure can take up to two hours, especially if you miss your connection. There is also bus service between Nice and San Remo, Italy.

## BY CAR

Major access to Monaco is along the A8 autoroute. Take **Monaco-Eze Exit #56.** You will pass through the new tunnel, which takes about ten minutes off your drive and avoids the two-lane take-your-breath-away La Turbie route, a scenic but hair-raising experience not recommended for wimp drivers. The locals who drive it hundreds of times a year speed around the hairpin corners at mach 8. To find current traffic information tune into 107.7 FM. Updates in English are given every 30 minutes during peak travel times, otherwise in French. Approximate travel times between Monaco using surface roads and: Nice: 35-45 mins., Antibes 60 mins., Cannes 90 mins. , St. Paul de Vence 60 mins., St. Tropez (3 hrs. + coast roads) ( 2 hrs. autoroute ), Lyon 5.5 hrs, and Paris 9 hrs. autoroute.

## THE CORNICHES

*You take the high road, I'll take the low road,*
*but the fastest road is the middle road, or Moyenne Corniche.*

The *Basse corniche,* the low road running along the coast, is the most scenic route. However, it is best avoided during prime beach times, mid-morning and late afternoon.

The *Moyenne corniche,* the middle road, is used by most locals and taxis because it is the fastest way except the autoroute to reach Nice. It gets a bit confusing around the Port area of Nice, though, as the Basse and Moyenne routes split off at the end of the Promenade des Anglais in the Old Port. Veer left toward the Moyenne, taking several short twists and turns until you head up the hill and east toward Monaco. Or if you want the scenic, slower-paced route, head straight-ahead past the Port up the hill, which becomes the coast route. The signs are well marked. Just follow the green sign post directions for Monaco that will take you to the Moyenne corniche.

The *Grande corniche,* or the high road that passes above Eze village and through **La Turbie,** is a safe bet to be the least traveled. It reaches a height of 1,679 feet (661 meters) above sea level and has spectacular views, but it's not the fastest way to travel to Monaco.

If you are traveling to Monaco from east to west, there are two routes: one that exits the autoroute A8, which drops you down at the **Vista Palace Hotel in Roquebrune Cap Martin**. If you have the time, it is a lovely place to stop. The other is the exit to Menton, from which you then take the Basse corniche to Monaco.

Once in Monaco be warned: if you are traveling on foreign license plates (**anything other than the cute white, red, and blue plates of Monaco or black and yellow French plates bearing the last two numbers of 06**) you will not be admitted to Monaco-Ville, which is the Palace area. So do not be surprised when the friendly policeman waves you on from this pedestrian area. In order to reach the *Musee* and *Palace* you should park in either *Parking des Pêcheurs,* or the *Parking de la Condamine* garage, where you can then either take the elevator or walk up to the Old Town area.

## GETTING AROUND
## BY TRAIN

If you are making major trips outside of Monaco, it is nice to know that all major trains stop in Monaco's new underground station. For **passenger information** and for advance bookings call toll free 08 3635-3535. It's best to make reservations and reserve your *couchette* in advance during the holiday periods to be assured of getting what you want. The general number of Monaco station is 9310-6015. American Express is an alternative to booking train tickets. They sometimes have seats on the TGV while the station has sold their allotment. Internet site is www.sncf.fr. For train information in English call 08-3635-3539. When calling from outside Monaco and France dial 33 and drop the initial 0. Approximate travel times from Monaco by train to: Nice 20 mins., Cannes 1 hr., Antibes 45 mins., and Menton 15 mins.

## BY BUS

Local Monaco bus service is the easiest way to get around this pretty Principality. You can buy individual tickets, but it is highly recommended that you buy a *carte de quatre*, a card of four one way trips or *huit*, a card of eight one way trips. To validate, punch the card into a box next to the bus driver or just on the left hand side of the isle.

The buses are safe, clean and the bus drivers are very helpful and understand basic transportation English and Italian. This is possibly the only place in the world where you can forget your purse or briefcase and with one phone call to Autobus de Monaco 9350-6241, have any possibility of getting it back intact. The author speaks from experience. There are five lines with departures approximately every 7 to 11 minutes Monday through Friday 7:00 AM until 9:00 PM. On Saturdays, Sundays and holidays, departures are every 20 minutes from 7:30 AM until 9:00 PM. There are well posted signs at every stop.

## BY TAXI

Taxis are recommended after the bus stops running (remember that's −21:00-9PM) or if you're dressed in a ball gown or you get too tired to hoof it. Your ride around Monaco will cost about 60FF (10€). The best places to get a taxi are the streets: (av. Monte Carlo) between the Opera and the Hotel de Paris, off the Place du Casino or near the train station. To call a taxi, phone 9350-5628 or radio taxis 24 hours a day at 9315-0101.
Taxi information at 9330-7153.

## BY TAXI-BUS

Seats between 8-13 people. Located at the train station, the taxi-bus is your answer if you have a larger group than a taxi will accommodate or lots of luggage. Telephone 9205-2557, 0607-933407 or 0607-935545. Regular taxis normally take only 3 persons. No up-front seat riding throughout Monaco and France is the usual rule.

## BY TOURIST TRAIN

**The Azur Express**                                        9205-6438

From February to November this miniature train painted in the national colors of red and white carries up to 54 passengers around The Rock for a guided tour. It takes you along the St. Martin Gardens, past the government buildings, winding its way along the city walls that overlook Port of Hercule before reaching the Palace Square. The train then heads down rue Colonel Bellando de Castro ending up at the Palais Justice and the Cathedral. Catch the express just in front of the Oceanographic Museum.

**The Port Azur Express**

Every day during July and August this little train makes its journey from the Port d' Hercule to the beaches of Larvotto, up to The Rock and then returns to the Port. You can pick it up Port side or Rock side for an enjoyable (save those feet for the Casino) ride.

## BY RENTED VEHICLE
## BUS RENTAL

**Rapetto**                                                 9330-1175
*9, rue Princesse Antoinette*
Has different sizes to handle your group's needs.
**Compagnie des Autobus de Monaco**                        9350-6241
*3, av. Président J.F. Kennedy*                        *Fax: 9325-3750*

## CAR RENTAL

Most people book their rental car when they make their plane reservations. However, if you haven't and decide to rent at the last minute, here are some recommended rental agencies with lower prices than your big name agencies.

**Century Car Rental**                          33 (0) 4 9227-0510
*Near Airport*                          *Fax: 33 (0) 4 9227-0511*
Atol Beach Residence, 10067 Promenade des Flots Bleu, St. Laurent du Var. They offer pick up and delivery service from airport. An economy car (Renault Twingo) with unlimited mileage is 1323FF or 201€ a week. There are also two-week rentals. They also rent vans and trucks. This is the cheapest car rental found so far.

**ML Rent A Car**                               33 (0) 4 9334-4800
*Galerie du Port, Rue Lucan, Antibes*
Monthly rentals start at 215FF (33€) a day or 3900FF (595€) a month for a Fiat Panda. They also rent vans and prestige cars such as Porches, BMW's Ferraris and Jaguar's. They have pick up and delivery from Nice Airport.

## CAR LEASING

If you are staying longer than two weeks, check into leasing a brand-new car from TT Car Transit, Aerogare #1, just as you leave customs. Tel: 33 (0) 4-9321-3974, Fax: 33 (0) 4 9321-4125. They lease new cars in England and Spain as well as France. Their head-quarters are 2, av. de la Porte St. Cloud, 75016, Paris, France. Tel: 33 (0) 1 4862-3753 Fax: 33 (0) 1 4862-1973. Their office in Nice is located at Nice airport office in Terminal # 1. Minimum rental is 17 days; prices are quoted from Paris. There are various drop-off and pick-up points in case you want to drive and see the sights between the Côte d' Azur and Paris.

| | |
|---|---|
| **Avis** | 9330-1753 |
| *9, av. d' Ostende* | |
| Also rents scooters. | |
| **Eurodollar** | 9205-9009 |
| Michel Limone | |
| *26, quai Jean-Charles Rey* | |
| **Calandres** | 9350-2525 |
| *6, Impasse de la Fontaine* | |
| **Europcar** | 9350-7495 |
| *47, av. du Grande Bretagne* | |
| *Heliport* | 9205-2575 |
| **Hertz** | 9350-7960 |
| *27, bd. Albert 1er* | |
| **Plaza International** | 9770-7044 |
| *4, av. des Citronnier* | |

## CHAUFFEURS, LIMOUSINES AND CITY TOURS

| | |
|---|---|
| **Auto-Locations Carlo** | 9350-3410 |
| 29, av. Hector Otto | |
| **British Motors** | 9205-8371 |
| 15, bd. Princesse Charlotte | |
| **Monte-Carlo Limousine** | 9350-8265 |
| *12, av.des Spélugues* | |
| *Heliport* | 9205-6600 |
| **Galaxie Limousines** | 9350-7950 |
| *1, av. Henry Dunant* | |
| **Limousine Tours Monte Carlo** | 9330-3014 |
| *3, rue Louis Auréglia* | Port: 0607-935793 |
| **Monaco Prestige Limousine** | 9350-4404 |
| **Monaco Sight Seeing Port.** | 0607-773537 |
| *Bd Princess Charlotte* | |
| **Star Limousine** | 797-3600 |
| *7, av. Grande-Bretagne* | |
| **Dream Tours** | Port: 0611-359292 |

## MOPEDS OR BICYCLES

Auto-Moto Garage       9330-2461
*7, rue de la Colle*
(see Avis)

## BOAT RENTAL

Charter & Charter       9330-0015
*9, av. Président J.F.Kennedy*
Camper & Nicholsons       9797-7700
*7, av. d'Ostende*
Monte Carlo Yachting       9325-3633
*40, rue Grimaldi*
Monte Carlo Offshore (Power Boat)       9325-7678
*14, quai Antoine 1*

## CHARTERING

Charter & Charter       9330-0015
*9, av. Président J.F.Kennedy*
Camper & Nicholsons       9797-7700
*7, av. d'Ostende*
Compagnie de Navigation et de Tourisme       9216-1515
*Quai des Etats-Unis*
Dahm International       9350-2586
*17, bd. Albert 1er*
Frazer Yachting       9205-6700
*8, quai Jean-Charles Rey*
Nigel Burgess       9350-2264
*57, rue Grimaldi*

## PUBLIC PARKING

The Principality has done a magnificent job in adding additional parking spaces to accommodate visitors currently 15,000 places. All garages have closed-circuit television or attendant surveillance. We highly recommend parking in a garage. Monaco - like most places - tickets, boots and tows illegally parked cars with regularity. You can park up to 60 minutes free in some garages, so check when you take your ticket. This is convenient if you're just running errands or picking something up. **Keep your parking ticket with you because you pay at the automated cashier before you return to your car.** If you don't have the correct change, there will be an attendant who can give you the proper amount (see map). Residents and people who work or spend time in Monaco should look into the *multi-parc card* that offers access to all garages at a discount. Receive up to a 35% reduction on a 500FF (77€) pre-paid card usable in any Monaco Parking garage.
For information call 9315-8824.

## CAMPING CARS

Special provisions have been made for those who are touring by camping cars and vans. Please note it is prohibited to park these vehicles on any of the public roads in the Principality. However, a special covered garage is easily accessible for them on the western side of Fontvieille called the *Parking des Ecoles*. It is open from 8 AM to 8 PM. Frequent bus service runs from it to all other points in Monaco and the main tourist attractions.

## ELEVATORS AND ESCALATORS

Older Monégasques are hardy and healthy, probably due to the millions of stairs they have climbed in their lifetime. However, modern visitors to Monaco who do not want to take the stairs have the use of many convenient elevators to take them to the alluring sites around the city. (see map). Clean and safe any time day or night, all lifts have video surveillance.

**Av. des Citronniers to Av. de Grande Bretagne**
**Av. de la Costa to Bd. Princesse Charlotte**
**Av. Président J-F.Kennedy to Parking de la Costa**
**Av. Pasteur** (hospital) **to Bd. du Jardin Exotique**
**Av. Princesse Grace** (National Museum-Beaches) **to Place des Moulins** (6.00-1.00)
**Bd. de Belgique to Bd. du Jardin Exotique**
**Bd. du Larvotto to Descente du Larvotto**
**Bd. Louis II** (C.C.A.M.) **to Terrasses du Casino**
**Centre Commercial de Fontvieille to Place d'Armes**
**Chemin des Pêcheurs** (car park) **to Av. St. Martin** (Oceanographic Museum)
**Place St. Dévote** (Port) **to Bd. de Belgique** (6.00-24.00)

## TRAVEL AGENCIES

Most travel agencies have multi-lingual personnel including English speakers.

| | |
|---|---|
| **American Express** | **9325-7445** |
| *35, bd. Princesse Charlotte* | *Fax: 9350-3729* |
| **Havas Voyages** | **9325-7373** |
| *4, rue des Iris* | *Fax: 9216-0573* |
| **Mercury Travel** | **9216-5260** |
| *1, av. Princesse Alice* | *Fax: 9330-6246* |
| **Hotel de Paris** | **9330-9069** |
| **Monaco Congrès et Tourisme** | **9325-5555** |
| *20, bd. Princesse Charlotte* | *Fax: 9216-0077* |
| **Monaco Voyages** | **9325-7990** |
| *57, rue Grimaldi* | *Fax: 9216-7073* |
| *15, bd. Princesse Charlotte* | **9325-7500** |
| | *Fax: 9216-0875* |

| | |
|---|---|
| **Monte Carlo Travel** | **9325-4700** |
| *Métropole Galerie* | *Fax: 9325-1279* |
| **Wagons-Lit Tourisme** | **9325-0105** |
| *2, av. de Monte Carlo* | *Fax: 9216-0249* |
| **Monte-Carlo Club Prestige** | **9205-9281** |
| *7, av. des Paplins* | *Fax: 9777-8002* |

## RULES OF THE ROAD; OR DON'T PANIC...
## YOU, TOO, CAN DRIVE LIKE A LOCAL

Be prepared for an adjustment period when driving. There is a high proportion of tourists who are unfamiliar with the area and native drivers in the South of France and Italy often show intolerance to indecisive driving behavior.

Try to get a rental car with the last two digits of 06, which indicates you're from the Alpes Maritimes area. Then local drivers will be a tiny bit less impatient. You may use your state or national driver's license for one year. However, you might like to obtain an international driver's license from your local automobile club back home before you leave. Members of most national automobile clubs, such as AAA in the United States or the RAC in Britain, will find that they are affiliated with the Monégasque, French and other European automobile clubs which will honor foreign membership cards for such privileges as maps and routing information.

## SAFETY TIPS

The low crime rate in Monaco does not exist in the surrounding areas so here are some safety tips:

• Stow all valuables out of sight, e.g. glove compartment or trunk. Do not have anything of value showing in your car.

• If someone on the road indicates they need assistance, do not stop. Even if it appears to be an accident, especially involving motorcycles. It's usually a trap to rob you.

• Keep your doors locked and windows partially up at stoplights where thieves can open the door and steal your purse.

• If your vehicle is bumped from behind or on other areas do not stop. Drive to the nearest well-lit pubic area or service station and call the police.

• If advised by another motorist of problems with your vehicle, do not stop until reaching a service station or well-populated area.

• Make sure that you are covered by insurance from your credit card or by the rental agency. In most cases car insurance from home doesn't cover you in Europe.

The legal driving age is 18 years old and in order to get a Monégasque driving license, you must have been issued your *Carte de Sejour.* You have one year in which to obtain your new driver's license and you will need the following: a medical certificate signed by a doctor in Monaco and a photograph. You must give up your former license and pass a written and road test. Classes and exams in English are given once a month or on an as needed basis. All residents must register their cars as well and pass *Service Technique* before receiving Monaco plates. This is handled at **Service de la Circulation** located in the Fontvieille Commercial Center. **Tel: 9215-8000**

## RIGHT OF WAY

The most important law to remember when driving in Monaco or France is that the driver coming from the right has priority unless an intersection is otherwise marked. Do not assume you have the right of way at any intersection just because the road you're on is a main thoroughfare. An example of this rule: coming down from *Boulevard de Jardin Exotique* where *Boulevard de Belgique* intersects you do not have the right of way even though *Boulevard du Jardin Exotique* is the main road.

## ROUNDABOUTS AND TRAFFIC CIRCLES

There is some confusion about these because in the past cars entering from the right had priority. Today cars already in the roundabouts have priority especially when they are coming from the left. When you see this sign upon entering the roundabout *"Vous n'avez pas la priorité"* means, **"you do not have the right of way."** It's always best to proceed with caution.

## ROAD SIGNS

The following signs are important:

You have the
right of way

You no longer have
the right of way

No parking and
no stopping

Intersection with right
of way from the right

Large white broken lines along the pavement indicates lanes for buses and taxis only. Smaller white broken lines can indicate a place to stop in order to make a left turn. Do not cross lanes if the line is solid.

# SPEEDING

It's hard to get caught for speeding in Monaco because there are just not enough straight-aways, but just after the Grand Prix Race pedestrians should beware while crossing any section along *Boulevard Albert 1er* because Grand Prix "wannabe's" might be fantasizing and zoom along the race course. Watch out when crossing *Avenue de la Porte Neuve* leading to the **Old Town.** This is a mini speedway for local residents, including the royal ones.

Radar is used in France to check speeds and fines for speeding are high. Signs are not normally posted to alert drivers. On coming traffic may flash their headlights to warn of a speed trap. Photographs are sometimes taken of speeding cars, recording the license plate numbers. The speeding fine is then mailed directly to the speeder. (It's been said that this "civilized" method is used to protect the "mistresses or lovers" of the offending speeder)

## MAXIMUM SPEED LIMITS

| | |
|---|---|
| Autoroute | 130 kph - 81 mph |
| *110 kph during bad weather conditions* | |
| Highways | 110 kph - 68 mph |
| Rural Roads | 90 kph - 56 mph |
| In Towns | 50 kph – 31 mph |
| Foggy conditions | 31 mph |

## SEAT BELTS AND MOTORCYCLE HELMETS

There is no seat belt law in Monaco, but one should buckle up when leaving the Principality since borders are a favorite place for the French police to catch the unbelted. In France all passengers are required to wear seat belts. Children under the age of 10 are required to ride in a rear seat except when there is no rear seat. One can be fined 250FF (38€), if caught. It is mandatory to wear a helmet while driving a motorcycle. In Monaco you will pay an on-the-spot fine of 150FF (23€) and in France up to 1,000FF or (152€) if you are caught without one.

## PORTABLE TELEPHONES

You can be fined up to 900FF (138€) on the spot if you are pulled over while using your cell telephone without an earpiece or a fixed portable phone holder in you car. This is also the case in France. You'll be in even bigger trouble if you cause a road accident while talking on the phone without handsfree aids.

## DRINKING AND DRIVING

There are frequent roadblocks to catch drunk drivers. Alcohol breath tests are mandatory when an accident involves injury or death or if you are suspected of being under the influence while driving. The limit in France is 0.5 grams per liter, which equals one aperitif or 2 glasses of wine per person. In Monaco it is 0.8 grams per liter or 2 aperitifs and a half a bottle of wine per person. Fines are between 2,000FF (305€) and 30,000 (4573€) and immediate confiscation of your driver's license. Causing a fatal accident carries a 2,000FF (304€) to 60,000FF (9146€) fine, permanent withdrawal of your license, and possibly jail.

## ACCIDENTS

**Don't panic** just because you don't speak French. First, request an accident form called a *"constat"* in English from the rental agency or your insurance agency. The police should be called to the scene of an accident only if there are any injuries, so it is necessary for both drivers to make out their own accident forms when the accident involves vehicles only. You and the other party to the accident fill out your constat, giving the details of how the accident happened. Both parties sign each *"constat"*. Above all be sure to get the number of the person's driver's license and plates. If you are unable to get an English constat write down exactly what happened in English. But don't sign the other person's constat unless you understand what you're signing. These forms are then sent to the respective insurance companies. If you own your own car you should take it to a garage or body shop where an expert will come look at it. You pay for the damage and get reimbursed by the insurance company. If you have a rental car, return it to the agency and they will deal with it.

## BREAKDOWNS

It is best to keep the number of your rental company handy in order to call from emergency call boxes on the autoroute if you have a problem. It should be your first call. Request a replacement car and take a taxi back to the agency to pick up the new car.

Key Phrases To Use In Case...

**My car is broken down.**
*Ma voiture est en panne.* (mah-vwah-tuwer-eh-tan-pahn)

**It doesn't work.**
*Elle ne marche pas.* (ehl-nuh-mahrsh-pah)

**Where is there a gas station?**
*Ou y-at-il une station-service?* (oo-ee-yahteel euwn- stasyohn sehr-veess?)

**I need gas.**
*J'ai besoin d'essence.* (j'zhay-buh-zwan deh-s-on-ss)

**Fill it up with unleaded please.**
*Faites-le plein sans plomb, s'il vous plait.* (feht-luh-plan san-pleh-om-b, seel-voo-pleh).

**Right is a droite** (a-drw-ah-t)
**Left is a gauche** (a-go-sh)
**Straight ahead is tout droit** (too-drw-ah-t)

Unleaded fuel is in green marked pumps having either a 95% or 98% octane rating. Unleaded gas costs about 7FF (1.10€) a liter or about $3.84 a gallon.

## AUTOMOBILE DEALERS

Often dealers have an English speaker to help you. Prices for dealer repairs are pretty standard all over the world. It costs the same to fix a Volkswagen here, the only difference being the additional 19.6% VAT tax.

ALFA ROMEO, LANCIA, MITSUBISHI, PORSCHE, HYUNDAI
**Monaco Mediterranée Motors**                 9350-0024
*13, bd. Charles III*

AUSTIN, BENTLEY, DAIMLER, JAGUAR,
LAND-ROVER, ROLLS ROYCE, ROVER
**British Motors**                              9325-6484
*15, bd. Princesse Charlotte*
BMW, NISSAN
**Rold**                                        9205-6970
*Stade Louis II*
**Garage Bristol Rold**                         9330-0376
*48, rue Grimaldi*
CITROEN, DAEWOO, SUBARU
**Garage Melchiorre**                           9350-6326
*Off bd. Princesse Charlotte north of Casino*
FERRARI, HONDA, MASERATI
**Monaco Motors**                               9330-2722
*11, rue Princesse Florestine*
FORD
**Riviera Auto**                                9325-5544
*23, bd. d'Italie*
MERCEDES BENZ
**Mercedes Benz Monaco**                        9325-2100
*7, av. Princesse Grace*
**Service**                                     9205-6565
LAMBORGHINI
**Lamborghini**                                 9770-8370
*49, bd. d'Italie*

OPEL, GM
**Monte Carlo Motors**                          9350-5492
*30, bd. Jardin Exotique*

PEUGEOT

**Splendid Garage**                                                9339-3040
*5, av. du Port*

RENAULT

**Nedo Del Bellino**                                               9315-0025
*5-8, rue des Açores*
**Service**                                                        9330-2525

TOYOTA, LEXUS

**E.D.A.M.**                                                       9325-2520
*27, bd. Princesse Charlotte*
**Service**                                                        9330-1005

VAG, AUDI, VOLKSWAGEN

**Koncept Auto Garage du Pont St. Dévote**                         9330-8203
*35, bd. Rainier III*

CHRYSLER, JEEP

**U.S. Automobiles**                                               9797-8955
*12, bd. Princesse Charlotte*
**Service**                                                        9797-8950

## PARKING REGULATIONS

People often double park for brief periods, even if it is not legal. Flashing signal lights mean the person will be back soon, you hope. If you find yourself blocked in that situation, beep your horn a few times and you should have fairly quick results. The French specialize in **"bumper parking"**; they gently kiss the rear and front end of cars to squeeze into small spots, so don't complain, they won't understand.

A broken yellow line on the curb means **No Parking** for all vehicles. However, you will find that people do park for very short times at the broken yellow line for deliveries or discharging passengers. A **solid yellow** line means no parking and no stopping. Parking tickets can be paid on the spot by putting the required amount in the envelope and depositing it in the red metal boxes located near the parking meters.

## THE BOOT, OR I CAN'T FIND MY CAR, "MA VOITURE A DISPARU"

Monaco has been using the **"Denver Boot"** for many years so *faites attention.* Be careful where you park because you will find your car either booted or towed. Car theft is rare in Monaco, under 10 cars a year, so if you can't find your car where you left it, then it's probably been towed. You can call the **Fourrière at 9315-3084**; the car pound is in Fontvieille in the *Parking des Ecoles* on *avenue des Guelfes.* Booting or towing is expensive and can cost between 900FF (150€) up to 2000FF (300€). It just doesn't pay to take a chance. Park in one of the convenient parking garages around town; the rates are reasonable with a 60 minute free grace period. *See map for list of locations.*

## GAS STATIONS

### MONTE CARLO
**Fina**                                                9330-7011
*3, av. de la Madone*
Close to the Hotel Métropole, open until 7:30 Monday through
Saturday. Closed all holidays.
**Total**                                               9330-3912
*Place des Moulins*
This is an underground station that is open until 8:00 PM. Closed
all holidays.

### LARVOTTO BEACH
**Station Service du Portier Agip**                     9315-9021
*4, av. Princesse Grace*
Down from Monte Carlo Grand Hotel, this underground station
is open until 9:00 PM. They have a car wash and rent snow tires
in the winter.
### FONTVIEILLE
**Esso**                                                9205-3939
*Stade Louis II, 15, av. Castellans*
Open until 11:00 P.M. Monday through Saturday and from 7:00
AM to 8:00 PM on Sundays and holidays. This station usually has
the most competitive gas prices in town. Many gas stations will
not accept American credit cards without a European computer-
type chip.
**Shell**                                               9205-9533
*Bd. Charles III on the Basse corniche heading towards Nice.*

## HITCHHIKING
Hitching is prohibited on the autoroutes; however, you may
thumb at entrance and exit points or at tollbooths. **Allostop** is a
nationwide organization whose aim is to connect hikers with drivers. You pay a registration fee and a contribution toward the gas.
Telephone 33 (0) 1 5320-4242 or toll free 0803-803636 or Riviera
Radio's Community Chest Line 9797-9494.

# 2
# ALL THE SIGHTS TO SEE

Monaco is divided into five areas **Monaco-Ville, La Condamine, Fontvieille, Monte Carlo and Jardin Exotique.** Among the locals an unofficial area is **Larvotto Beach,** the section east of Monte Carlo. Knowing these sections is the fastest way to find your way around for sightseeing and just about anything else.

## MONACO-VILLE

The area with the most scenic attractions is Monaco-Ville, which also is referred to as **The Rock, Le Rocher, or Old Town.** This can be reached by the *Rampe Major*, located at the bottom of the hill *(Place d'Armes)* connecting La Condamine and the Place du Palais *(Palace Square)*. The ramp is paved with red bricks and lies between two 16th-century gateways. It is a gradual and scenic climb that will take you over a hundred steps to the Palace square. There you will encounter one of the early historic figures in the long dynasty of the Grimaldis, a larger than life bronze statue of *"Maliza"* Grimaldi, who first claimed the fortress disguised as a monk in 1297. If you don't want the exercise, take bus line (1) or (2) from the bottom, which will drop you off in front of the Lycée Albert 1er. Follow the well-marked signs to the **Palace** or to **Oceanographic Museum** (more later).

## THE PRINCE'S PALACE

The palace was built on the site of a fortress erected by Italians from Genoa in 1215. The **main courtyard** is paved with three million white and colored pebbles forming immense geometrical patterns. In the center is a 17th-century double revolution staircase in Carrara marble. This area was once the central part of the fortress started early in the 13th century. Both the courtyard and staircase are home to Monaco's famous summer concerts. Next, you visit the **Italian style gallery** alongside the south facade. This is where you may walk through to the state apartments, a journey that will take you back in time from the Guelfs and Ghibellines to the Napoleonic period. In the 16th-century Genovese artists, painted lovely frescoes, depicting mythological scenes, around the palace courtyard. The palace apartments are beautifully appointed with French period furniture and famous paintings. The **Louis XV Room** is done in a stunning regal blue and gold decor. The **Mazarin Room** is paneled in multi-colored wood with arabesque motifs. The famous **York Room** is where the Duke of York died while on a trip to visit his mistress in Italy. The **Throne Room** with a large Renaissance fireplace has been the scene of historic ceremonies since the 16th century. Outside the north door is the 17th century **Palatine Chapel** where the Royal family attends mass.

Prince Albert I built the **Clock Tower Sainte Marie** with white flagstone from nearby La Turbie. The Prince's standard flies from the top of this tower when the Prince is in residence; however, it always flies on Sundays whether the Prince is there or not. The palace tour takes 35 to 40 minutes and is open June to October 9:30 AM to 6:30 PM.

## THE PLACE DU PALAIS

Lined with cannons cast under **Louis XIV**, the **Palace Square** offers a spectacular panorama over Monte Carlo and the harbor and as far as the Cape of Bordighera in Italy. To the northwest, the scene takes in Mount Agel and the Tête de Chien (head of the dog), then east to Fontvieille, Cap d'Ail and St. Jean Cap Ferrat.

**The Changing of the Guard** takes place at precisely 11:55 AM every day in front of the main entrance to the palace. The ceremony is performed in full dress uniform (black in the winter, white in the summer) and has not changed for more than 100 years.

Responsible for guarding the Sovereign Prince 24 hours a day and providing him with escort and ceremonial services are the *Prince's Compagnie des Carabiniers*. These are highly trained and qualified French Army men. They also provide assistance to the Monégasque Red Cross and ensure security to those who take part in sporting events in the Principality.

From earliest times, regimental bands employing a variety of instruments have served Monaco's Sovereign Family. In 1966 Prince Rainier III created a dedicated ceremonial group of 12 musicians called the *Fanfare de la Compagnie des Carabiniers*. The Fanfare recruits young carabiniers with solid musical training and today, numbering 26 musicians, it has attained an international reputation. Within the Fanfare there is also a smaller orchestra with an extensive repertoire of popular music, jazz, religious music; and a brass ensemble.

**The Museum of Napoleon Souvenirs and Historic Archives of the Palace** is situated on the ground floor in the south wing of the palace. This fascinating museum contains more than a thousand objects and documents relating to the First Empire; objects belonging to Emperor Napoléon I, garments of the King of Rome, and religious souvenirs. Do not miss the displays of the Charter of Independence of Monaco, signed by King Louis XII of France; a letter written by Louis XIV to Prince Antoine I and uniforms of past Prince's Guards. Open every day except Monday 9:30 AM to 6:30 PM.

## IN THE HEART OF THE OLD TOWN

Wander down narrow streets, inter-connected by vaulted passageways, flanked with houses dating from the 12th and 13th centuries, many retaining their medieval character. This is the feel of the old Monaco, with none of the glitter of the modern.

Recommended viewing in this area: *The Chapelle de la Paix* in the gardens near the Place de la Visitation where spouses of non-Royal members are buried. *The Placette Bosio* (on rue Comte Félix Gastaldi) named for the famous Monégasque sculptor **Joseph Bosio,** official sculptor to the Emperor Napoleon I. *The Palais de Justice* (Court House), across from the Cathedral, built in 1930s Italian Gothic style. Visitors are not allowed into the building except on the day the court convenes for the new law year in September. However, the dual staircase is an excellent photo spot. *The Place St. Nicolas,* behind the Palais Justice next to the Cathedral, is one of the most picturesque squares in the Old Town with a charming fountain of St. Nicolas, patron saint of sailors and children.

**The St. Martin Garden** facing the sea contain aleppo pines, agaves, aloes, fountains, a pergola and graceful bronze statues that include a monument to Prince Albert I. It was in these gardens between 1887-89 that the poet *Guillaume Apollinaire* found inspiration. And it isn't difficult to see why. This is a garden of special delights, perfect to sit and enjoy the views, or find solitude to think or read, or smell the bursts of flowers, the pines, magnolias and eucalyptus trees. At the end closest to the palace is a child's playground. Please note picnicking or picking flowers is strictly forbidden. There is a dog station near the Oceanographic Museum.

## THE MONACO CATHEDRAL

The cathedral was built in 1875 in the *Romanesque-Byzantine* style from stone taken from nearby La Turbie. It contains the tombs of the former royalty of Monaco. Important paintings from the 1500s by the famous Nice painter **Louis Brea** are located on the right side of the transept. The high altar and episcopal throne are made from white Carrara marble. The bell from the original *Church St. Nicolas* dating to the 1200's was re-hung on the northwest nave of the cathedral in 1993. Pontifical services are held on the major liturgical feast days, like St. Dévote in January and on the national holiday in November. A magnificent four-keyboard organ accompanies the service and frequent organ concerts are given throughout the year. From September through June, a Mass is sung every Sunday at 10:00 A.M. by *Les Petits Chanteurs de Monaco* and the singers of the Cathedral Choir School. The Cathedral steps offer another photo opportunity.

## THE PRINCES OF MONACO WAX MUSEUM

Located on rue Basse, this museum depicts historical episodes in the Grimaldi dynasty from the late 13th century to the present day. The life-size figures wear authentic period costumes. The tour takes between 20 to 30 minutes. Open daily 9:30 AM to 6:00 PM. Tel: 9330-3905

## THE MUSEUM OF OLD MONACO

Located on rue Emile de Loth in the heart of the Old Town. The National Committee of Monégasque Traditions presents a collection of souvenirs from the history of the Rock. The exhibits include paintings, books, pottery, old photographs, costumes and artifacts evoking an earlier time. Allow approximately 30 minutes for this visit. Tel: 9350-5728

## THE CHAPEL OF MERCY (MISÉRICORDE)

Across from the Mairie (mayor's office), this pink and white chapel was built in 1646 by the Brotherhood of Black Penitents, whose first Prior was Prince Honoré II. Among the religious art treasures is a Christ statue carved out of wood by Joseph Bosio. On Good Friday this statue is carried through the streets of the Old Town. Above the entrance is a magnificent 19th-century ceramic scene.

## MUSÉE CHAPELLE DE LA VISITATION

*Place de la Visitation*

This beautiful Baroque chapel adjacent to the bus stop will surprise visitors with its collection of oil paintings, sculptures and tapestry by such great masters as Rubens, Zurbaran, Bononi, Cantarini, and Jusepe De Ribera. The art is graciously on loan from the American collection of Mrs. Barbara Piasecka Johnson. Open daily except Mondays 10:00 AM to 4:00 PM. Tel: 9350-0700.

## THE PRINCESSE GRACE IRISH LIBRARY

Located at 9, rue Princesse Marie de Lorraine (first floor) this small but unique library was established by Prince Rainier III in 1984. It is dedicated to Irish literature and houses the personal collection of Irish books and Irish sheet music of Princess Grace. Lectures, play readings, musical evenings and international conferences are part of its community activities. English-language publications in pamphlet and book form are available to the public as well as to academics on all continents. Visiting hours from 9:00 AM to 4:00 PM. Monday through Friday. Tel: 9350-1225 Fax: 9350-6665, Web site: www.monaco.mc/pglib  E-mail: pglib@monaco.mc

## THE OCEANOGRAPHIC MUSEUM AND AQUARIUM

Prince Albert I opened the doors in 1910 to this exceptional museum of marine sciences. The building alone is a masterpiece of architecture. The first two floors contain the remarkable collections of marine fauna gathered by Prince Albert I, a passionate oceanographer. There are many specimens of sea creatures here, including a **70-foot whale, and a 43-foot giant squid** caught off the coast of Newfoundland. In addition, the museum displays models of the **Prince's ships laboratory.** Here, also, are the famous scientific research laboratories where they grow and clone coral from all over the world used for elaborate bone grafting and other scientific purposes. Films about the sea, made for television by Commander Jacques Yves Cousteau, are screened in the acoustically advanced conference hall, which can seat up to 300 persons. Catch the **Micro-Aquarium** show where they magnify sea water and sea creatures on a giant screen, or during the summer whale season watch them frolic via a live underwater camera placed in their migration area.

The highlight of the Oceanographic is in the basement. Its famous Aquarium is home to more than **90 tanks of rare species of fish** from all the seas of the world. This is a must for both adults and children.

The restaurant terrace of the Museum has a splendid panoramic view and is a favorite photo spot for visitors. Looking east is the Italian Riviera, to the west the Esterel Mountain range. You should plan to spend at least an hour or as much as three hours for a comprehensive visit to this Museum. Open every day July through August 9:30 AM to 9:00 PM; from April to June and October 9:00 AM to 7:00 PM; from October to March 10 AM to 6:00 PM. Musee restaurant terrace is another photo spot.
Tel: 9315-3600 Fax: 9350-5297 or E-mail: rela@oceano.org or musee@easynet.fr

## THE MONTE CARLO STORY

**Housed in the Parking des Pêcheurs complex.** You take the escalators next to the Oceanographic Museum, then elevators to the next floor. This multi-vision show recreates the fascinating history of the lords and princes of Monaco. Headphones can be tuned to five different languages. This 35-minute presentation shouldn't be missed if you want to understand the long and singular historical past of the Principality of Monaco. Open every day 11:00 AM to 5:00 PM. Subject to change. Closed December 1 through 20. Tel: 9325-3233 Web site:www.cyber.monaco.mc/setav E-mail mcstory@cyber-monaco.mc

## FORT ANTOINE THEATRE

Built by Prince Antoine I in the 18th century it is located at the northeast end of The Rock. This ancient fortress with arrow slits covered in myrtle and clumps of thyme is today an enchanting outdoor theater seating up to 350 persons for summer classical music concerts by well-known artists. Its ramparts offer terrific views for the summer fireworks displays. For more information. Tel: 9315-8000

# THE AZUR EXPRESS

From February to November this miniature train painted in the national colors red and white carries up to 54 passengers around The Old Town for a guided tour. Its route takes you along the **St. Martin Gardens**, past the government buildings, then winds its way along the city walls that overlook the *Port d'Hercule* before reaching the Palace Square. The train then heads down rue *Colonel Bellando de Castro* ending up at the Palais de Justice and the Cathedral. Catch the express just in front of the Oceanographic Museum. You can also catch it at the Port during July and August. (See La Condamine and Fontvieille next section). Operates daily 10:30 AM to 6:00 PM.

# LA CONDAMINE

La Condamine is the second-oldest area in Monaco; the name comes from the Middle Ages and means the **cultivable land** at the foot of a village or castle. Today La Condamine is a combination of old and very new extending from The Rock to Monte Carlo, including Port d'Hercule. Bustling with shops and restaurants, its old buildings reflect the architecture of the Belle Epoque with wrought iron balconies and beautiful tiles, its new buildings are designed to blend in with the red-tiled roofs of old villas.

# THE CHURCH OF SAINT DÉVOTE

This chapel is dedicated to the Patron Saint of the Principality and to the Royal Family. Saint Dévote was martyred in Corsica in the 3rd century when, according to tradition, the skiff carrying her body was caught in a terrific storm and was guided by a dove toward the French coast, finally landing at Monaco. In the Middle Ages relics of the saint were stolen, but the thieves were caught and their ship burned. Every January 26th a ceremony takes place in front of the church when a ship is burned followed the next day by a religious procession. The chapel was restored and enlarged in 1870 during the reign of Prince Charles III. Length of visit: 15 to 30 minutes.

# PORT D'HERCULE (THE OLD HARBOR)
**Aquavision Monte Carlo Catamaran**
Offers guided tours all year round of the Mediterranean coastline, with a stop at Cap Martin or at the far end of the Douaniers in Cap d'Ail to allow viewing of the underwater landscape. Maximum capacity is 200 persons; tours last 55 minutes. Tel: 9216-1515

# THE PORT AZUR EXPRESS

Every day during July and August this little train makes its journey from the Port d'Hercule to the beaches of Larvotto, up to The Rock, and then returns to the port. You can pick it up portside or rock side for an enjoyable (save those feet for the Casino) ride. Tel: 9205-6438

## CHOCOLATERIE DE MONACO

Chocolate lovers will be thrilled to learn that Monaco is the home of one of the best chocolate makers in Europe. It has been making over 78 kinds of chocolate treats for more than 80 years. Their factory is located at 7, rue Biovès, with an additional boutique in the Place de la Visitation in the Old Town. Tours by appointment can be arranged by calling 9797-8888 Open year round. Closed on Sunday.

## FONTVIEILLE

This new area on the southwest side of The Rock, opposite La Condamine, was built up during the 70s and 80s from land reclaimed from the sea. It is an environmentally planned community with a new private harbor, shopping center, luxury apartments, soccer stadium, low-income housing, light industry, the Heliport and plenty of green space.

## THE ZOO

Walking from Place d'Armes west toward Fontvieille is the Zoo and its gardens. There are numerous species of tropical and African plants, monkeys, reptiles and multicolored tropical birds to delight your children. Open from June from September from 9:00 to 12:00 AM and 2:00 to 7:00 PM; October to February from 10:00 to 12:00 AM then from 2:00 to 5:00 PM; March to May from 10:00 to 12:00 AM to 2:00 to 6:00 PM. Length of visit: 1 hour. Tel: 9325-1831

## THE LOUIS II STADIUM

One of the worlds finest sports complexes, completed in 1985. It is home to the popular Monaco Football Team (soccer), with a seating capacity of 20,000. There is an Olympic-size indoor swimming pool, basketball court, athletic track, and workout room and parking garage. The exterior of the building contains government and business offices. Be sure to look for the correct *entrée* (entrance) when trying to locate a business or office; they start alphabetically with A. Tours are given at 3:00 and 4:30 every day. Length of visit is 45 minutes. Call to check times Tel: 9205-4011.

## THE PRINCESSE GRACE ROSE GARDEN

Surrounding the Rose Garden is a magnificent park with plants and shrubs from around the world, a charming little pond with ducks, swans, turtles and koi fish. The Royal Family inaugurated the garden in 1984. This quiet spot is where one can sit and admire the beauty of more than 4,000 rose bushes and trees of more than 150 varieties. Some famous celebrity friends of the late Princess Grace have donated their favorite roses in her honor. In the center of the garden there is a bronze statue of Princess Grace providing **excellent photo opportunities.**

The best time to visit the garden is during the month of May and June when the garden is at its peak of colorful blossoms.

## THE PRIVATE AUTOMOBILE COLLECTION OF H.S.H. PRINCE RAINIER III

Located on the terraces of the Fontvieille Commercial Center. An enthusiastic collector of vintage cars for 30 years, Prince Rainier's collection consists of more than 85 models built by the best-known manufacturers in both Europe and the U.S.A. The first and oldest car is a 1903 De Dion Bouton. Others models are: Renault Torpedo 1911, Panhard Levasseur 1913, Ford Model T 1924, Peugeot Quadrilette Convertible 1924, Hispano-Suiza 1934, Packard 1935, Cadillac 1953, Chrysler 1956, as well as Maserati, Jaguar, Mercedes and Rolls Royce. A particular favorite is Prince Louis II's Ford hunting-break and a London taxi re-fitted and used by Princess Grace. Open daily except Friday, 10:00 AM to 12:00 and 1:00 to 6:00 PM. Tel: 9205-2856, Fax: 9205-9609.

## MONACO NAVAL MUSEUM

Just around the corner from the Automobile Collection is an exhibition of model ships from around the world. Models include modern aircraft carriers, submarines, merchant ships, war ships and ancient sailing ships. Model ship builders will be delighted by their visit. Open every day from 10:00 AM to 6:00 PM. Children under 8 are free. Tel: 9205-2848

## THE STAMP AND COIN MUSEUM

One of the first things that distinguishes a country's independence is the creation of it's own stamps and money. Prince Charles, in 1885, decided to create the first stamps of the Principality and mint the first coins. Monaco's stamps have won many awards for their design and beauty. They are world famous and sought after by collectors. The exhibition showing the history of Monaco and world events thorough its stamps is well worth the visit. Remember that blocks of stamps make a wonderful souvenir gift at a reasonable price. For information on new issue subscriptions, (see Les Basics under Stamps). Located near the Prince's Automobile Collection. Open daily 10:00 AM - to 12:00 and 1:00 PM to 5:00 PM to 6:00 PM in the summer. Tel: 9315-4150.

## THE MONACO PORCELAIN MANUFACTURING COMPANY
### (Manufacture de Porcelaine de Monaco)

Yes, Monaco has its own high quality porcelain manufacturer. Their factory is located in Fontvieille at 5, rue Gabian while their boutique is located in the Métropole shopping Galerie. Free guided tours are given by appointment. Call Mr. Joram Rozewicz at 9205-7755. Open year round M-F 9:00 AM to 4:00 PM. Web site: www.mdpm.com. E-mail: info@mdpm.com

## JARDIN EXOTIQUE
## EXOTIQUE GARDEN

The magnificent Exotic Garden cascades down the sheer faces of rock. Take a stroll along footbridges with fantastic views over the Principality and surrounding coast areas. Monaco's microclimate lends itself to the growth of cacti and succulents, and the Principality has collected 7,000 varieties of these plants from all over the world. Especially impressive are the 100-year-old Mexican and South American cacti and the 45-foot African Euphorbia.

The **Observatory Caves** have several chambers with illuminated limestone stalagmites and stalagmites. Excavations have revealed signs of prehistoric habitation, which are on display in the **Museum of Prehistoric Anthropology**. Besides tools and prehistoric animal bones, there are some interesting antiquities on display here, including the famous treasure discovered in la Condamine comprised of Punic coins, late Roman coins, gold medals, vases, lamps and Roman jewelry. One showcase displays prehistoric figurines; Grimaldi Venus, mammoth, horse and other Bronze age items. There is an impressive collection of skeletons including the remains of ancient Grimaldi ancestors, Cro-Magnon man, and collective burials. There are also prehistoric animals such as reindeer, mammoths, cave bears, elephants, and hippopotami that roamed the Riviera. Take bus line # 2. The gardens are located in the northwestern part of Monaco Tel: 9315-2980 Web site: www.monte-carlo.mc/jardinexotique or E-Mail: jardin-exotique@monte-carlo.mc Open daily from 9:00 AM to sunset.

## MONTE CARLO

## THE CASINO

Charles Garnier, the architect of the Opera House in Paris, built The Casino in 1878, it is the centerpiece of Casino Square. Its atrium is paved in marble and is surrounded by 28 Ionic onyx columns. From the atrium you can reach the Opéra, called the *Salle Garnier,* which is decorated in luxurious red brocade and gold leaf, many bas-reliefs, frescoes and sculptures. (See A Petite History section for more detail). The gaming rooms are a succession of rooms with stained glass windows, sumptuous decoration, sculpture, allegorical paintings, and bronze lamps. Please note entrance is limited to those over 21, so have proof ready. (See Entertainment section for further information on gaming).

## THE CASINO GARDENS AND TERRACES

In front of the Casino are magnificent flowerbeds, fountains, ponds where reeds and water lilies grow. This gently sloping upward park leads to *boulevard des Moulins*, one of the **wonderful shopping streets of the Principality**, and the **Métropole Galerie shopping arcade**. Behind the Casino, facing the sea, is the **Bar du Soleil**, terraces, sculptures, and the colorful geometrical tiled **Vasarely roof** of the Convention Center and Auditorium. **Great photo opportunities**, especially the *Botero* statue of *Adam and Eve*.

## THE NATIONAL DOLL MUSEUM

This beautiful villa along avenue Princesse Grace by the sea was built by Charles Garnier and houses a collection of 400 antique dolls and automata (animated dolls) created by Madame de Galea. A charming terraced rose garden with sculptures surrounds the grounds. Open every day 10:00 AM to 12:15 and 2:30 PM to 6:30 PM. Take Bus Line #6 or # 4. Tel: 9330-9126

## THE JAPANESE GARDEN

Looking for peace, serenity, and tranquility, a place where you can reflect on life? Take a stroll, sit and listen to the cascading water, admire the artistic placement of shrubs and trees in the second-largest Japanese garden outside of Japan. This garden was carefully designed and planted by Japanese craftsmen and gardeners who traveled across the seas to spin their magic. Open daily from 9:00 AM until sunset.

# THE BEST MONACO PHOTO OPPORTUNITY SPOTS

## MONACO-VILLE

- Coming up the Rampe Major with the port and casino in the background.

- The bronze statue of Miliza Grimaldi.

- The Palace Square with views east or west, or in front of the Palace.

- Staircase in front of the Palais de Justice (courthouse) next to the Cathedral.

- The Cathedral staircase.

- The rooftop terrace of the Oceanographic Museum.

- In front of the Jacques Cousteau's yellow submarine.

- Just about anywhere in the St. Martin Garden.

## LA CONDAMINE

- In the port in front of any large Yacht.

## FONTVIEILLE

- The Princesse Grace Rose Garden.

## MONTE CARLO-LARVOTTO

- Anywhere in the casino square or casino garden with the casino as the background.

- Behind the casino on the terrace near the Botero sculpture.

- The Japanese Garden.

The **best birds eye view of Monaco** is from the Vista Palace hotel and the road going down from it.

# 3
# DINING IN THE PRINCIPALITY

Monaco has everything from Tex-Mex to Japanese, from sublime dining in the Louis XV to port-side cafés. Be sure to try some of the Monégasque specialties like **barbagiuan**, a delicious tidbit of rice, spinach, leek and cheese, served as an appetizer. Current favorites for a 'lite snack' sandwiches are toasted *paninis, foccacia* and open faced *bruschettas* found in the Old Town. The following list caters to every taste, but the budget minded should check out *Monaco on a Shoestring chapter* for all the $ listings. The prices include tax, service but not drinks. Best values are the lunch menus. Just choose. Bon Appetit.

Key: Prices per person not including drinks:

| | | | |
|---|---|---|---|
| $ | Best Value | 60-120FF, | 9-18€ |
| $$ | Moderate | 130-240FF, | 19-36€ |
| $$$ | Expensive | 250-300FF, | 38-45€ |
| $$$$ | Very Expensive | 350-1000FF, | 53-152€ |

The best places to find reasonable food is at **snack bars** where you can get a good sandwich on French bread, or you can graze appetizers. Most foreign travelers have trouble adjusting to eating on the European time schedule. So if hunger strikes after 3 PM go directly to a snack bar, crêperie, or café. This will hold you over. Most restaurants do not start their evening service until **7 PM** at the earliest. Many restaurants are closed on Sunday evening, so always call ahead and check the times, or pick up a restaurant guide from the tourist office or your hotel.

   The best bet for value is ordering the "**formule**", which is a fixed priced meal. This usually offers you a **starter** *(entrée)*, **main dish** *(plat)* and **dessert**, but generally does not include beverages. Restaurants give you several offerings to choose from on their fixed menu. House wines are usually excellent and a lot cheaper than soda. Or you might order mineral water "*avec gaz*" (**with bubbles**) or "*sans gaz*" (**without bubbles**). Generally don't expect to substitute anything different. If you want a bigger choice, you must select from what is called "**la carte.**" If you order a meat dish, you may be asked how you like it cooked-*quelle cuisson?* **Saignant**-rare, *à point*-**medium rare**, and *bien cuit*-**well done**. Locals generally prefer their meat very rare, so it's better to overcompensate if you don't like rare meat.

   To get the most out of the following section, figure out what area you're in or decide where you feel like dining. **Monte Carlo? Larvotto Beach? La Condamine?** Then check the restaurants in that area within your price range. For the budget minded, see Monaco on a Shoestring-restaurants for a list of lower priced fare.

# MONTE CARLO

**Argentin**         $$$         9350-6500
*Monte Carlo Grand Hotel*
By far the best steaks in town. South American atmosphere. They have a mini menu after 12 PM and serve until 4 AM. Live music.

**La Belle Epoque**         $$$         9216-4001
*Hotel Hermitage*
Dining here is a turn-of-the-century experience. Noted for their Bollito Misto, an Italian boiled meat and vegetable specialty that is served only six times a year. Otherwise open for special theme dinner evenings.

**Borsalino**         $ Lunch $$ Dinner         9350-6692
*4, bd. des Moulins*
Not far from the Tourist Office. This is a good spot to get a pizza or plate of spaghetti.

**Bistroquet**         $$-Lunch $$$ Dinner     9350-6503
*Galerie Charles III*
Just around the corner from the Casino, the Bistroquet has a mixed tourist menu. A good post-late-night spot to quench your jet lag hunger pangs. Live music after dinner when it becomes Club Sabor Latin.

**Café de la Mer**         $$         9350-6500
Monte Carlo Grand Hotel
The restaurant has delightful panoramic views of Italy. Excellent for eggs benedict, salads, sole and specials of the day. You can eat light here.

**Café de Paris**         $$         9216-2020
*Place du Casino*
No trip to Monaco is complete without at least a drink at the café just next to the Casino and across the street from the Hotel de Paris. This is the premiere 'see and be seen' spot, whether sitting outside or dining inside. There is a lively mix of locals and visitors in a French brasserie atmosphere. The menu has an international flavor. Daily specials are always good; favorites are steak tartar and fresh oysters in season.

**Capocaccia by day**         $         9325-5952
**Caposushi by night**         $$
*6, impasse de la Fontaine (Park Palace Galerie complex)*
Italian pannini by day and sushi by night. Order your sushi in advance for either take out or eat in.

**Ciao**         $$         9325-7868
*7, rue du Portier*
A locals' favorite for Italian food. Favorite picks are slightly spicy penne arrabbiata, tagliolini with salmon or with tomato basil. Good mixed salad and delicious country bread.

*Dining In The Principality*

**Costa La Crémaillère**   $$        9350-5524
*Place de la Crémaillère*
This little brasserie has fresh pasta and fish. Atrium dining in winter becomes open air dining in summer.

**Côté Jardin**   $$        9316-6844
*Hotel de Paris*
Here's the place for your power breakfast or discrete lunch in a charming, sun-filled room or on the garden terrace. Mixed menu, pleasant atmosphere.

**Fuji**   $$ Lunch $$$ Dinner   9330-4011
*Métropole Galerie*
The Fuji is Monaco's first Japanese restaurant for connoisseurs of sushi and sake. During the summer months it moves to the Sporting d'Ete where it overlooks the gardens, sea and Monte Carlo.

**Giacomo**   $$$$        9325-2030
*17, av. des Spélugues*
Upscale Italian just down from Rampoldi. In season white truffle risotto can't be beat.

**L'Albatros**   $$$        9330-9880
*Le Meridien Beach Plaza Hotel*
Av. Princesse Grace
Chef Bernard Cuq plies his talents over this cozy seafood restaurant. Excellent sea-bass cooked in fennel and rock salt - and the Crepe-Suzette can't be beat.

**L'Ascot**   $ Lunch $$ Dinner   9770-6406
*1, av. des Citronniers*
Watch horse racing while enjoying a open faced "bruchetta" for lunch. Also serving dinner, live music on the weekends.

**L'Hirondelle**   $$ Lunch   9216-4930
**Thermes des Marins Spa**
Part of the spa complex, this restaurant can help you cut calories in the most satisfactory way.

**La Coupole**   $$$        9216-6565
*Hotel Mirabeau*
Chef Michel de Mattteis presides over this one star restaurant, and his classic gourmet French cuisine will delight you. He has worked with some of the best chef's in France. Check to see if they are offering any of their special theme lunch or dinner menus. Usually featuring a regional specialty.

**La Pizza**   $$        9350-4700
*9, rue du Portier*
More fine northern Italian dinning.

**La Salle Empire**   $$$$        9216-2952
*Hotel de Paris*
Inside or out on the terrace, elegant gourmet dining at its "*be and be seen*" best. The Salle Empire is often used for balls and large dinners, and is an unforgettable experience.

**Le Grill**                    $$$$                    9216-3002
*Hotel de Paris*
On the rooftop of the Hotel de Paris, Le Grill has one of the best views of Monaco and in the summer the roof opens. By far one of the Best Restaurants in Monaco; rated one star by the Michelin Guide. Chef Mario Muratore works his gastronomic magic here and as well in the Salle Empire and Côté Jardin.

**Le Raja**                    $$                    9350-1714
*27, bis rue Portier*
Monaco's only Indian restaurant.

**Le Saint-Benoit**                    $$                    9325-0234
*10, av. de la Costa*
Located behind the Hotel Balmoral overlooking the port. This is a romantic dinning spot with excellent seafood specialties. It is one of Monaco's best values, but stick with the set menu. Convenient parking under the building.

**Le Train Blue**                    $$$                    9216-2211
*Place du Casino*
Travel back to the Belle-Epoque era in an elegant gourmet restaurant modeled after the Orient Express. Located inside the Casino so you must pay the entrance fee.

**Le Vistamar**                    $$$                    9216-2772
*Hotel Hermitage*
The old bar that was one of the best spots in Monte Carlo has been expanded to include a new enclosed terrace restaurant. Done in a nautical theme, you dine on the terrace in the summer and in the atrium during the winter. Perhaps the only restaurant advertising fresh fish caught by Monaco's last commercial fishermen M. Rinaldi. A wonderful spot where the discreet meet and business deals are made. The kitchen is presided over by chef Joel Garault, who won his first Michelin star at the Palme d'Or in Cannes in 1985.

**Louis XV**                    $$$$                    9216-3001
*Hotel de Paris*
Transports the diner back in time to the beauty and luxury of European royalty. Three-star chef Alain Ducasse creates food magic to make this dining experience unforgettable! Reserve as soon as possible as seating is limited. The best values are the "tasting" menu - available at lunch only - including wine 500FF (77€) per person. The **"vegetarian"** menu for 860FF (132€) and the **"gourmet"** menu for 980FF (150€) per person for lunch and dinner.

**Loga Café**          $$ Lunch $$$ Dinner  9330-8792
*25, bd. des Moulins*
Memorable French cuisine, cozy atmosphere.

**Maison du Caviar**                    $$                    9330-8006
*1, av. St. Charles*
As the name implies, a place to indulge in caviar and fine dining.

**Maxim's de Paris**                    $$$$                    9797-8460

*20, av. de la Costa*
The name is already famous and you won't be disappointed with this charming turn of the century setting and its excellent food. Service in the indoor atrium or under the stained glass ceiling of the dining room. Pierre Cardin owns this gem of a restaurant.

**Monty's**                                **$$**                           **9770-6880**
*3, av. St. Laurent*
A popular business men's lunch spot. You must order pasta for two. Associated with Zepter next door.

**Périgordin**                **$ Lunch $$ Dinner**            **9330-0602**
*5, rue des Oliviers*
Duck, duck, duck and foie gras! Traditional country cooking from the Périgord region in southwest France. Located on a small street below the Métropole off a cul-de-sac from avenue des Spélugues.

**Polpetta**                               **$$**                           **9350-6784**
*2, rue Paradis*
A hot spot for locals and celebrities alike. Frequented by Shirly Bassey, Roger Moore and Sean Connery. You guessed it! Excellent Italian food, friendly service, and wonderful complimentary lemon grappa after dinner. Always busy so reserve early.

**Pont Superior**                          **$$**                           **9350-6500**
*Monte Carlo Grand Hotel*
Summer terrace dining at its best with panoramic views and bountiful buffet. Open from mid-June to mid-September . A romantic dinner dining spot.

**Piedra Del Sol**                         **$$**                           **9350-6213**
*2, rue du Portier*
Serving Cocina Latina on a large terrace. Outdoor bar and Mexican specialties.

**Pulcinella**                             **$$**                           **9330-7361**
*17, rue du Portier*
Located on Italian restaurant row, Pulcinella has a warm and friendly atmosphere with your basic Italian menu. Frequented by locals and visitors.

**Rampoldi**                              **$$$$**                          **9330-7065**
*3, av. des Spélugues*
Celebrity watching here. On a recent night John Forsythe, Sharon Stone, Kirk Kerkorian and Nigel Mansell were seen eating the restaurant's excellent Italian food.

**Rigoletto**                              **$$**                           **9325-2428**
*11, rue du Portier*
Excellent Italian cuisine in booths or on the terrace.  Good seafood, veal and pasta al dente.

**Sans Souci**                            **$$$**                           **9350-1424**
*42, bd. d'Italie*
The best Italian food in this part of town.  This is a favorite with the locals.  Everything cooked to order.  Lovely choice of country breads.

**Santa Lucia**          **$$**                    9350-9677
*11, av. des Spélugues*
Old World charm makes this Italian eatery a Monaco mainstay on
restaurant row.

**Sam's Place**          **$ Lunch $$ Dinner**     9350-8933
*1, av. Henry Dunant*
Your basic no-thrills steak place. Reliable food at moderate prices.
Good chili.

**Il Terrazzino**        **$$**                    9350-2427
*2, rue des Iris*
An intimate non-smoking restaurant serving home-made-dishes
from Sicily. Bring a group and sample the antipasto bar.

**Il Triangolo**         **$ Lunch $$ Dinner**     9330-6730
*1, av. de la Madone*
A local's pizza and calezone spot for after the movies. Close to
Casino square.

**Tip Top**              **$ Lunch $$ Dinner**     9350-6913
*1, av. des Spélugues*
A late-night eating spot with diner-type menu located on restaurant row.

**Toum**                 **$$$**                   9216-6363
*Le Casino*
Well-known chef Toum presides in a cozy niche in the Casino
atrium. Discover the best Thai, Indonesian and Malay recipes.

## LARVOTTO BEACH

**Bar et Boeuf**         **$$$**                   9216-6060
*Sporting d'Eté*
Three star chef Alain Ducasse latest addition to the Principality.
The restaurant offers only fresh bar (Atlantic sea bass) and beef
served in the fashion that only a chef of his reputation can create.
Dining on a large wood deck with the sounds of fountains below
and Monte Carlo's sparkling lights in the background make this a
magical place. Open May thought October.

**Bombay Frigo**         **$$**                    9325-5700
*3, av. Princesse Grace*
Décor suggests an Indian Frigate, but restaurant features conti-
nental cuisine. Open for croissants, brunch, lunch and dinner.

**Costa à l' Ariston**   **$$**                    9330-9989
*39, av. Princesse Grace*
Dining on the sidewalk terrace attracts the lunch crowd. Very tasty
veal Milanese and salads.

**Chez Gianni**          **$$$**                   9330-4633
*39, av. Princesse Grace*
More superb Italian food.

**Fuji** $$ Lunch $$$ Dinner 9350-0545
*Sporting d'Eté*
The Fuji is Monaco's first Japanese restaurant for the connoisseur of sushi and sake. During the summer months it moves to the Sporting d'Ete where it overlooks the gardens, sea and Monte Carlo.

**La Pontinère** $$ 9797-5243
*Monte Carlo Beach Hotel*
More fresh fish al fresco. Open in the summer only.

**La Spiaggia** $ Lunch $$ Dinner 9350-5080
*Larvotto Beach next to the Sea Club*
This snack bar is the latest contender for the 'in' spot on the beach. Best place to get into a pick-up game of volleyball or badminton.

**La Vigie** $$$ 9797-5244
*Monte Carlo Beach Hotel*
This outdoor restaurant is set on a promontory jutting out into the blue Mediterranean waters. Accessible by foot or by boat.

**Les Pergolas** $$ 9330-9880
*Le Meridien Beach Plaza Hotel*
Traditional cuisine and pasta with a panoramic sea view. Al fresco dinning in the summer. Here's where you can find many sports stars when they are in town.

**Le Rivage** $$ 9797-5242
*Monte Carlo Beach Hotel*
More fine dinning at the Monte Carlo Beach Hotel. Open in the summer only.

**Miami** $ Lunch $$ Dinner 9350-9416
*Larvotto Beach*
On the beach, this is another local favorite for lunch.

**Sass Café** $$$ 9325-5200
*11, av. Princesse Grace*
Interior atrium with traditional and Italian cuisine. The piano bar is the place where different generations and nationalities mix it up for fun. A definite meeting spot; bar area is small and crowded. Dining on the sidewalk during the summer.

## LA CONDAMINE

**Chez Bacco** $$ 9350-1331
*25, bd. Albert 1er*
Italian cuisine; service is usually very slow.

**La Cigale** $$ 9330-1614
*18, rue de Millo*
A locals' favorite for homemade pasta served wonderfully al dente. Small terrace located on a quaint street in the Condamine.

**La Rascasse**               $$$                    9325-5690
*1, quai Albert 1 er*
International menu with dining under the stars. Their specialty is
Rascasse, a hearty bouillabaisse fish soup. Live music in the
downstairs bar. The bar is a definite late night **"in"** spot and great
place to be during the Grand Prix.

**La Strega**                 $$                     9205-6777
*4, rue de la Colle*
A standard local's spot for pizza, pasta and veal.

**Le Botticelli**        $$ Lunch $$$ Dinner    9325-3905
Situated in the heart of the port with terrific views. Offering traditional French and Italian cuisine.

**Le Calypso**           $ Lunch $$ Dinner     9315-0777
*Jetty Nord (on the Port)*
The only restaurant that's literally on the water in Monaco.
Hidden below the north port sea wall, it provides diners with a
great view of topless bathers and other fireworks in the summer.
Fresh fish specialties and traditional continental cuisine.

**Le Texan**                  $$                     9330-3454
*4, rue Suffren Reymond*
This is one of the best Tex-Mex Anglo-American restaurants and
watering holes in Monaco. Long on down-home American
friendliness that attracts the rich, the famous, and just about eve-
ryone in town. The easiest way to meet people is around the
Alamo bar. Open 7 days a week.

**My Sushi**                  $$                     9770-6767
*2, rue des Oranges*
The décor is minimalist white and neon lights. A surprising find
and the newest addition to Japanese cuisine. Also has take away.

**Porte d'Or**                $$                     9325-1415
*9, rue Grimaldi*
The best Chinese and Vietnamese food in town. Excellent shrimp
dim sum, and Chinese soups. Has home delivery.

**Quai des Artistes**         $$                     9797-9777
*4, quai Antoine 1er*
The newest addition to the port, looks set to be the next 'in' spot with
its open space and large bar area. Traditional French cuisine and
spit-roasted specials.

**Restaurant du Port**        $$                     9350-7721
*On the Port*
The best quai-side restaurant. Great view along the port, good
food and people watching.

**Stars and Bars**            $$                     9350-8575
*6, quai Antoine 1er*
Sports bar and restaurant with American food. Dining on port
side terrace in the summer. Brunch and lots of games to entertain
the kiddies. Live music and disco at night.

**Vecchia Firenze**          $$          9330-2720
*4, av Prince Pierre*
Always busy, this is another local's favorite with Mediterranean fare.
**Venezia American Bar**     $ Lunch $$ Dinner     9315-9727
*27, bd. Albert 1er*
Started out as a snack and pastry bar with the best expresso and
cappuccino in town, now serves a variety of food.

## MONACO-VILLE (THE OLD TOWN)

**Castelroc**          $$ Lunch $$$ Dinner     9330-2617
Place du Palais
One of the best-kept secrets in Monaco. The restaurant, only open
during lunch in the winters, is now serving dinner in the summer.
It offers the largest selection of Monégasque specialties. The
Loup (sea Bass) in rock salt is especially wonderful. Varied daily
menu, fish, pasta or meat. Great place after watching the changing
of the guard at 11:55 AM.
**Cavagnetu**          $ Lunch $$ Dinner     9330-3580
*14, rue Comte Félix Gastaldi*
This restaurant has a traditional menu and also features
Monegasque specialties. Well frequented by tourists.
**Da Sergio**          $ Lunch $$ Dinner     9330-3415
*22, rue Basse*
Whitewashed cellar walls, good daily specials and pizza.
**D'Avuta**          $ Lunch $$ Dinner     9330-7199
*1, rue Col. Bellando de Castro*
Courtyard dining, basic fare.
**Fredy's International Grill**     $$          9330-3776
*6, rue de l'Eglise*
Next to the Cathedral on Place St. Nicolas, offers a mixed tourist
menu.
**L'Express**          $ Lunch $$ Dinner     9330-4393
*22, rue Comte Félix Gastaldi*
Al fresco dining behind the Cathedral. Pizza, salads and basic fare.
**Pasta Roca**          $ Lunch $$ Dinner     9330-4422
*23, rue Comte Félix Gastaldi*
Good value for money.
**Pinocchio**          $$          9330-9620
*30, rue Comte Félix Gastaldi*
Located around the corner from the Palace, this place has some of
the best fresh pasta around. Favorites are the sage ravioli and paper-
thin prosciutto and melon. This is another celebrity-watching spot.
**St. Nicolas**          $$          9330-3041
*6, rue de l'Eglise*
On Place St. Nicolas next to the Cathedral. Old World charm and
traditional French cuisine at affordable prices. Wonderful place to
take the kids to wander in the courtyard and play with the pigeons.
Try the sandwich shop across the street.

# FONTVIEILLE

**Amici Miei**       **$$**       9305-9214
*16 quai Jean-Charles Rey*
Italian cuisine; outdoor terrace dining.

**Asia**       **$$**       9205-6068
*32, quai Jean-Charles Rey*
Asian cuisine, usually slow service. Outdoor terrace.

**Brasserie l'Offshore**       **$$$**       9205-9099
*22, quai Jean-Charles Rey*
A popular seafood and steak restaurant along the new port in
Fontvieille. Friendly, sleek nautical atmosphere. Good for lunch or
dinner.

**La Bodega**       **$ Lunch $$ Dinner**       9205-2618
Situated next to the Commercial Center, this is a busy steak and
pizza place. Open from 7:00 AM til 11:00 PM.

**Gerhard's Café**       **$ Lunch $$ Dinner**       9205-2579
*42, quai Jean-Charles Rey*
Snack bar and tea room

**L' Orangeraie**       **$$**       9205-6737
*42, quai Jean-Charles Rey*
Continental cuisine and fish specialties.

**McDonalds**       **$**       9205-3990
*Commercial Center*
Undoubtedly one of McDs best views, situated on a spot overlooking
the harbor. Pirate playship for kids. Will satisfy any craving for
American junk food. Credit cards accepted

**Michelangelo**       **$$**       9205-7733
*8, quai Jean-Charles Rey*
Charming Italian restaurant with terrace. Good businessmen's
lunch spot.

**La Salière**       **$$**       9205-2582
*14, quai Jean-Charles Rey*
Best antipasto in town. Lively atmosphere.

# RESTAURANTS IN THE NEIGHBORHOOD

Just across the border in France, a five-minute walk from the
Casino, you'll find some small local restaurants. In **BEAUSOLEIL**
there is an excellent Indian restaurant called **New Indian** at *10, bd.
de la Republique* **33 (0) 4 9378-1789**, open for lunch, dinner and
carry out. Service is a bit slow; all dishes are cooked to order. The
**Grain de Riz** on **33 (0) 4-9378-8820** for Asian cuisine.

    In **CAP D'AIL** to the west of Monaco try **La Pinède 33
(0) 4 9378-3710** for fresh fish al fresco on an olive branch shaded
terrace overlooking the Mediterranean. Other restaurants include
**Pizza Chez Michel 33 (0) 4 9378-3710**, *on Plage Mala (see day trip
section)*, **La Reserve 33 (0) 4 9378-1706**, **Tahiti Beach 33 (0) 4
9378-8899** or **La Coquille 33 (0) 4 9341-9049**.

About 3 miles east along the *Basse Corniche* on the south side there is **Le Roquebrune 33 (0) 4-9335-0016**. This two-generation family run restaurant will make you feel as if you've been invited to their home for lunch or supper. Overlooking the Mediterranean. Doorman to park your car.

# 4
# ACCOMMODATIONS

You can pamper yourself in some of the world's most fabulous hotel rooms with stunning views and romantic decor. You can watch satellite television on a hi-definition plasma screen while you relax in your own jacuzzi. If you're here on business, the Monte Carlo Grand boasts 2 telephone lines in every bedroom plus a phone in the bathroom. However, if you're on a modest travel budget you can also find comfortable rooms at affordable prices at the smaller hotels. Two new hotels are scheduled to open in 2001: a 300 room, 4★★★★ hotel next to the Sporting d' Eté and a top-end 50 suite deluxe hotel port side run by the Forresthills Hotels & Resorts, former managers of London's, Lanesborough and Dallas Mansion of Turtle Creek fame.

## THE TOP-OF-THE-LINE
### 4★★★★ (LUXE)

Four-star hotel prices start in the low season between 1,200FF (185€)for a single and 1,400FF (215€) for a double; in high season 1,850FF (285€) for single and 2,500FF (385€) for a double. Suites and apartments run between 3,000FF (460€) and 6,500FF (1000€).

An asterisk (*) indicates S.B.M. (Société des Bains de Mer) hotels that present a *Carte d'Or* or **gold card** to guests. This card entitles you to reduced entrance fees to all S.B.M. properties such as the Monte Carlo Beach Hotel pool, the Monte Carlo Tennis Club, Golf Club and the Monte Carlo Casinos.

## MONTE CARLO

**Hotel de Paris\***  9216-3000
*Place du Casino*  *Fax: 9216-3849*

For more than a century, The Hotel de Paris has been one of the world's great hotels. It is the home of the well-known Louis XV restaurant (*See restaurants*); as well as The Grill; the Terrace of the Salle Empire and the Côté Jardin. Wine cellars boast more than 300,000 bottles. 135 rooms, 43 suite-appartments and 19 junior suites. It has some wonderful period rooms overlooking the port or the Casino Square. The Churchill suite is perfect for celebrities or others seeking the ultimate in privacy; its rooms can be locked off. Or the famous Sarah Bernhart suite. AC, pool, all credit cards. (For good luck, be sure to rub the equestrian statue of Louis XV as you enter).

Web site: www.montecarloresort.com  E-mail: hp@sbm.mc

**Hotel Hermitage***       9216-4000
*Square Beaumarchais*       *Fax: 9216-3852*
This Belle Époque hotel is for the discriminating traveler who wants luxurious period rooms overlooking the harbor. Its main restaurant is decorated Versailles style with frescoes, shimmering crystal chandeliers and pink marble Corinthian columns. 196 rooms; 17 suite-apartments and 17 junior suites. AC, pool, all credit cards. Web site:www.montecarloresorts.com.
E-mail: hh@sbm.mc

**Monte Carlo Grand Hotel**       9350-6500
*12, av. des Spélugues*       *Fax: 9330-0157*
The Monte Carlo Grand offers the finest in European hospitality and luxury with a blend of American facilities and efficiency. Each room has 2 telephone lines and 3 phones. Its state of the art fitness center overlooks the Grand Prix circuit. The rooftop's fresh water heated pool with panoramic views is open all year round. A world-class resort hotel that can handle conventions, business executives and families in style. There are four specialty restaurants, 619 rooms and suites with AC, all amenities.
Web site: www.montecarlograndhotel.com
E-mail: grandhotel@monaco.mc

**Métropole Palace**       9315-1515
*4, av. de la Madone*       *Fax: 9325-2444*
A symbol of excellence and quality in the heart of Monte Carlo, the Métropole has been the home to European aristocracy and artists for more than a century. The lobby has magnificent crystal chandeliers, frescos and ornate Italian marble. There are 170 rooms, 12 suites, and 45 junior suites all lavishly appointed. A gourmet roof top restaurant and dinning in Le Jardin in the summer. Conference facilities and meeting room for 200 are available AC, and pool. Web site: www.monaco.mc/metropole/index.html
E- mail: metropole@monaco.mc

**Hotel Mirabeau***       9216-6565
*1, av. Princesse Grace*       *Fax: 9350-8485*
The Mirabeau trademarks are ultra-modern comfort, balconies and fine one star Michelin dining at La Coupole. It caters to businessmen and conventions. It is centrally located near the Casino, facing the sea and Japanese gardens. There are 89 rooms and 14 junior suites, AC, and pool.
Web site: www.montecarloresorts.com E-mail: mi@sbm.mc

## LARVOTTO BEACH
**Monte Carlo Beach Hotel***       9328-6666
*Av. Princesse Grace-St. Roman*       *Fax: 9350-2314*
Set in a picturesque cove, The Monte Carlo Beach hotel is perfect for seaside pleasures. (also a romantic honeymoon spot) The rooms are decorated in southern Italian style. Terrific people

watching poolside. For privacy, they have cabanas for rent. For dining, their La Vigie is an open-air restaurant on the peninsula; La Potinière features Mediterranean specialties around the Olympic size pool; and the Le Rivage is the convenient snack bar. The hotel has 41 rooms, 2 junior suites, 1 duplex apartment with terrace. AC, pool. Open February through November.
Web site: www.montecarloresort.com   E-mail: bh@monaco.mc

**Le Meridien Beach Plaza Hotel**                    9330-9880
*22, av. Princesse Grace*                      *Fax: 9350-2314*
This modern hotel is the only one in Monaco situated on its own exclusive beach. The open-air lobby and spacious guestrooms are decorated in nouvelle Mediterranean with vivid Provençal terra cotta colors. 333 rooms, each with E-mail access through the television via an infra red keyboard. In addition, there are 24 luxury roof top suites with a personal concierge and food service. Two out-door and one heated indoor pool, and a workout room with a sea view. The hotel hosts the men's professional tennis players for the Tennis Masters Monte Carlo during the third week in April. Extensive meeting and conference facilities with the attached Sea Club next door. Three excellent restaurants.
Web site: www.lemeridien.com
E-mail: resa@lemeridien.montecarlo.com

## THE BEST FOR THE REST OF US
### 3★★★
Moderately priced hotels start at 500FF (77€) for a single and 650FF (100€) for a double in low season, and 650FF (100€) for a single to 800FF (123€) for a double in high season. All take credit cards.

## MONTE CARLO
**Hotel Alexandra**                              9350-6313
*35, bd. Princesse Charlotte*                  *Fax: 9350-4712*
Situated in the heart of Monte Carlo, good for shopping along the boulevard des Moulins, this restored turn-of-the-century hotel is a find. 56 rooms all with air-conditioning and sound proofed.

**Hotel Balmoral**                               9350-6237
*12, av. de la Costa*                          *Fax: 9315-0869*
Older hotel with superb port views situated next to the Hotel Hermitage. Very centrally located. Some rooms have a balcony and others have air-conditioning. 54 rooms 7 junior suites and 5 apartments. Web site: www.hotel-balmoral.mc
E-mail: balmoral@cyber-monaco.mc

**Hotel du Louvre**                              9350-6525
*16, bd. des Moulins*                          *Fax: 9330-2368*
Centrally located with easy access to buses, this traditional small hotel will meet your needs and make your stay enjoyable. Some rooms have sea views No pets allowed. 33 sound proofed rooms, most with AC. Web site: www.monte-carlo.mc/louvre
E-mail: hotel-louvre@monte-carlo.mc

### La Masion d'Or
*21, rue du Portier*

9350-6666
*Fax: 9330-7600*

This small charming hotel is decorated in the style of a 19th century palace. Located on Italian restaurant row, close to sea and Casino. There are 8 rooms and suites all beautifully decorated in a different color. AC. Web site: www.hotelmaisondor.com
E-mail: monica@hotelmaisondor.com

## LA CONDAMINE

### Hotel Miramar
*1, av. Président J.F. Kennedy*

9330-8648
*Fax: 9330-2633*

The only hotel right on the port. 12 modern rooms with showers, 8 with AC. Panoramic bar and terrace. Racing fans take note; it is directly on the Grand Prix track.

### Hotel Ambassador-Monaco
*10, av. Prince Pierre*

9330-2556
*Fax: 9330-0372*

Located conveniently in the Condamine and close to parking, bus service, shopping and sightseeing. Its 35 comfortable rooms have been soundproofed and air-conditioned.
Web site: www.monte-carlo.mc/ambassador
E-mail: ambassador@monte-carlo.mc

### Tulip Inn Monaco Terminus
*9, av. Prince Pierre*

9205-6300
*Fax: 9205-2010*

The rooms were refurbished in 1999 in bright and cheerful modern provençal style and are good value. La Sariette serves provençal dishes, and Le Corail offers seafood and tapas. 54 soundproofed rooms, 12 with sea view.
Web site: www.terminus.monte-carlo.mc
E-mail: tupipinn-terminus@monte-carlo.mc

## FONTVIEILLE

### Abela Hotel
*23, av. des Paplins*

9205-9000
*Fax: 9205-9167*

This hotel built in 1989 is another excellent value and as a consequence caters to the business traveler and is usually booked in advance. The 192 contemporary California-style rooms are soundproofed and air-conditioned with sea, port and mountain views. There are 9 rooms adapted for handicapped persons, 18 suites, 10 businesswomen rooms and one whole floor dedicated to non-smokers. Most rooms have terraces. Outside pool
E-mail: abela-hotel@monte-carlo.mc

## BUDGET LODGING
### 2★★

Room prices are 310FF (48€) for a single to 400FF (62€) for a double in low season and 500FF (76€) for a single and 700FF (107€) for a double during high season.

# LA CONDAMINE

**Hotel de France**                                        9330-2464
*6, rue de la Turbie*                              *Fax: 9216-1334*
A clean modern hotel of 26 rooms, each with shower, TV and direct telephone lines. An excellent location for the port and old town. Parking and transportation are close by.
Web site: www.monte-carlo.mc/france
E-mail: hotel-france@monte-carlo.mc

**Hotel Helvetia**                                        9330-2171
*1, bis rue Grimaldi*                             *Fax: 9216-7051*
The Helvetia has 25 rooms, 21 of which come with bath or shower. Perfect for the no-frill traveler.
Web site: www.monte-carlo.mc/helvetia.
E-mail: hotel-helvetia@monaco.mc

**Hotel le Versailles**                                   9350-7934
*4, av. Prince Pierre*                            *Fax: 9325-5364*
A moderate priced hotel with 15 rooms, all with bath or shower, TV and direct dial phones. Well placed for sight seeing, transportation and parking. A popular French-Italian restaurant next door.
Web site: www.monte-carlo.mc/versailles
E-mail: hotel-versailles@monte-carlo.mc

**Hotel Cosmopolite**                                     9330-1695
*4, rue de la Turbie*                             *Fax: 9330-2305*
The only one-star hotel in the Principality is naturally the least expensive. It has 24 rooms, 5 with shower. Good location.
E-mail: hotel-cosmopolite@monte-carlo.mc

**Princesse Stephanie Youth Hostel**                      9350-8320
*24, av. Prince Pierre*                           *Fax: 9325-2984*
Basic youth hostel accommodation for travelers between 16 and 31 years old. Stays are on a first come, first serve basis, and for 3 nights only in the summer.

# HOTELS IN THE NEIGHBORHOOD

Hotels in France are less expensive because the price of land is cheaper. Rates for a double room in a **2★★** hotel run between 120FF (18€) to 720FF (110€), **3★★★** double rooms 230FF (35€) to 2,000FF (308€) and **4★★★★** 450FF (69€) to 6,500FF (1000€).   Bordering Monaco is **BEAUSOLEIL, which is a five-minute walk** to the Casino, shopping and convenient parking at several new garages. The following is a list of good budget hotels in Beausoleil that are always in demand.

**Hotel Olympia**                                33 (0) 4 9378-1270
*17, bis bd. Général Leclerc*        *Fax: 33 (0) 4 9341-8505*
Money saver hotel with 32 rooms. AC, TV and mini bar.

**Hotel Diana**                                  33 (0) 4 9378-4758
*17, bd Général Leclerc*             *Fax: 33 (0) 4 9341-8894*
35 agreeable rooms with TV.

**Hotel Cosmopolite**                              33 (0) 4 9378-3600
*19, bd. Général Leclerc*                    *Fax: 33 (0) 4 9341-8422*
19 rooms with showers, T.V. and A.C.
**Forum**                                            33 (0) 4 9378-9636
*Place des Monéghetti*                       *Fax: 33 (0) 4 9378-9638*
A 3 star hotel that is good value for money 39 rooms, AC and parking.
**Residence Pierre & Vacances**              33 (0) 4 9241-2000
*Palais Josephine,*                          *Fax: 33 (0) 4 9241-2001*
*2A, av du General de Gaulle*
A residence hotel with studios up to 3 bedrooms that sleep 5 or 6 people - roof-top pool, open for 1 year. Short or long stays. A 3★★★ good value next door to Monaco. 130 rooms. AC.

On the western border are **CAP D'AIL** and its port. It is adjacent to Monaco's Football stadium, Stade Louis II in Fontvieille. There is frequent bus service between Monaco, Nice and the airport.

**Marriott Cap d'Ail**                               33 (0) 4 9210-6767
*Port of Cap d'Ail*                          *Fax: 33 (0) 4 9210-6700*
Rooms have splendid views either facing the yacht harbor or the mountains. The hotel has 174 tastefully appointed guestrooms and 12 suites and AC. There is an outdoor pool; it's a short walk to the beach and tennis courts, and an in-house fitness center. US and Canada toll free number 1-800-228-9290, U.K.0800-221-222, and in France the toll free number is 0800-908-333.
Web site: www.marriott.com

In the town of **CAP D'AIL,** here are two moderate priced hotels:
**Edmonds Hotel**                                    33 (0) 4 9378-0855
*87, av. du 3rd September*
Run by a British-French couple, it has a well-attended restaurant. 10 rooms.
**Hotel Normandy**                                   33 (0) 4 9378-7777
*6, allée des Oranger*                       *Fax: 33 (0) 4 9378-4826*
21 rooms, some with sea views.
**International Youth Hostel**                       33 (0) 4937-81858
*Villa Thalassa, in Cap d'Ail*
A student favorite.
**Residence Pierre & Vacances**              33 (0) 4 9341-7300
*Av du General de Gaulle*                    *Fax: 33 (0) 4 9341-7477*
A residence hotel that has studios and sleeps up up to 5 or 6 people in three bedrooms. Pool, AC., 174 rooms. Best to have a car if you choose to stay here. Magnificent sea views.

To the east is **ROQUEBRUNE CAP MATIN** where there are several smaller hotels and restaurants. (See day trips). Frequent bus service to and from Monaco, Nice and airport.

**Hotel Westminster**                    **33 (0) 4 9335 0068**
*14, av. Louis Laurens-Cabbeé*        *Fax: 33 (0) 4 9328-8850*
Small hotel not far from Monaco and Roquebrune Cap Matin beach. This is a favorite of tennis journalists and photographers during the tennis tournament. 31 rooms.

**Alexandra**                    **33 (0) 4 9335-6545**
*93, av. Winston Churchill, Cap Matin*    *Fax: 33 (0) 4 9357-9651*
40 rooms with AC, parking and allows dogs.

**Victoria**                    **33 (0) 4 9336-6590**
*7, Promenade du Cap Martin*        *Fax: 33 (0) 4 9328-7202*
30 rooms with AC, parking and allows dogs.

# 5
# ENTERTAINMENT

Here are the **"in"** spots ... the discos, the best meeting places, best piano bars, the best places to **"see and to be seen"** and a guide to all the gambling establishments. Of course, we recommend you check out some of the cultural activities for which Monaco is justly famous.

## CULTURAL ACTIVITIES

Monaco has had a long history of supporting the arts, so it isn't surprising that it has its own symphony orchestra and opera and ballet companies. These cultural institutions rival the best of larger countries. Here is a rundown of the Monte Carlo Opera, Ballet, Philharmonic Orchestra, the Princess Grace Theater, Dance Academy, the Prince Rainier III Music Academy, Fort Antoine Theater, the School of Plastic Arts, the Prince Pierre and Princess Grace Foundations. If you love classical music, then you must get tickets to the summer concerts in the Palace Courtyard. Ticket information for the ballet, opera and orchestra: Box Office Atrium du Casino, Place du Casino Tel: 9216-2299, Fax: 9216-3837. The ticket office is open every day except Monday from 10:00 AM to 12:30 PM and 2:00 PM to 5:00 PM. Or at FNAC in the Métropole Galerie. E-mail www.fnac.fr. Please note that some performances of the Philharmonic, Ballet and Opera will be performed in the new Forum Grimaldi located on Ave. Princesse Grace.

## THE MONTE CARLO OPERA
## SALLE GARNIER

For over the last hundred years the Salle Garnier has been the setting for Monaco's most prestigious performances in music and dance. Just sitting in this jewel of an opera house, you can easily fantasize what life must have been like in a gentler world at the turn of the century. You enter through the atrium, a large hall flanked by twenty-eight ionic columns by Gustave Jundt. The interior of the opera house is decorated with frescoes by Chabaud and on the ceiling, images representing instrumental music, comedy, dance and song. Sitting inside is like being inside a Fabergé Egg, and one cannot help visualizing the past performances by all the great singers, dancers, and conductors who performed there.

Original works by Georges Bizet, Charles Gounod, Camille Saint Saens, "The Damnation of Faust" by Berlioz, "Don Quichote" by Jules Massenet, "L'Enfant et les Sortiléges" by Ravel, and Puccini were premiered here. World-famous singers such as Enrico Caruso, Placido Domingo, Luciano Pavarotti, Julia Migenes and Barbara Hendricks have enchanted audiences in unforgettable performances. Opera Director **John Mordler** has continued the innovative traditions with the commission of new operas such as "The Picture of Dorian Gray" and the recent set design of "The Regiment's Daughter" by the renown artist Botero. The company tours the world when not performing in Monaco. The opera season in Monaco runs from January until March. Ticket sales begin the last week of November.

## THE MONTE CARLO BALLET

Ballet started in Monte Carlo in 1911 when Impresario Serge de Diaghilev left Russia with the Russian Imperial Ballet and established his famous "Ballets Russes" in Monaco. The Salle Garnier has always been a pioneer in ballet with premiers of such famous ballets as "Le Spectre de la Rose," "Petruchka', and "Prelude aˆ l'Apres-Midi d'un Faune." The world renowned artists Bakst, Benois, Picasso, Braque and Matisse created magical stage sets for Diaghilev and famous choreographers, among them Nijinsky, George Balanchine, Margot Fonteyn, Rudolph Nureyev and Maria Tallchief. The Monte Carlo Ballet is currently under the direction of **Jean-Christophe Maillot**, who has brought a new vitality to the ballet company. Nowadays, The Monte Carlo Ballet divides its time between Monaco and other cities around the world. They are in Monaco for Christmas, the spring arts festival and during part of the summer, they provide some dazzling evenings of dance on the terrace behind the Opera. Look for an International Dance Forum to be staged in December in the Grimaldi Forum.

## THE MONTE CARLO PHILHARMONIC ORCHESTRA

The forerunner of the current orchestra was the *"Cercle des Etrangers Orchestra"* formed in 1856, which premiered "L'Arlésienne" by George Bizet. Today the orchestra is composed of eighty-six musicians and performs symphonic and lyric works. It also accompanies the ballet and opera productions. The orchestra has been conducted by some of the great conductors: Toscanini, Paul Paray, Edouard Van Remoortel, Leonard Bernstein, Igor Markovitch, Sir Neville Mariner, Walter Weller, Lawrence Foster and James Priest. International artists such as Rubinstein, Horowitz and Rostroprovitch have performed with the orchestra. The orchestra's recordings are known and sold throughout the world. The Philharmonic season begins every autumn and continues into the spring. In July and August, the orchestra plays in the Prince's Palace courtyard. Be sure to add this highlight to your musical agenda. Tickets also go on sale at 4:00 PM before the performance at the Centre de Congrès Auditorium (C.C.A.M.) which is behind and below (take the elevators) the Place du Casino. Any available tickets to Palace

Courtyard concerts will be for sale at 7:30 PM the evening of the concert so it's wise to be first in line at the ticket booth on the Place du Palais.

## PRINCESSE GRACE THEATER

The Beaux-Arts Theater, built in 1930 by the Société des Bains de Mer, originally housed a stage and movie screen. One could see plays written by famous authors like Sacha Guitry and Marcel Pagnol and performed by well-known actors. Because of Princess Grace's interest in theatrical arts, the old theater was renovated and renamed after her. Today one can see the best of French plays during the autumn and winter season. The amateur English Drama Group puts on plays in English in the fall and spring. For further information and reservations call Tel: 9325-3227. Ticket sales begin one week ahead of each performance Monday through Saturday, except Sunday from 10:00 AM to 12:30 PM and from 3:00 to 6:30 PM, at 12 av. d'Ostende

## SALLES DES VARIÉTÉS

This theater offers recitals, chamber music and film screenings. 1, bd. Albert 1er (La Condamine) Tel: 9216-2000

## FORT ANTOINE THEATER

Have performances during July and August of chamber music, recitals, poetry, brass quintets and other music ensembles. For further information contact the Direction of Cultural Affairs at Tel: 9315-8303. There is no advance booking. Tickets available 45 minutes before the performance at the Fort Antoine Theatre.

Since the reign of Prince Antoine I, Monaco has appreciated and sponsored the arts. Today it is home to a fine ballet school, a music academy, a school of plastic arts, the Prince Pierre Foundation and the Princess Grace Foundation.

## THE PRINCESSE GRACE ACADEMY OF CLASSIC DANCE

Created in 1975 by Princess Grace and run by Marika Besobrasova, the school is housed in a small Florentine Villa overlooking the port of Monaco. Students come from all over the world to study ballet based on the great Russian tradition of academic dancing. The school offers a complete professional education in dance with a wide range of subjects such as the history of dance, jazz dance, pas de deux and contemporary dance. Its graduates have gone on to dance professionally in eminent ballet companies. For further information call Tel: 9330-7040.

## PRINCE RAINIER III FOUNDATION OF MUSIC ACADEMY

Originally established in 1922 as a municipal music school, it has been transformed into this thoroughly modern music academy with more than 775 students and 45 instructors. Subjects include musical formation, harmony, stringed instruments, and all wind instruments except the tuba. Chamber music, organ, mandolin, harp, classic guitar, saxophone, classic accordion, flute, harpsichord and percussion instruments. Group classes include a jazz and stringed instruments workshop and folk music. For further information call Tel: 9315-2891.

## THE SCHOOL OF PLASTIC ARTS

A one-or two-year program for 30 full-time students that prepares them for other highly qualified National Art School programs. Classes are also held for other Monaco school children and adults. Subjects taught include French art history, painting, drawing, perspective, engraving, photography, video, bookbinding and pottery. Students have access to the library's books, magazines, slides and videocassettes. For more information call Tel: 9330-1839.

## THE PRINCE PIERRE FOUNDATION

This foundation was created in February of 1966 by His Serene Highness Prince Rainier III in tribute to his father, who was a great patron of the arts. The foundation's purpose is to promote culture and the arts through the creation and awarding of prizes. These are "The Prince Pierre of Monaco Literary Prize," which pays tribute to a French writer or any well-known author who writes in French; and "The Prince Pierre of Monaco Musical Composition Prize," awarded to a contemporary music work. "The International Contemporary Art Prize" is given as part of a contemporary art exhibition. The Foundation's lectures and programs begin in the fall.

## THE PRINCESSE GRACE FOUNDATION

Established by Princess Grace in 1964 with the purpose of promoting humanitarian aid and cultural goals. Now under the direction of H.R.H. The Princess of Hanover, the foundation has continued to expand and achieve her mother's goals. It is the expressed wish of The Princess of Hanover to focus on the needs of helping children in distress. The foundation supports The Academy of Classical Dance, The Princesse Grace Irish Library, The Boutique du Rocher and many charitable organizations such as Oeuvre de Soeur-Marie, and a Youth Hot Line. Each year in March the "Bal de la Rose" takes place in Monte Carlo and brings close to one thousand guests together to support the Foundation's fund-raising efforts. In the United States, the Princess Grace

Foundation USA (not to be confused with the one in Monaco) discovers and awards grants to young artists in the applied arts. Many celebrity friends of the late Princess Grace contribute to this fund-raising effort. For more information about the foundation in Monaco call Tel: 9315-8262. Or for ticket information for the Bal de la Rose contact the S.B.M. Tel: 9216-3636.

## GAMING

Who was "The Man Who Broke the Bank in Monte Carlo?" He was Charles Deville Wells, and in 1891 he parlayed $600 (625€) into $60,000 (62,500€) over a period of three days. Using no apparent system other than increasing his bets when he was losing on the roulette wheel, he put even money bets on red and black, winning nearly every time until he finally exceeded the $20,000-(20,833€) franc "bank" allocated to each table at that time. In those days, it was customary to cover the table with a black cloth when its allotment was reached and close it for the rest of the day. The third and last day that Wells appeared at the Casino, he placed his opening bet on number 5 at odds of 35:1 and won. Then he left his original bet on number 5 and added his winnings to it. Number 5 won again and then again for another five times in succession. At the end of the night, Wells claimed his winnings and left Monte Carlo – never to be seen again. As far as it is known, his win was an honest one.

Well, you might not be so lucky, but here are a few pointers when trying your luck at any of the casinos. People who plan to play more than 100,000FF (15,385€) should approach the manager for discounts on hotel, restaurant and complimentary show tickets. A few words of caution. In the game rooms, don't loan out money and be careful where you put your purse. If you think you've won a jackpot, don't move from your machine: Someone will come around to assist you. Many machines have credit meters and you may have won more than you know. Cameras or recording devices are not allowed in casinos, so check them at the door. Card counters beware. There are professionals on staff just waiting to catch you. Cheats are put in jail. Play with your head and don't spend more than you can afford to lose. All good players set their limits and walk away when they've reached it.

The hottest games are the progressives with big pay-offs, and poker. Craps is always the most exciting game. The best play for your money is at the Café de Paris where the machines have a high turnover. The house holds the least, so the player has a better advantage. There is no tax on winnings.

All the casinos are set up for credit lines. When you show your I.D., they will check to see if you are on the barred list. Plan ahead, they don't set up credit lines overnight. The casino will keep track of your plays so don't expect the red carpet treatment unless you're an established world VIP high roller. Free drinks are not given at the slots. The legal age for gambling is 21. No native Monégasque is allowed to gamble in the Casinos.

# MONTE CARLO

### Casino de Monte Carlo                                        9216-2300
The beginning and the end in "civilized" European Gambling with a capital G. A passport or identity card is absolutely necessary to be admitted to the European and private rooms, plus an admission fee and appropriate dress (no t-shirts or shorts allowed). The 50FF (8€) admission fee is waived for SBM hotel guests and Carte d'Or holders. But one will have to pay an additional 100FF (15€) to play in the salons privés (private rooms). Just inside the entrance are slot machines open without admission from 10:00 AM daily. Web site: www.casino-monte-carlo.com

In the Private Salon Touzeta you'll find European and English roulette, trente-quarante (30-40), chemin de fer, black jack, craps starting around 3:00P.M (4:00 PM in the summer).  Pai gow poker starts from 10:30 PM . Opening hours noon Monday through Thursday, Friday, Saturday, Sunday and bank holidays. Closing time is usually 5:00 AM but depends on the action.

### Café de Paris  (SBM)                                        9216-2300
*The American Gaming Room*
Just next door to the Old Casino is the American gaming room, where you will find American roulette, craps, black jack and every kind of electronic slot and video machine and game.

### Salon Grand Siècle                                         9216-6316
Slot machines, horse racing machines, and video poker. Admission is free. Slots are open from 10 AM other games from 5:00 PM.

### Sun Casino          (SBM)                                  9216-2080
*Monte Carlo Grand Hotel*
Here is where to come for fast "Las Vegas"-style action. A lively atmosphere and good people watching, especially Euro-Italians. Bonne chance. Slots, craps, black jack and American roulette. Slots open from 11:00 AM; the rest of the games open Monday through Thursday from 5:00 PM and Friday, Saturday, Sunday, bank holidays from 4:00 PM.

# LARVOTTO BEACH

### Salle Des Palmiers (SBM)                                   9216-2300
*Monte Carlo Sporting d'Eté Complex*
Open summers only July to mid-September. Just the spot after the floor show or Jimmy'z to indulge in some gaming. English and European roulette, trente-quarante (30-40), chemin de fer, craps, black jack; play begins after 10:00 PM.

## NIGHT LIFE
## FLOOR SHOWS

If you missed the leggy dancers at the Crazy Horse, the Folies
Bergères or the Lido in Paris don't despair. Just book for a dinner
or late show at the following:

## MONTE CARLO

| | |
|---|---|
| Le Cabaret | 9216-2200 |
| Old Casino | 9216-3636 |

Has imported the best dancers from Paris so you can't go wrong.
Show begins at 10:30 P.M. Closed Mondays and from the end of
June to mid-September. Jacket and tie but no evening dress required.

## LARVOTTO BEACH

**La Salle des Etoiles** 9216-2244
*Sporting d'Eté av. Princesse Grace*

Top-notch entertainment from July through September. This is our
pick if you only have one night and like who is performing. The
Salle des Etoiles (Salon of the Stars) lit with twinkling lights gives
you that out-of-this-world feeling. Breathtaking views and fireworks cap off the evening. Previous headliners: Tina Turner,
Whitney Houston, Tony Bennett, M. C. Hammer, Paul Anka,
Barry White, James Brown and a equal number of celebrated
European entertainers. Book for dinner at 9:00 PM or just the show
at 10:45 PM. Call for the schedule and book early because tickets
for the best shows don't last long. For reservations call: 9216-3636.

## DISCOS
## MONTE CARLO

**Tiffany's** 9350-5313
*3, av. des Spélugues*

It is located a half a block from the Casino. Open every evening
from 11:00 PM, except Monday and Tuesday from October to
April. Mainly Italians between 20 to 30's.

**L'X Club** 9330-7055
*13, av. des Spélugues*

Every evening from 11:00 PM year round. Mostly a hangout for
the young trendy French set.

**Sparco Café** 9330-4106
*19, Galerie Charles III*

Adjacent to the Metropole Galerie this Formula 1 designed restaurant and nightclub caters to 16 year olds and over.

**Symbol** 9325-0925
*7, rue Portier*

Open every evening, except Monday, from 11:00 PM. Cozy intimate disco with an older, later crowd.

# LARVOTTO BEACH

**Jimmy'z**                                                    9216-2277

In the Sporting d'Eté Club complex. The "Cadillac" of discos. A luxurious, exotic setting with open walls in the summer, facing a pond and waterfalls. Opens at 11:00 PM, but doesn't really start going until 12:30 or 1:00 AM, giving you plenty of time for dinner or a snooze. This is where the "elite" meet and separate the men from the boys! Be prepared. All drinks are 250FF (38€), even beer. Call Frank early for a good table and buy a bottle, which runs around 1500FF (230€). If you don't finish it, they print your name on it for your next visit.

Like Cigars? Try some of Cuba's best in the new Cigar room. This disco is frequented by a mixed group of older Italians, Euros, locals, celebrities, sports stars and conventioneers. Singles circle around the dance floor looking for Ms. or Mr. Right. Dancing etiquette demands that single men and women dance free form on the floor. When you make heavy eye contact with your target and it's returned, they'll start drifting toward you. You've just been asked to dance and accepted the offer. Men generally do not ask women verbally to dance.

**Le Box**                                                    9330-1522

*39, av. Princesse Grace*

Open from 10:30 PM all year round.

# LA CONDAMINE

**Stars and Bars**                                            9350-9595

*6, quai Antoine 1er*

On the south side of the port, an American "less is more" garage warehouse-style sports bar, Internet café, restaurant and nightclub. Features live bands, electronic games, American shuffleboard, and things to keep the kiddies entertained. Open air terrace in the summer.

# MEETING PLACES, BARS AND PUBS
# MONTE CARLO

**The Living Room**                                           9350-8031

*7, av. des Spélugues*

A piano bar-disco that caters to the older and the late set. If you want to unwind after the Jimmy'z, this is the spot. Open every evening from 11:00 PM until the last person leaves.

**Cherie's Café**                                             9330-3099

*9, av. des Spélugues*

Late nightspot with piano bar, and live music.

**Lobby Lounge Bar**                                          9350-6500

*Monte Carlo Grand Hotel*

Sweeping views and melodic sounds will entertain you here. The "in" spot when there is a convention in town or to read the Sunday papers. Excellent people watching.

### Café de Paris                          9216-2020
*Place du Casino*

The number one place to be seen in Monte Carlo, with restaurant and gaming area. Most of the year the outdoor terrace is packed, especially in the late afternoon. During the winter months part of the terrace is enclosed, and there is a fresh oyster bar. Legend has it that the famous chef Escoffier was preparing a special dessert for Edward VII, reputedly a womanizer, and the dessert accidentally caught fire. Edward's companion at the time was Suzette so the flambé was christened crêpe Suzette in her honor.

### American Bar                          9216-3000
*Hotel de Paris*

For Old World charm, try the American Bar. A great place for late afternoon tea or cocktails. Grab a table facing the Place du Casino for people watching. You might be lucky enough to be there when visiting celebrities stop in for a libation. Piano bar and occasional special jazz evenings.

### Le Vistamar Terrace Bar                9216-4000
*Hotel Hermitage*

This is where the very "discrete" meet. Tucked away, this gem of a restaurant-bar is where you can hold those high-level discussions or romantic encounters without everyone in Monaco knowing it. Their terrace is one of the best spots to view the Grand Prix and summer fireworks.

### Flashman's Pub                         9330-0903
*7, av. Princesse Alice*

Home to Brits, Aussies, Dutch and Scando-Anglophiles. It is better known to locals as Club Au Pair. You can catch the after-work business crowd in the late afternoon, and from then on it's a mixed bag. Lots of yachties in the summer.

## LARVOTTO BEACH

### McCarthy's Pub                         9250-8767
*7, rue du Portier*

This Irish pub has reasonable prices, live music DJ and doors that open onto the sidewalk terrace in the summer.

### Bombay Frigo                           9325-5700
*3, av. Princesse Grace*

A restaurant that serves croissants, as well as cocktails; a good place to meet up.

### Sass Café                             9325-5200
*11, av. Princesse Grace*

This restaurant piano bar is a late-night spot for Euro's, Italians and locals. The bar area is small and usually jammed; however the action spills over to the sidewalk terrace in the summer.

**Le Meridien Beach Hotel Bar**                                9330-9880
*22, av. Princesse Grace*
Another spot for that discreet meeting away from the crowds and
definitely the spot to see tennis stars during the Tennis Master
Series Monte Carlo in April.

## LA CONDAMINE

**Le Texan**                                                   9330-3454
*4, rue Suffren Reymond*
Everyone who's anyone sips margaritas at the Alamo Bar, a top
watering hole. It was chosen as one of the best bars in the world
by Newsweek magazine in 1997. The celebrities that have passed
thorough these doors are too long to list. Open daily mid-day to
2:00 AM.

**La Rascasse**                                                9325-5690
*1, quai Albert ler*
Located on the Grand Prix circuit, the downstairs bar features live
music and attracts the 20 to 30 somethings. Catch Julian Lennon
or the Scorpions when they are in town. Open until 5:00 AM.

**Stars and Bars**
See Disco section

**Quai des Artistes**                                          9797-9777
*4, quai Antoine ler*
This looks set to become one of the new 'hot in' meeting spots,
and conveniently located across the street from La Rascasse. Large
open bar area with brasserie atmosphere.

## FONTVIEILLE

**Ship and Castle**                                            9205-7672
*42, quai Jean-Charles Rey*
This port side restaurant is the Brits' favorite choice for old-time
English ale, fish and chips.

**La Bodega**                                                  9205-2618
*Commercial Center*
Steak, pizza, salad, and bar popular with the Fontvieille locals.
Open 7-midnight

## MOVIE THEATERS, CINÉMAS

**Cinéma Le Sporting d' Hiver**                                9325-3681
Located in the building on the street next to the Hotel de Paris. It
is a three-plex cinema with English-language films shown daily. If
you see V.O. after the title of a film it means that it's in Version
Original, its native language with French subtitles. Most of the
time the original language is English, but not always. All other
screenings are dubbed in French. If you are staying in Monaco for
a protracted time, the best value is to buy a card of 10 movies.
Popcorn is either salted *"salé"* or sweetened *"sucré"* with **sugar.**

For the past 50 years Monaco enjoyed one of the only 'walk-in-sit-down' English cinemas on the Riviera. From July through mid-September an English feature length film was screened in the open air near the Sporting d'Eté each evening. This was certainly one of the 'in' spots frequented by everyone who happened to be in town. The cinema has been closed for construction of a new 300-room hotel and the powers that be are deciding where to relocate one of Monaco's most popular landmarks.

## YOUR ENTERTAINMENT RATINGS

# MONACO
## Classic Week
### 700<sup>èmes</sup> Nautiques

Exposition
et Concours
de Yachts et Canots
automobiles
12-21 Septembre 1997

# 6
# THE BIG EVENT CALENDAR

Monaco is known for its special events and holidays, so it's a good idea to see if anything special is going on during your visit. Here is the general social calendar of principal attractions each month. We advise you to check the monthly *Bienvenue* guide for specific ticket information and other happenings as new events come up all the time and these listings may be rescheduled to other months.

## JANUARY

### JANUARY 1                                                 NEW YEARS DAY

New Year's Day is often celebrated in a restaurant with a special menu. We suggest you reserve early. New Years cards are exchanged with friends and neighbors instead of Christmas cards. People wish everyone a Happy New Year *(Bonne Année et Sante)* and good health until January 31.

### JANUARY 6                                                       EPIPHANY

Epiphany is the *Fête des Rois* or **Feast of the Three Kings**, the wise men who visited Jesus. A special cake called *galette couronne des rois* is served on this day. This traditional cake has a paper crown on it and contains a small prize, or fève, a small ceramic figurine. Whoever finds the prize gets to choose a consort to become king and queen for the day. Be careful that the figurine, Good Luck that it may be, doesn't cause you to chip a tooth.

### JANUARY 27                                            FÊTE SAINT DÉVOTE

Celebrates the patron saint of Monaco. The legend is based in part on reality. During the 3rd century, the Governor of Corsica, under Roman influence (which was anti-Christian), tortured a young girl named Dévote. Christians who wanted her to have a proper burial put her in a small fishing boat and prayed that favorable winds would bring her home. A storm came up, forcing the boat along the coast of Provence and finally to the shores of Monaco. Then out of the mouth of Dévote came a dove. The Christians saw this as a miracle and erected a chapel in her honor. Over the years, thieves came by sea to steal the relics in the chapel. When they were caught, they were put in jail and their boats burned. To commemorate this legend, on the evening of every January 26, a fishing boat is set ablaze by the Prince, and on January 27, there is a 'Te Deum' at the Cathedral followed by a procession through the streets of the Old Town. The spirit of St. Dévote has galvanized the spirits of the Monégasques through many a hard time. Even today one can hear 'Merci St. Dévote' on the lips of locals.

## MONTE CARLO OPERA

## MONTE CARLO PHILHARMONIC ORCHESTRA

### THE PRINCESSE GRACE THEATER
See page 79 for ticket information for the Monte Carlo Ballet, Opera , Orchestra and the Princess Grace Theater.

### RUSSIAN CHRISTMAS
Candlelight dinner with dancing and other entertainment; call Société des Bains de Mer (S.B.M.) Tel: 9216-3636 and the Métropole Hotel on Tel: 9315-1515.

### THE MONTE CARLO CAR RALLYE
Usually held the last two weeks of January. This international event is more than 60 years old and spectators from all parts of Europe gather around the course to get a close look at the fantastic Rallye cars. This competition is part of the world championship for car manufacturers and drivers. All competitors end in Monaco for the last race, followed by a gala dinner and awards ceremony. Call the Automobile Club of Monaco for further information Tel: 9315-3600.

### THE MONTE CARLO HISTORIC CAR RALLYE
Call the Automobile Club de Monaco for further information Tel: 9315-3600.

### INTERNATIONAL JUDO TOURNAMENT
Held in the 'Salle Omnisports Gaston Médecin' Stade Louis II. For information call Tel: 9205-4000. Some times held in June.

# FEBRUARY

### FEBRUARY 2                    CANDLEMANS OR LADY DAY
Lighted candles celebrate the day the Virgin Mary went to the temple to be purified after the birth of Christ. It is considered good luck to eat crêpes on this day. Tradition requires that a person holds a gold coin in one hand and a crêpe pan in the other, and if the crêpe is successfully flipped in the pan, the person will be wealthy all year.

### MONTE CARLO INTERNATIONAL CIRCUS FESTIVAL
This grand event takes place the last week of January and/or the first week of February. The best circus acts from around the world compete for Gold and Silver Clown awards. Top internationally known artists vie for honors, and the whole week culminates in the spectacular "Winners Show." Don't miss it if you're in the area. The Monte-Carlo Grand Hotel does a circus tent restaurant, where you can see your favorite clowns and lion-tamers while

enjoying a delicious meal. Reservations required. The circus tent is located close to the Espace Fontvieille Circus tent. For tickets call Tel: 9205-2345, or Fax: 9205-2622. By mail Monte Carlo Festivals 5, av des Ligures MC 98000 Monaco

## PREMIERE RAMPE
International competition for Circus Schools held in the Espace Fontvieille. The competition is usually held in February after the Circus Festival but could also be held in November or Espace Fontvieille

### MONTE CARLO INTERNATIONAL TELEVISION FESTIVAL
A competition for the best fictional and current affairs programs judged by a panel of internationally recognized celebrities, directors and producers. This is partly a trade show where television execs show their wares. The market is not open to the public, but the Television Festival is. Located in the (C.C.A.M.) Convention Center under the Monte Carlo Grand Hotel. There are public viewing rooms set up for watching a wide range of programs from all over the world. For more information contact Festival de Television de Monte-Carlo 4, bd. du Jardin Exotique MC 98000 Monaco.
Tel: 9310-8438/68 Fax: 9310-8533 E-mail: info@tvfestival.com

### IMAGINA
An international meeting of television, film, computer graphics and special effects experts that was created in 1981. In 1999, the Innovation Village was added, along with the awarding of the Pixel-INA prize. This area showcases the most amazing digital productions, applications and prototypes selected from around the world. Set to move into the Forum Grimaldi. For more information contact Festival de Television de Monte-Carlo 4, bd. du Jardin Exotique MC 98000 Monaco. Tel: 9310-8438/68
Fax: 9310-8533
E-mail: info@tvfestival.com  Web site: www.imagina.fr

## MONTE CARLO PHILHARMONIC

## MONTE CARLO OPERA

## PRINCESSE GRACE THEATER

## PRIMO CUP SAILING REGATTA
Usually held in the first two weekends in February
Contact the Monaco Yacht Club at Tel: 9310-6300
Fax: 9350-8088 or E-mail: ycm@yacht-club-monaco.mc

# MARCH

## MARDI GRAS                               SHROVE TUESDAY
The last day before the start of Lent, traditionally celebrated by parades and fancy dress. People come from around the world to see the Carnival in Nice, which lasts for two weeks. (Note: this may begin in February).

## GOOD FRIDAY
Good Friday processions have been taking place in Monaco since the 1300s. Organized by the Brotherhood of the Black Penitents, Monaco's modern day procession winds through the Old Town with a statue of the dead Christ, horses, a band and Roman gladiators on foot and horseback.

## EASTER SUNDAY
Celebrated with church services, family meals, Easter egg hunts with decorated hard-boiled eggs and chocolate rabbits.

## MONTE CARLO PHILHARMONIC

## MONTE CARLO OPERA

## PRINCESSE GRACE THEATER

## MARCH 17                                ST. PATRICK'S DAY
History suggests that St. Patrick resided for a while in the monastery on the Ille des Lerins (Lerin Islands) off Cannes. In modern day Monaco, bars gear up for St. Patrick's Day and, of course, the Princess Grace Irish Library celebrates with a special activity each year.

## BAL DE LA ROSE
This is one of the major charity events in Monaco. Created in 1954, it benefits the Princess Grace Foundation. Each year H.R.H. The Princess of Hanover selects a new theme. But there are always ravishing bouquets of over 25,000 roses to decorate the Salle des Etoiles in the Sporting d'Eté complex. Top-name performers delight the audience, most of them dressed to the 'nines' in designer gowns. The public is welcome to join this prestigious event. For further information call SBM. Tel: 9216-3636.

## AUTOMOBILE SHOW
Espace Fontvieille

# APRIL

## APRIL 1                                 POISSON D'AVRIL
Instead of April Fool's Day, practical jokers here try to pin a paper fish onto the victim's back.

## MONTE CARLO INTERNATIONAL JUMPING
The Monte Carlo International Jumping competition has become a 'must' on the international horse show calendar. Taking place in

the Espace Fontvieille, the intimate distance between the audience and the competitors allows the public to become totally involved in the action of horse and rider. This event brings the best international riders as well as some glittering personalities to the Principality. For more information and tickets contact BCM on Tel: 9350-9560 Fax 9350-9561.

## PRO-CELEBRITY PENTATHLON

Brings together some of the best athletes to compete in 5 tough events with celebrities like Dolph Lungren, Angela Bassett and Harrison Ford for charity. The event consists of 10 meter air pistol shooting fencing, 200 meter relay swim, an equestrian obstacle course, and a 1500 meter relay run.

## INTERNATIONAL DOG SHOW

Held in the Espace Fontvieille during the last week of March or the first week of April.

## HOME INTERIOR DESIGN AND GARDEN EXHIBITION

Held in the Espace Fontvieille.

## TENNIS MASTERS SERIES MONTE CARLO

Represents the best in top men's tennis for the 21st century. The Tennis Masters Series – Monte Carlo replaces the former Monte Carlo Tennis Open. It is always held in the third week in April on clay courts of the Monte Carlo Country Club. This is one of the most beautiful clubs in the world perched high above the glittering Mediterranean Sea. In this intimate setting you can rub shoulders with some of the best players in tennis. Reserve a table for lunch on the terrace where you might find yourself sitting next to Michael Coulthard, Goldie Hawn, Kurt Russell, Sharon Stone and any number of other celebrities who happen to be in the vicinity. For tickets and group ticket information contact the Monte Carlo Country Club B.P. 342 98006 Monaco CEDEX or call 33 (0) 4 9341-7200. Fax Reservations to 33 (0) 4 9378-1204. For information phone 33 (0) 4 9341-3015 or visit the Web site: www.mcopen.org. E-mail inquiries to: info@mcopen.org.

Conveniently the ATP Tour (Professional Men's Tennis Circuit) European headquarters is located in Monte Carlo. During the fall of each year they hold an ATP Tour University for all the new and up and coming young players. The University's focus is on training the players in media and communication skills, tennis history, correct court behavior, tennis rules and financial management of their winnings. Just about any time during the year, when they are between tournaments, you can catch some top men's players at the tennis club. (Many of them live in Monaco). For more information about the ATP Tour their Web site: www.atptour.com or ATP Tour 74, bd. de Italie Tel: 9797-0404 Fax: 9797-0400

## SPRING ARTS FESTIVAL (PRINTEMPS DES ARTS)

Created in 1984 by H.R.H. The Princess of Hanover, this festival features young new talent in ballets, concerts, recitals and operas. The festival also shows art and film exhibitions. Check Bienvenue or the Tourist Office for a list of their activities that take place April through May, or call the Direction Affaires Culturelles Tel: 9315-8303

## MONACO YACHT CLUB TALL SHIPS

Some of the world's biggest tall ships visit the port of Monaco. At that time, it is usually possible to tour the boats. For more information contact. Yacht Club de Monaco Tel: 9310-6300

## MINI GRAND PRIX FOR RADIO CONTROLLED CARS

Port d' Hercule

# MAY

## MAY 1       FÊTE DU TRAVAIL

The Lily of the Valley or muguet, sold on most street corners, symbolizes Labor Day. The flowers are given to family and friends for good luck and happiness.

## MONACO INTERNATIONAL FLOWER SHOW

Held in the beginning of May behind the Opera on the terrace.

## MONTE CARLO WORLD MUSIC AWARDS

All the top international names in music convene at the Salle des Etoiles to receive awards at this big event. In the past, honorees have been Michael Jackson, Sting, UB40, Prince and Whitney Houston. For ticket information call S.B.M. Tel: 9216-3636

## MONACO HISTORIC GRAND PRIX

Run every few years, the Historic Grand Prix brings the glorious old classic racing cars back to Monaco. On the same circuit as the Grand Prix, these beautiful older cars compete with each other at high speeds. The first Grand Prix of this kind was inaugurated in 1997 in honor of the 700-year anniversary of the Grimaldi reign. It proved such a success that they have brought it back for the year 2000. In 1997 Bugattis were flying around the course, and old model Ferraris competed with each other in their class. Because no seat belts were used in antique car racing models, one driver was thrown out of his car on a tight turn. Luckily he was not injured. For more information and the exact date one week before the regular Grand Prix, contact the Monaco Automobile Club at Tel: 9315-2600 or Fax 9325-8008.

## MONACO FORMULA ONE GRAND PRIX

This is the third most important international sporting event after the Olympics and the Soccer World Cup. At this time, Monaco becomes a mecca for Formula I fans from the Four Corners of the world. Join in the fun watching the fastest cars race on the world's most beautiful street course. That's if you can take your eyes off the beautiful women and handsome drivers. During some years the Cannes Film Festival overlaps the Grand Prix and many celebrities come to Monaco to watch the race. It is held around Ascension Day weekend usually the last weekend in May.

The royal box marks the start and finish line on Boulevard Albert 1er along the port. The royal family watches the beginning and the finish from there but retreats to a private party in an apartment high above the race circuit. The noise is deafening as the race cars careen along the two and one-half mile course. First there is the straightaway up toward the Casino, past the Métropole following the chicane down past the Monte Carlo Grand Hotel, then another straightaway through the tunnel and port to another chicane at the Rascasse Restaurant. Thrilling!

The Monaco Automobile Club organizes the race each year. There are more than 30,000 seats available for sale on the circuit. To order tickets or receive information regarding ticket ordering contact the Automobile Club de Monaco, 23, blvd. Albert 1er, MC 98000 Monaco or Fax 9325-8008. They start sending out information in November. Tickets also are available from ticket booths set up during the race. Prices for tickets run anywhere from 300FF (46€) to more than 2100FF (323€) for really good seats. For latecomers and those on a budget, pack a picnic and buy space on the hillside lawns just below the Palace. Spots (secteur Rocher) go for about 200FF (30€) apiece and offer a panoramic Monte Carlo view, but bring your own blanket and picnic. Even if you have a seat in the stands, we suggest bringing a small pillow to cushion your backside.

Hotel rooms are hard to come by in Monaco during the Grand Prix. Most rooms are booked on a yearly basis, so either reserve as much as six months in advance or stay in Menton, Nice, or other nearby towns and take the train or bus in. There is boat service from the St. Jean Cap Ferrat port. Under no circumstances try to drive into Monaco during the four days of racing. Access is very restricted and parking is non-existent. Many residents rent out their terraces, but prepare to pay a minimum of 31,000FF (4769€) to 62,000FF (9538€) for the four days. A track side villa with six double bedrooms, terraces, a large garden and private parking can be rented for 5 days for 650,000FF (100,000€). If you have a large group or are a corporation this may be one of the most economical ways to go. People advertise in the International Herald Tribune, Nice Matin Monaco edition or on Riviera Radio's Community Chest.

Other alternatives: Sprint Communication, a Monaco-based company that offers a 4 day package aboard the Club Med II cruise ship that is moored in the harbor. Package includes transfer to and from Nice Airport via helicopter, accommodations, all food either on the terrace or on the boat. Cost: 25,935FF (3990€) per person. (For those with the budget, this may be one of the best bargains to see the Grand Prix in style.) Visit the Sprint web site at www.sprint.mc or phone Euan Postel at 9777-8191. Grand Prix Tours in the US, contact Cherry Cooper at Tel: 949-717-333, Fax 949-717-3344 Web site: www.gptours.com E-mail: Ccooper@gptours.com and mention Inside Monaco to either of these companies.

## OTHER IDEAS FOR GETTING A ROOM

The reason why there are so few hotel rooms available (and if there are any, there is usually a minimum stay of 5-6 nights required) is because they are pre-sold by the hotels to travel packagers. However, if the rooms are unsold, then they are returned to the hotel several weeks before the race. So you might want to put your name on a hotel waiting list with a credit card number guaranteeing the reservation. It pays to check around at various large hotels a week or two in advance. Sometimes they have cancellations and you might be the lucky one. Delta Vacations has packages offered in conjunction with the Monte Carlo Grand Hotel. Be sure to check out the Internet for other possible package deals.

Restaurants and hotels along the course offer special (expensive) lunch menus that include watching the race from their terraces. This is a way to get a seat for the race and eat a meal. Prices vary from 620FF (95€) to 3000FF (461€) on race day.

Don't be put off by price or discouraged by lack of accommodations. We haven't met anyone who didn't get a ticket or spot on the grass if they wanted one. There are lots of people selling tickets on the streets around the authorized ticket booths, but try the ticket booths first. Be sure to get a map of the circuit so you can see the spot where the seat is located. **The best seats are in Sections A1, A4, V, Z1, Z2, and O.** Prior to race day, the course is closed to normal traffic for practice sessions, qualifying and other races. Many events are free. Note: There is no entry charge to watch Friday's half day time trials. See you there and don't forget your earplugs.

## PRESTIGE CAR AUCTION

Often held during the day before the Grand Prix in the Espace Fontvieille. This auction offers luxurious and sought after collector cars to the public. For more information check with the Automobile Club.

## MOTHER'S DAY                                    FÊTE DES MERES
Last Sunday in May.

# JUNE

FÊTE DIEU                                    PENTECOST MONDAY
Celebrated since 1260, the Corpus Christi procession takes place
through the streets of the Old Town and culminates at the Palace.
The Bishop of Monaco gives his blessing.

## BAL DE L'ÉTÉ
This event brings together many of the young (25-40 year old)
from European royal and prestigious families to support the
Monegasque Sovereign Order of Malta and the World
Association of Children's Friends (A.M.A.D.E.). For more
information on the 2-day event contact: S.B.M. on Tel: 9216-
3636 or Princess Catherine Colonna de Stigliano by Fax 33 (0) 1
4640-1747.

## MONTE CARLO INTERNATIONAL
## SWIMMING MEET
Top international swimmers compete against one another at the
Centre Nautique in the Stade Louis II Fontvieille. The public is
welcome. The press and swimming coaches look for potential
champions at this first-rate event. For information call Tel: 9205-
4213.

## MIDSUMMER NIGHT'S FESTIVAL
Held in Monaco-Ville and Monte Carlo, it features folk groups,
children's activities, magicians, fire-eaters and local craftsmen.

## JUNE 21                                  FÊTE DE LA MUSIQUE
Various musicians play throughout Monaco and France.

## JUNE 23                                       FÊTE SAINT JOHN
The Palatine Chapel
in the palace is
dedicated to St. John
the Baptist, and
every year a local
group, La
Palladienne, dresses
in native costumes to
sing and dance
traditional songs and

dances in the Palace square. A salute to the Holy Sacrament is
sung in the presence of the Sovereign family and Monégasque
authorities followed by the lighting of a huge bonfire in the Place
du Palais. Everyone is invited to join in the circle dance around the
fire. Local color.

## JUNE 24          LA FÊTE DE LA MER

Celebrated by the Yacht Club of Monaco with regattas, parades and other activities to honor St. Nicolas, the patron saint of sailors.

## PRINCE RAINIER III MUSIC ACADEMY CONCERT

Held at the Centre de Congrès Auditiorium (C.C.A.M.) with the Monte Carlo Philharmonic Orchestra. For information contact the Academy or ticket office in the Casino atrium.

## PALACE GUARDS CONCERT SEASON BEGINS

Fanfare de la Compagnie des Carabiniers of Monaco.
For details check Bienvenue guide. Held throughout July and August.

## FATHER'S DAY          FÊTE DES PÈRES

Last Sunday in June

# JULY

## THE MONTE CARLO BALLET

The troupe, weather permitting, performs on the Casino terrace
For dance aficionados this is a magical evening under the stars.

## WORLD BACKGAMMON CHAMPIONSHIPS

Held at the Monte Carlo Grand Hotel

## MONTE CARLO INTERNATIONAL FIREWORKS FESTIVAL

This free event attracts thousands from the area to view some of the most beautiful, original and noisy fireworks around. The competition has been held since 1966 and brings pyrotechnic specialists from countries around the world to show off their talent. Fireworks begin around 9:30 PM or when it's dark. Good viewing from several locations: along the port sitting at a café, from the palace area or along the ramparts of Fort Antoine, and just off the Casino Terrace. Competition continues through the month of August and the winner returns November 18th to create the fireworks display on the evening before the National Fête Day.

## SHOWBOATS RENDEZVOUS AND BAL DE LA MER

The Rendezvous brings the largest private luxurious super yachts in the world to Monaco during the first weekend in July. The event is sponsored by the magazine Showboats International. A gala evening, the Bal de la Mer, raises money for the Oceanographic Museum's Coral Reef Foundation and other projects related to saving the sea. For event ticket information in Monaco call Tel: 9330-7832 or Showboats International in Ft. Lauderdale at 1-954-525-8626, E-mail: showboats @aol.com. Sorry, no private boat tours, but admiring them doesn't cost a dime. A Yacht parade is held off the Oceanographic Museum on the first Sunday morning in July and offers a wonderful photo opportunity.

## JULY 14                                  BASTILLE DAY
French Independence Day celebrated with parades, festivals, street dances and fireworks. Please note: This holiday is not celebrated in Monaco.

## CONCERTS AT FORT ANTOINE THEATER
Schedule in Bienvenue. Held during July and August. For information and tickets call Tel: 9315-8303. No advance bookings. Seats on sale at the reservation office of the Theatre 45 minutes before the start of each performance.

## CONCERTS IN THE COURTYARD OF THE PRINCE'S PALACE

The Monte Carlo Philharmonic Orchestra plays in the courtyard of the palace. You enter through the main gates and for a few dreamy hours you can conjure up images of life in a palace while listening to enchanting music. A definite must for your classical music agenda. Tickets are sold at the Casino atrium and at ticket booths just outside the palace one-hour before the concert. The concert starts at 9:30 PM July through mid-August.

# AUGUST

## THE MONÉGASQUE RED CROSS BALL

Held under the patronage of H.S.H. Prince Albert, at the Sporting d' Eté Club in the Salle des Etoiles the first weekend in August. This annual fund-raiser brings out scores of international celebrities for a good cause. Elegantly prepared meal, top-name entertainers such as Whitney Houston, Tina Turner, Liza Minnelli, and Stevie Wonder perform and a display of ballgowns that will knock your eyes out. For reservations and ticket information call S.B.M. Tel: 9216-3636

## HERCULIS INTERNATIONAL ATHLETICS MEETING
Major international track and field stars compete in this prestigious event. For ticket information contact Tel: 9205-4108 or purchase at Stade Louis II. Web site:www.fma.mc

## PALACE GUARD CONCERTS
See June

## CONCERTS FORT ANTOINE
See July

### PALACE COURTYARD CONCERTS
See July

### MONTE CARLO PHILHARMONIC ORCHESTRA CONCERTS
See July

### BI-ANNUAL ANTIQUE SHOW
Sporting d' Eté every other year.

### MONTE CARLO ANTIQUE FAIR
International Trade Fair for Antique Dealers
Espace Fontvieille

### MONTE CARLO BIG GAME FISHING TOURNAMENT
Here is where the fishing elite meet to try their skills against the
Mediterranean biggest game fish. For more information contact
the Monaco Yacht Club Tel: 9310-6300.

## SEPTEMBER

### INTERNATIONAL BOB-SLEIGH CONTEST
More than 27 countries from around the world compete against the
clock. Held on the port, entrance is free. Watch some of the best-
built men in between pushes that attract some beautiful woman!

### MONACO PRO-BEACH SOCCER AND VOLLEYBALL
These two events are additions to the social event calendar. The
Beach Volleyball tournament attracts the very best players and is
played in a specially built arena on the port.  Pro-Beach Soccer
follows the volleyball and brings together some of the sport's top
retired world soccer players such as Eric Cantona, Glen Hoddle
and former Brazilians players. The speed of play is fast and furious
due to the small playing field, which makes it a great spectator
sport. Entrance is free.

### MONACO YACHT SHOW
Looking for a big Yacht? Then the Monaco Yacht show is the
place to view the best Monte Carlo has to offer for sale. This show
will celebrate its 10th anniversary and has almost outgrown the
port with 65- 20 meter (60 ft plus boats) and 150 exhibitors. For
more information contact Luc Pettavino on Tel: 9310-4170
Fax: 9310-4171. Web Site: www.monacoyachtshow.org

### PIANO MASTERS COMPETITION
Held in the Salle Garnier, for tickets Casino atrium.

### MONTE CARLO PHILHARMONIC ORCHESTRA CONCERTS

### PRINCESS GRACE THEATER
Held in C.C.A.M.

## MONTE CARLO INTERNATIONAL CAT SHOW
Held in the Espace Fontvieille.

## MONTE CARLO CLASSIC CAR RALLYE

The best antique cars compete for the winner's cup. For information contact the Monaco Automobile Club. Tel: 9315-2600.

## PRO-CELEBRITY GOLF TOURNAMENT
Held at the breathtaking Mont Agel golf course, this event attracts the best senior European golfers as well as celebrities. The public is welcome to watch. For more information contact the Monte Carlo Golf Club at Tel: 33 (0) 4 9341-0911 or S.B.M. for gala reservations held in the Salle des Etoiles Tel: 9216-3636.

## MONACO CLASSIC WEEK (BI-ANNUAL)
Organized since 1994 by the Monaco Yacht Club in association with the Prada Trophy, this event brings vintage powerboats, antique motor-yachts and traditional sailing yachts from all over the globe to Port Hercule. Regattas, nautical trials, like challenges and elegance competitions are just some of the planned activities. There are also yacht parades with period costumes and exhibitions by craftsmen all week long, culminating with a Gala evening. For more information contact Monaco Yacht Club on Tel: 9310-6300 or E-mail: ycm@yacht-club-monaco.mc.

## MONTE CARLO SQUASH CLASSIC
Stadium Louis II For more information Monaco Tourist Office.

# OCTOBER

## MONACO HERITAGE DAY OPEN HOUSE DAY
Usually held the first Sunday in October. All the museums, except the Oceanographic, are open free for the day. Also the Casino, the Salle Garnier, Villa Miraflores (the headquarters of the International Amateur Athletic Association), the International Atomic Energy Marine Lab, the Bibilotheque (Library) Louis Notari, the National Conseil, Academie of Monégasque Language, the Ateliers d' Artistes and the Palais du Justice (Court House). Each gives tours or lectures. It's a wonderful opportunity to see Monaco if you are in town. The conferences and tours are in French.

## MONTE CARLO PHILHARMONIC ORCHESTRA CONCERTS

## THEATER PRINCESS GRACE

## MONACO KART CUP
Go-Karts invade Monaco's Port Hercule. Join the spectators around the track and watch future Forumla 1 drivers hone their skills.

## MONTE CARLO MAGIC STARS

An international magic show with magicians from everywhere competing for the Gold and Silver Wand. Held in the Princesse Grace Theater. For more information call Tel: 9350-0345.

## CHILDREN'S' EXHIBITION

Children's exhibition held in the Espace Fontvieille. Features many children's play activities, special shows and clowns.

## MONTE CARLO INTERNATIONAL FAIR

An international trade, industry and services fair held in the Espace Fontvieille. This Fair shows off many interesting companies doing business in Monaco. Highlighting a different foreign country each year, it has over 150 exhibitors offering wine, champagne and foie gras tasting, Italian specialties, lacquer boxes from Russia and interesting new products every year. Admission is free during the weekdays.

## MONACO WORLD CUP TRIATHLON

For information contact the Tourist Office Tel: 9216-6166.

## ENVIRONMENT DAY                              OCTOBER 16

Special events and activities. Check Bienvenue for details.

## BAROQUE MUSIC FESTIVAL

Monaco spotlights some of the excellent musicians of the Baroque. Concerts are held in an appropriate setting, the Chapelle de la Visitation in Monaco-Ville. Tickets in Casino Atrium or at the door before the concert. Concerts start at 9:00 PM.

## MONTE CARLO CUP FOR M CLASS AND 12MJ1 RADIO CONTROLLED YACHTS

Held in Port Hercule

# NOVEMBER

## SPORTEL

This international event brings together sports personalities and sports television production companies from over 60 countries, and more than 1200 sports television buyers for 3 days of exposure to the latest in sports television programming. This growing convention is set to move to the Grimaldi Forum. For more information Tel: 9330-2032 Fax: 9330-2033.

## MONTE CARLO PHILHARMONIC ORCHESTRA CONCERTS

## THEATER PRINCESS GRACE

## MONTE CARLO INTERNATIONAL BRIDGE TOURNAMENT
Monte Carlo Sporting Club. For information call S.B.M. Tel: 9216-3636.

## NOVEMBER 19                                   NATIONAL FÊTE DAY

A wonderful time to be in Monaco to see red and white flags flying to celebrate the Prince's Saint Day. Activities include spectacular fireworks over the port the night before and a mass in the Cathedral the next morning. This is an opportunity to see the pomp and circumstance of the Principality. The Knights of Malta, distinguished ambassadors, consuls and state officials are decked out in medal-laden uniforms as they congregate in the Place St. Nicolas after the mass. Follow the pageantry to the Place du Palais. At 11:30 AM you will see the royal family wave to the onlookers from the windows of the palace and then present loyal and deserving subjects with such honors, as the Order of St. Charles medal. A grand national holiday.

## MONTE CARLO GASTRONMIE
An exhibition for fine dinning and tableware held in the Espace Fontvieille.

## NOUVEAU BEAUJOLAIS DAY
Around November 18th, restaurants feature menus to complement the young nouveau beaujolais wine.

## EUROPEAN J24 SAILING CHAMPIONSHIPS
Contact the Yacht Club of Monaco Tel: 9310-6310

## INTERNATIONAL MEN'S AND WOMEN'S FENCING CHAMPIONSHIPS
Held in the Salle Omnisports Stade Louis II.

# DECEMBER

## INTERNATIONAL STAMP COLLECTING EXHIBITION
Held in the Salon du Canton and the Museum of Stamps and Coins
A top the Fontvieille Commercial Center

## MONTE CARLO PHILHARMONIC ORCHESTRA CONCERTS

## THEATER PRINCESS GRACE

### MONTE CARLO BALLET
Performances during Christmas

### MONACO DANCE FORUM
Grimaldi Forum
Ballets, exhibitions and the Monaco
World Dance Awards.

### DECEMBER 25

**NOËL**

The Christmas Eve dinner, or Réveillon de Noël, is a very important occasion in Monaco. It is a sumptuous meal that may include oysters, lobster, foie gras, turkey with chestnut stuffing and bûche de Noël (yule log cake). As for New Year's Eve, restaurants feature specially priced menus for the meal. Children place wooden shoes or sabots near the fireplace or tree to be filled by Santa. See church services posted in Nice Matin-Monaco.

### MONTE CARLO INTERNATIONAL ANTIQUES FAIR
Grimaldi Forum.

---

## NOTES

# TICKET INFORMATION

| | |
|---|---|
| **Monte Carlo Ballet, Opera and Concerts** | 9216-2299 |

**Monte Carlo Spring Arts Festival**
(Printemps des Arts de Monte Carlo)
*Atrium du Casino Box Office*
Open daily except Monday from 10 AM to 5:30 PM

| | |
|---|---|
| **Princesse Grace Theater** | 9325-3227 |

*12, av. d'Ostende, MC 98000 Monaco*
Open daily except Sunday 10 AM to 12:30 PM and 3 PM to 6:30 PM

**ARTISTIC EVENINGS (SOIRÉES ARTISTIQUES)**

| | |
|---|---|
| **Fort Antoine** | 9315-8303 |

*Direction des Affaires Culturelles*
*4, bd. des Moulins, MC 98000 Monaco*
No advanced seats, ticket sales begin 45 minutes before the concert.

| | |
|---|---|
| **Monte Carlo International Circus Festival** | 9205-2345 |

*5, av. des Ligures, MC 98000 Monaco*

| | |
|---|---|
| **Galas (Black Tie Balls)** | 9216-2000 |
| **S.B.M. Société des Bains de Mer,** *Place du Casino* | 9216-3636 |

# NOTES

# 7
# LES SPORTS

The world of sports and Monaco have been closely linked since 1886 when François Blanc, founder of Société des Bains de Mer (S.B.M.), introduced lawn tennis to Monte Carlo. The year 1910 saw the opening of the Mont Agel golf course, the first air race was held in 1914 and the first Grand Prix rumbled through the streets of Monaco in 1929. Famous boxing matches, international track meets, gymnastics competitions, swimming meets and the Dream Team is all part of spectator sports in Monaco. Prince Albert, an enthusiastic athlete, is a member of the International Olympic Committee. His Monaco Bob-Sleigh team has competed in the last four winter Olympics. Little wonder that the Principality provides a wide selection of sports activities for its guests.

## BOULES OR BOWLES
A great family game that everyone can learn to play. It is the European take on horse shoes pitching, but with lots of nuance. This game is played throughout the region and competition is cut-throat among the professionals.

**Club Bouliste de Monaco**     9205-6247
*1, rue de l'Industrie*
Located in Fontvieille near the Stade Louis II.
**Club Bouliste du Rocher**     9330-4273
*Av. des Pins*

## CYCLING AND MOPEDS
**Auto-Moto Garage**     9330-2461
*7, rue de la Colle*
Bicycle and moped rental. Open Monday through Friday 8:30 to 12:30 PM and 2:00 to 7:00 PM, Saturdays 9:00 to 12:00 .
**Avis**     9330-1753
*9, av. d'Ostende*
Also rents motor scooters

## MOUNTAIN BIKING
Like other places in the world, the mountain biking craze has caught on in Monaco. There are even several competitions. Mountain bikes of velo tout terrain (VTT) and protective gear can be rented. If you are interested in buying one, prices are favorable.

## FISHING
See Boat Rentals Transportation section.

## GOLF

**Monte Carlo Golf Club**                    33 (0) 4 9241-5070

One of the most spectacular mountaintop-view golf courses in the world. Located on Mont Agel straight up past La Turbie. This is an 18-hole par 71 course. The bar and restaurant are open to the public, but are closed on Mondays from October to June. Course and practice green open all year. Holders of the SBM 'Carte d'Or' receive a 50% reduction on green fees.

**Golf School**                             33 (0) 4 9378-2045

Contact the Monte Carlo Country Club, St. Roman. Open every day except Sundays and public holidays from November to May.

**Miniature Golf**                                9330-6387

*Parc Princesse Antoinette, 54 bis, bd. du Jardin Exotique.*

Open all year except September. Hours July and August from 2:00 PM to midnight except Mondays. October to June from 10:00 AM to noon and from 2:00 PM until 6:00 PM on Wednesday, Saturday, Sunday, public holidays and school holidays.

## HANG GLIDING AND PARAPENT

Take-off is in the Mont Agel area and landings are on Roquebrune Beach. For more information call:

**Monaco Voltige**                                9330-5919
**Roquebrune'Aile**                         33 (0) 4 9335-0068
*14, av. Louis Laurens*              *Fax: 33 (0) 4 9328-8850*
*06190 Roquebrune-Cap-Matin*

Web site: www.imaginet.fr E:mail:westmins.@imaginet.fr

This is a paragliding school open between Sept.-June 30. Min. age 18.

**ABC d'Air Para Gliding School**           33 (0) 4 9304-0515
*1, av. Jean Medecin*                 *Fax: 33 (0) 9208-4672*
*06380 Sospel*

Open all year round, depending on weather and air conditions. Min. age 14. Web site: www.parapente@ infonie.fr

## HIKING

The hinterland behind the coast, the national parks of the Mercantour and the mountains offer superb opportunities for hikers. All the main footpaths in France form part of the national network of long-distance footpaths, sentiers de grandes randonnées (GR). The major footpath in our region is the GR5, which goes from Nice all the way to Amsterdam. The GR1 runs from Theoule to Castellar, overlooking the coast; the GR52 from Menton to the Vallée des Merveilles, and the GR4 to the Gorges du Verdun.

Footpaths of Europe, a series of books published in English by Robertson-McCarta, are based on French guides. They also furnish maps and information about accommodations along the way. A list of state-qualified guides working in the area is available from Association des Guides et Accompagnateurs des la Haute-Vestubie c/o Otto Bruc Sports, rue Cagnoli, 06459 St. Martin-Vesubie, France Tel: 33 (0) 4 9303-2660 Fax: 33 (0) 4 9303-4918 or Syndicate National des Accompagnateurs du Val des Merveilles B.P. 12, 06430 Tende, France Tel: 33 (0) 4 9304-7773. Open from June to September. Also refer to Rafting and Canyoning for more companies that organize trips.

## AROUND MONACO, TRY THESE ROUTES:
**From Monte Carlo Beach to Cap Martin,** via a very picturesque path along the coastline. Round trip: 3 hours. Jogging is possible.

**From Monte Carlo Beach to the Port of Monaco**, along the coast via the square overlooking Larvotto Beach, the Portier embankment and Boulevard Louis II. Length: Approximately 40 minutes. Jogging is possible.

**The Casino Terraces and the Spélugues property center**, which connects the Princess Grace Theatre in the west with the Monte Carlo Grand Hotel in the East.

**From Fontvieille to Cap d'Ail (Mala Beach),** via a path which starts along the edge of the sea. Round trip: 3 hours. Jogging is possible.

**The Saint-Martin Garden,** in Monaco-Ville, with peaceful and shady pathways among the Mediterranean flora. Walk.

**The Princess Antoinette Garden,** with 100-year-old olive groves. Entrance in Boulevard de Belgique or Boulevard du Jardin Exotique. Walk.

**The scenic Parc Fontvieille** where you will find a vast range of green plants and shrubs from all over the world. The Princess Grace Rose Garden with over 4,000 rose plants is here.

## HORSEBACK RIDING
**Denis Longfellow**                         **Tel-Fax 33 (0) 4 9303-3023**
*4950, rte. De l'Armee des Alpes, 06500  St. Agnes*
St. Agnes open from Sept. 15-June 15, Boreon open June 15-Sept. 15 Trail riding excursions by appointment. 4 pers. min-8 max.
**Cercle Hippique St. Georges**              **33 (0) 4 9320-9964**
*2359, rte. De Grasse*                 *Fax: 33 (0) 4 9322-4227*
*06270 Villeneuve-Loubet*
Open all year round 8A.M.-8 P.M. Closed Thursday, 5 arena's, 2000 meters of sandy trails, 4 cross-country trails, 250 horse stalls, and tack shop.

## HUNTING
Departmental Fédération of Hunters, Alpes Maritimes,
*46, rue Pégurier, Nice*                    33 (0) 4 9383-8239
## JET SKIING
Plage Larvotto                                      9350-8645
Monte Carlo Beach Hotel                33 (0) 4 9348-6666

## JUDO
Judo Club of Monaco                            9205-4074
*Stade Louis II*
Adults Tuesday and Friday, from 7:30 PM to 9:00 PM.
Children Monday to Friday, from 5:00 PM. to 7:15 PM.

## KARATE
Karate Club-Shotokan                           9330-4774
*Ecole des Révoires Gym, 63, bd. du Jardin Exotique*
Open Monday through Friday from 7:30 PM to 9:30 PM.

## PARA SAILING KITING
Monte Carlo Beach Hotel                33 (0) 4 9328-6666
*Av. Princesse Grace*

## PARCOURS
Parcours Sante (Health and Fitness Course)
*Bd. du Jardin Exotique*
A 1.1-mile (2.5km) route through the heart of an ancient olive
grove, with a succession of gymnastics points with the necessary
sport equipment. Open daily. Free.

## RAFTING AND CANYONING
Rafting outfitters offer courses and trips for a day or longer. Many
of the rafting outfitters also offer canyoning, a combination of
rock climbing, diving and caving. Participants find themselves
sailing down waterfalls one minute and swimming in mountain
pools the next. Normally done in-groups with experienced guides.
Here is a list of companies that offer multi-sports services:
**Acro Adventure,** *88 Corniche Fleurie, 06200 Nice* Tel: 33 (0) 4
9383-3733 *Fax: 33 (0) 4 9372-3302,* **Loca Adventure** *in Nice* at
Tel: 33 (0) 4 9356-1467 *Fax at 33 (0) 4 9356-7572.* **Association
Lou Pais** in *Seranon* Tel: 33 (0) 4 9360-3451 *Fax: 33 (0) 4 9360-3445,*
**Deambule** in *Sospel* Tel-Fax: 33 (0) 4 9304-2075
E-mail: deambule@infonie.fr, **Destination Nature** in *Cagnes-sur-
Mer* Tel-Fax: 33 (0) 9213-2402 www.aaacom.com/pdg, **Escapade**
(Mercantor Guides) in Menton Tel-Fax: 33 (0) 4 9357-5271.

## ROCK CLIMBING

Try route de La Turbie underneath the Tête de Chien. See also canyoning, above.

## ROLLER SKATING, ROLLER BLADING, INLINE SKATING AND SKATE BOARDING

Permitted only on the boardwalk area of Larvotto Beach and the Port. Not allowed on sidewalks or streets as a means of transportation.

## RUNNING

A new cushioned running pavement has been put down alongside boulevard du Larvotto, which runs parallel to avenue Princesse Grace and the beach. This is an easy-to-find circuit from most of the hotels around the Casino area. See also Hiking.

## SAILING

**Yacht Club of Monaco**                                    9310-6300
*16, quai Antoine 1er*
**Sailing School**                                              9350-5839
*Ecole de Voile Juniors*
Sailing classes for adolescents and adults. See Les Basics A-Z, Yacht Club.

## SKIING AND WINTER SPORTS

A little known fact to most visitors is the close availability of skiing in the winter months, from late December through March. Just an hour-and-a-half away, beautiful local ski resorts offer a full day of skiing close enough for you to return to Monaco for the night.

**Isola 2000** at 8,700 feet (2651m) with 75 miles (120km) of alpine trail-7 green, 18 blue, 16 red, and 5 black; 25 lifts and a 10-mile (16km) nordic track. Information on 33 (0) 4 9323-1515 Fax: 33 (0) 4 9323-1425  Web Site: www.skifrance.fr/~isola2000

**Auron** at 7,300 feet (2395m)) has 80 miles (128km) of trails, 26 lifts serving 36 slopes: 4 green, 13 blue, 16 red, and 11 black, and 10 off trail runs. For more information: 33 (0) 4 9323-0002 Fax: 33 (0) 4 9323-0509

**Valberg** at 6,300 feet (1920m) is linked to Beuil and has more than 50 miles (80km) of nordic skiing, 55 miles (88km) of alpine skiing with 27 ski lifts 58 slopes 11 green, 13 blue, 22 red and 11 black trails. For information: 33 (0) 4 9323-2425 Fax: 33 (0) 4 9302-5227 Central reservations: 33 (0) 4 9323-2432

## SNOW TIRE RENTAL

Snow tires and chains are mandatory during snowstorms. You can obtain them from:

**AGIP Gas Station du Portier**                    9315-9021
*4, av. Princesse Grace*
Open until 9:00 PM.

## SNOWSHOE WALKING

For a more sedate form of winter sport that requires no particular training or skill, try walking on snowshoes. This sport has become increasingly popular and there are various groups who arrange tours: **Montagne et Ski**, 05330 Serre-Chevalier Tel: 33 (0) 4 9224-4575. **A.E.T. Nature** in Breil-Sur-Roya Tel-Fax: 33 (0) 4 9304-4764 contact Michel Rostagni open year round business hours. Roya Evasion in Breil-Sur-Roya Tel-Fax 33 (0) 4 9304-9146 open year round business hours (Also see Escapade, Deambule, and Destination Nature in Canyoning section).

## DOG-SLED DRIVING

Looking for some adventure, something you have never tried? How about dog sledding? Now recognized as a competitive sport, the Hautes Alpes hosts an annual international competition in Valberg. If you want to try your hand, contact the following for instruction or excursions: **Apaq**, 05460, Abries 33 (0) 4 9246-7407 or **L'Etape de Seqineq**, 05310 Fressiniers 33 (0) 4 9220-9391.

## SKIING (WATER)

**Larvotto Plage (Beach)**                          9350-8645
July and August.
*Monte-Carlo Beach Hotel*                   33 (0) 4 9328-6666

## SKIN DIVING

**Monégasque Sub-Aqua**                              9777-8017
**Club d'Exploration Sous-Marine**                   9205-9178
Diving is permitted, with air cylinders, along the shore. No skin diving in the harbor or the Monaco underwater reserve. *See map.*

## SNOOKER OR BILLIARDS

**Hip Hop Café**                                     9205-2860
16 quai Jean-Charles Rey
Open 8:00 AM until 3:00 AM.

## SNORKELING

Permitted along shore and in Monaco's underwater reserve; it is against the law to harpoon, net fish, or remove specimens or samples from the protected marine environment.

# SQUASH

Monte Carlo  Squash Racket Club                9205-4222
Four courts, open all year.
Monte Carlo Country Club            .         33 (0) 4 9341-3015
Two courts, open all year.

# SWIMMING

Public Outdoor Pool
Stade Nautique Rainier III`                    9330-6483
Located in the middle of the port. An Olympic-size heated seawater pool is open from May to October 9:00 AM to 8:00 PM. A
very popular pool, with snack bar; a good place to do laps and
people watch.

# PUBLIC INDOOR POOLS

*Centre Nautique*
Stade Louis II, Fontvieille                    9205-4213
Top-of-the-line Olympic-size freshwater heated pool. Especially
good for serious swimmers. Open Monday, Tuesday, Thursday and
Friday from 7:30 AM. to 2:30 PM, Saturday from 2:00 AM to
6:00 PM, Sunday from 9:00 AM to 1:00 PM. Closed every
Wednesday September to July, and closed during August.
The Saint Charles Swimming Pool                9216-0422
*7, av. St. Charles*
Heated freshwater pool. Lap swimming and all kinds of lessons,
including aquagym and pre-and post-natal swimming classes.
Open Mondays 4:00 PM to 6:00 PM, Tuesday and Thursday
10:00 AM to 3:00 PM. Wednesday from 9:00 AM to 12:30 PM
and 1:00 to 8:00 PM, Friday 9:00 AM to 12:30 and 1:30 to 7:00
PM, Saturday 8:00 AM to 3:00 PM. Closed in August and from
December 23 to January 2nd.

# PUBLIC BEACHES

PLAGE DU LARVOTTO
9330-6384
Located along avenue Princesse Grace, this is a great place to
check out the bikinis and thongs, and soak up the rays at one of
the many beach restaurant clubs with curbside service. Pick-up volleyball games played on the eastern end of the beach. The private
beach clubs charge, choice of half or full day, for sun mattresses and
parasols. In public areas, you can bring your own beach mat.

THE JETTY'S
Large rocks form a sea wall at the south end of the port on both
sides. You get there via the Calypso and Yacht Club. "Sun lizards"
arrive early to choose their favorite flat rock.

## PLAGE DES PÊCHEURS

Just behind the Parking des Pêcheurs. Residents of the 'Le Rocher' may think of it as their private beach, but it is open to the public. It is a small rock beach with a steep drop-off into the azure waters. Be sure to bring your own mat and refreshments, as there is no curbside service.

There are wonderful pools in the many fine hotels throughout Monaco open to the public for a fee. You might check the following places:

## PRIVATE BEACHES

**Monte Carlo Beach Hotel**        33 (0) 4 9328-6666
*End of avenue Princesse Grace*
The 'crème de la crème' in bathing spots, especially if you're looking for romance, action or privacy. The place has atmosphere but with environmental soundness. Where else can you find an Olympic outdoor heated seawater pool with 'ozone' filtering! For privacy, rent one of the exclusive bathing bungalows as the Royal family and visiting celebrities do. Bungalows have access to a private beach. Three restaurants. Open from April to October. Free admission to S.B.M. guests or holders of the Carte d'Or.

**Le Meridien Beach Plaza Sea Club**      9330-9880
*22, av. Princesse Grace*
The only hotel in Monaco with its own private beach. There are two open-air seawater swimming pools, one heated. Open May to September. Children love feeding the huge fish that swim up for breadcrumbs.

## SPA

**Les Thermes Marins Spa**       9216-4040
*2, av. d' Ostende*
A luxurious center of thalassotherapy. This treatment is the use of seawater, seaweed and mud under medical supervision to prevent or alleviate various ailments. Programs have been specially designed to treat stress, tobacco withdrawal, weight-loss, sports rehabilitation, lower back pain, circulatory problems and menopause. The spa also offers cardio-vascular strengthening and a program for new mothers. If you have no physical problems, just lie back and enjoy the beauty treatments, massage or workouts in the gym. The spa, directly accessible from the Hotel de Paris or the Hermitage Hotel, has a large recreational swimming pool, a special diet restaurant and a traditional restaurant. It is open to the public on a daily basis, or on a weekly basis with hotel packages.

## SURFING

Believe it or not, during the winter months storms kick up three to four foot waves along the beach next to the port of Cap d'Ail. So, hang loose and hang five!

# TENNIS

**Monte Carlo Country Club**          33 (0) 4 9341-3015

This is home to the Tennis Masters Series Monte Carlo played the third week in April each year. Put this club on your list of must-play. You can mingle with the likes of Pete Sampras, and Andre Agassi and other celebrities. This is one of the most beautiful tennis clubs in the world with 19 clay courts, 5 lighted, 4 plexipave courts and 1 clay-covered court perched high over the blue Mediterranean. The clubhouse, bar and restaurant are open to the public year round. The club is owned by S.B.M. so guests with the SBM *'Carte d'Or'* receive 50% off entrance fee.

Web site: www.mcopen.org  E-mail: info@mcopen.org.

**Tennis Club of Monaco**          9330-0102

*27-29, bd. de Belgique*

Five lighted clay courts and eight plexipave courts. Clubhouse, bar, open year round from 8:00 AM to 8:00 PM.

# TARGET SHOOTING

**Ranier III Shooting Range**          9205-3030

*5, rue Gabian*

Located in Fontvieille. Open year round

# WIND SURFING

**Monte Carlo Beach Hotel**          33 (0) 4 9328-6666

*Avenue Princesse Grace.*

Open April to October

**Le Meridien Beach Plaza Hotel**          9330-9880

*22, av. Princesse Grace.*

Open May to September

# WORKOUTS AT THE GYM

## LA CONDAMINE

**Centre d'Esthétique Corporelle**          9330-2335

*Located next to the Olympic pool* in the port, this gym offers aerobic and gymnastic classes, free weights and weight training equipment but not for the serious pumper. UVA tanning. Open Monday to Friday 8:45 AM to 8:30 PM, Saturday form 10:30 AM to 1:00 PM.

## LARVOTTO

**Columbia Tonus Center**          9325-0327

*Located at 7, avenue Princesse Grace in the Columbia Palace.*

The gym offers a variety of impact and low-impact aerobic classes, free weights and workout equipment, sauna, UVA tanning, beauty treatments and thalassotherapy. Open Monday to Friday 9:00 AM to 9:00 PM, and Saturday from 9:00 AM to 2:00 PM. Closed Sundays.

## FONTVIEILLE
**Stade Louis II**                                              **9205-4213**
The best Monaco has to offer in the way of weight training equipment and free weights. Various exercise classes. Open to the public.

## MONTE CARLO
**Monte Carlo Grand Health Spa**                               **9350-6500**
Exercise classes, workout equipment, free weights, and Stairmaster. They have upgraded their workout equipment. Hours 8:00 AM to 10:00 PM, open to members and hotel guests.

**Monte Carlo Gym**                                            **9325-8558**
*Located in the Le Montaigne Building, 6, boulevard des Moulins*
Exercise classes, low-impact aerobics, cardio funk, weight training, and UVA tanning. Hours Monday through Friday 9:00 AM to 8:30 PM, Saturday 9:30 AM to 12:30 PM and 4:00 PM to 6:00 PM. Closed on Sundays.

**Baby Boom 2000**                                             **0686925986**
Anette Shine Galantino organizes gym classes for new mothers and their baby's.

# YOGA

**Valerie Medecin**                                            **9350-7743**
*16 bis, rue Bel Respiro*
By appointment

# 8
# SHOPPING

From haute couture to souvenirs, there's something for everyone who is shopping in Monaco. The best way to use this section is to determine what you're looking for, whether it's gifts, clothes, jewelry, antiques or groceries. Shopping areas are broken down by location, then by shops. No doubt about it, you can drop a bundle in many of the high fashion designer boutiques or fine jewelry stores in Monaco. But let's dispel the myth that only millionaires can shop here. The fact is there are stores carrying a large array of items at moderate and reasonable prices. There is even a women's and men's European designer clothes discount boutique. Take time to window shop or stock up on T-shirts, souvenirs or world-famous Monaco stamps. For information regarding exchange rates and Euros. (see Les Basics)

## SHOPPING HOURS

Shops are open from 9:00 AM (10 for boutiques) to noon, and from 3:00 PM to 6:00- 7:30 PM except Sundays and bank holidays. However, some shops are closed Saturday afternoon or Monday morning. Smaller shops have a two- to four-week annual closing called *fermeture annuelle* between November and March. Call ahead to make sure they are open if it's a special trip. Just prior to Christmas most shops have extended hours and are open on Sundays.

## RETURN AND EXCHANGE POLICIES

Buyer Beware! Make sure that the item you purchase fits properly and is exactly what you want because in most small boutiques and shops there are no cash or credit-card refunds. You will receive a store credit. Be sure to bring the credit slip with you when you want to redeem the credit since some stores do not keep accurate records and will not acknowledge the credit without the store receipt. Some larger stores like Carrefour will give cash refunds with proof of purchase. This is true for France as well.

## SALES (SOLDES)

January and July are the two big sales months, when merchandise is reduced as much as 50 to 60 percent. Sale items and your VAT refund mean big savings for travelers. If you see something that you like, buy it. Don't hesitate since most shops have limited inventories and things are rarely restocked.

## CLOTHING SIZES

MEN: Suits To change American suit sizes to French suit sizes, add 10 to the American suit size. To change French suit sizes to American suit sizes, subtract 10 from the French suit size.

**Shirts:** To change American shirt sizes to French shirt sizes, multiply the American shirt size by 2 and add 8. To change French shirt sizes to American shirt sizes, subtract 8 from the French shirt size and divide by 2.

**WOMEN: Dresses and Coats:** To change U.S. dress/coat sizes to French dress/coat sizes, add 28 to the U.S. dress/coat size. To change French dress/coat sizes to U.S. dress/coat sizes, subtract 28 from the French dress/coat size.

**Blouses and Sweaters:** To change U.S. blouse/sweater sizes to French blouse/sweater sizes, add 8 to the U.S. blouse/sweater size. To change French blouse/sweater sizes to U.S. blouse/sweater sizes, subtract 8 from the French blouse/sweater size.

**Shoes:** To change U.S. shoe sizes to French shoe sizes, add 32 to the U.S. shoe size. To change French shoe sizes to U.S. shoe sizes, subtract 32 from the French shoe size.

## SHOPPING AREAS

The main shopping areas are:

**MONTE CARLO** Along *boulevard des Moulins* (keep walking east on the same street as the Tourist Bureau), the *Métropole Galerie* (avenue de la Madone, east side of park, in front of Casino), *Park Palace Galerie* (avenue de la Costa, on west side, top of park, in front of Casino), *avenue des Beaux Arts* (between the Hotel de Paris and the Sporting d'Hiver) and behind the Hotel de Paris is the *avenue de Monte Carlo*.

**LA CONDAMINE** Rue Grimaldi and rue Princesse Caroline. Here you will find stores for teens, children, young adults and reasonable prices.

**MONACO-VILLE** The quaint streets of the Old Town is the best place to find all those great Monaco T-shirts and tourist souvenirs. If you missed the Grand Prix, you might find one of the official T-shirts here.

**FONTVIEILLE** "See you at the mall". Here you'll find Ronald McDonald, excellent men's and women's clothing chains at affordable prices, and of course the Carrefour Hypermarket, with the cheapest prices in town.

## SHOPPING IN ITALY

(See Day Trips section)

## ANTIQUES

Antiques or antiquaire indicates high-quality stock with appropriate prices. You should be able to get a certificate guaranteeing authenticity from such shops. *Brocante*, on the other hand, can be anything from good antique furniture to *"bric-à-brac"* or junk.

*Depôt-vente* is the term used for consignment stock. Christie's and Sotheby's hold sales in October, December, April, and June, and offer paintings, furniture, and jewelry. All dealers "expect" to reduce their prices by 15 to 20 percent, especially if you pay cash, *argent liquide*, and many will make deliveries.

(See Day Trips for list of Brocante markets)

## MONTE CARLO

| | |
|---|---|
| Sotheby's | 9330-8880 |
| *Sporting d'Hiver* | |
| Fersen | 9350-9177 |
| *Sporting d'Hiver* | |
| Czarina | 9216-1989 |
| *Sporting d'Hiver* | |
| Christie's | 9797-1100 |
| *Park Palace Galerie* | |
| *5 bis, av. Saint Michel* | |
| Monte Carlo Star Decors | 9770-8540 |
| *Park Palace Galerie* | |
| *27, av. de la Costa* | |
| Art Conseil | 9770-8336 |
| *3, av. St. Michel* | |
| Templier | 9325-0043 |
| *3, av. St. Michel* | |
| Monaco Art and Auction | 9350-0080 |
| *5, av. St Michel* | |
| Battifoglio Galerie | 9330-8885 |
| *6, av. St. Michel* | |
| Antiquitiés-Curiosités | 9350-2050 |
| *11, av. St. Michel* | |
| Adriano Ribolzi | 9330-2717 |
| *Palais de la Scala* | |
| *1, av. Henry Dunant* | |
| Fredric Bravard | 9350-3659 |
| *15, av. Princesse Charlotte* | |
| Galerie d'Art Ancien et Moderne | 9330-7622 |
| *21, bd. Princesse Charlotte* | |
| Galerie St. Germain | 9350-9466 |
| *Metropole Galerie* | |
| SAPJO | 9350-5434 |
| *16, bd. des Moulins* | |
| Monte Carlo Antiquities | 9330-8261 |
| *27, bd. des Moulins* | |
| Galerie 41 | 9330-8128 |
| *41, bd.des Moulins* | |

## LARVOTTO

| | |
|---|---|
| Gismondi J. Pastor | 9325-2714 |
| *11, av. Princesse Grace* | |

Rabel          9350-9306
*21, av. Princesse Grace*

## LA CONDAMINE
Gaggino          9330-4626
*41, rue Grimaldi*
Carpe Diem          9770-7343
*16, rue de Millo*
Antiquities Bourgoin          9330-5442
*17, rue de Millo*
Monaco Art          9770-8950
*5, rue Baron St. Suzanne*

## FONTVIEILLE
Le Verandah          9205-2401
*31, quai Jean-Charles Rey*

## JARDIN EXOTIQUE
Zebrak          9216-0001
*1, bd. du Jardin Exotique*
Walpole Galleries          9330-7014
*15, bd. du Jardin Exotique*

## MONACO-VILLE
Le Vieux Ramparts
*17, rue Basse*

# ART GALLERIES

## MONTE CARLO
Galerie Monaco Fine Arts          9350-7438
*Sporting d' Hiver*
Galerie Battifoglio          9330-8885
*6, av. St. Michel*
Galerie Henri Bronne          9325-2439
*6, av. St. Michel*
Galerie Start          9770-7057
*1, av. Henry Dunant*
In & Out          9770-8190
*Métropole Galerie*
C & C Art Gallery          9330-2822
*Métropole Galerie*
Noor Arts          9350-1255
*Métropole Galerie*
Galerie Trianon          9325-1122
*6, bd. des Moulins*

| | |
|---|---|
| Arts Contemporains | 9325-6768 |
| *23, bd. des Moulins* | |
| Galerie d'Art | 9330-6140 |
| *31, bd. des Moulins* | |
| Galerie Shanaz | 9315-0508 |
| *2, bd. d' Italie* | |

## LARVOTTO
| | |
|---|---|
| Pastor & Gismondi | 9325-2714 |
| *11, av. Princesse Grace* | |
| Galerie du Forum Kamil Art | 9350-3640 |
| *3, av. Princesse Grace* | |

## LA CONDAMINE
| | |
|---|---|
| Galerie Pierre Nouvion | 9325-7075 |
| *11, bd. Albert 1er* | |
| Galerie Ricadonna | 9350-8646 |
| *7, rue Grimaldi* | |

## MONACO-VILLE (OLD TOWN)
| | |
|---|---|
| Galerie de la Cathédrale | 9350-0705 |
| *7, rue Emile de Loth* | |
| Galerie Berrino | 9216-7484 |
| *19, rue Basse* | |

## FONTVIEILLE
| | |
|---|---|
| MonaLisa | 9205-7005 |
| *20, quai Jean-Charles Rey* | |

Specializes in Automobile and Formula 1 art.

*Note some antique shops also carry pictures.

## AUCTIONS

Auctions, or *salles des ventes*, are an excellent way to buy antiques, paintings, rugs and decorative objects if you're in town and can handle French numbers. Look in Sunday's local **Nice Matin** newspaper, in the back section under *Ventes Publiques* or *Ventes aux Enchères*. Monaco, Menton, Antibes and Cannes have several auction houses or *Hôtel des Ventes*. Previews usually are held a day or two before the auction. There is a 10 percent premium above the auction price as a general rule. This is where the dealers buy, so prices escalate for good items. Don't overbid! You'll be guaranteed to have lots of fun and shocked at the reasonable prices.

## AUDIO CASSETTES, CDS

### MONTE CARLO
FNAC       9331-8181
*Métropole Galerie*

### LA CONDAMINE
International Video Group       9325-1025
*The Port*

### FONTVIEILLE
Nuggets       9205-5785
*Fontvieille Commercial Center*
Carrefour       9205-5700

## WOMEN'S CLOTHES
## WOMEN'S DESIGNER HAUTE COUTURE

### MONTE CARLO
Céline       9330-9278
*Av. des Beaux Arts*
Chanel       9350-5555
*Av. des Beaux Arts*
Lanvin       9330-0453
*Av. des Beaux Arts*
Odile       9325-7313
*Place du Casino*
Sonia Rykiel       9325-8370
*Place du Casino*
A.K.R.I.S.       9325-3404
*Avenue des Beaux Arts*
Christian Dior       9350-9204
*Avenue des Beaux Arts*
Givenchy       9325-3404
*Avenue des Beaux Arts*
Yves Saint Laurent       9325-0132
*Avenue des Beaux Arts*
Prada       9797-9410
*Avenue de Monte Carlo*
Gucci       9797-3434
*Avenue de Monte Carlo*
Hermès       9350-6489
*Avenue de Monte Carlo*
Valentino       9325-1263
*Avenue de Monte Carlo*
Salvatore Ferrgamo       9325-1221
*Hotel Hermitage*

Linea Nuovo                                        9350-2780
*Park Palace Galerie*
**Atmosphère**                                     9325-0003
*Park Palace Galerie*
Stizzoli                                           9315-0479
*Park Palace Galerie*
Escada                                             9797-1242
*Park Palace Galerie*
Gianfranco Ferre                                   9325-6105
*Park Palace Galerie*
Laurel                                             9325-0435
*Park Palace Galerie*
Oscar Cadence                                      9315-9015
*Métropole Galerie*
Triangle                                           9350-1026
*Métropole Galerie*
Ichthy's                                           9330-7515
*Monte Carlo Grand Hotel*
*43, Place des Moulins*                            9350-3932
Loris Azzaro                                       9330-0062
*19, bd. des Moulins*

## LARVOTTO BEACH
Adonis                                             9350-5704
*39, av.. Princesse Grace*
Karen Millen                                       9325-5040
*39, av. Princesse Grace*
D.K.N.Y.                                           9325-2508
*39, av. Princesse Grace*

## MONACO-VILLE
Isabelle Kristensen
*18 rue Princesse Marie de Lorraine*

# WOMEN'S BOUTIQUES,
## MODERATELY PRICED CLASSIC FASHION

## MONTE CARLO
Charlotte                                          9350-5389
*21, bd. des Moulins*
Marlène Mode                                       9350-1757
*Métropole Galerie*
Monique                                            9330-7387
*26, bd. des Moulins*
Rive Droite                                        9325-1106
*46, bd. des Moulins*
Tender                                             9325-4170
*29, bd. des Moulins*

## LA CONDAMINE
**Yveline Garnier** 9330-3381
*57, rue Grimaldi*
**Flore et Claire** 9330-1334
*27, rue Grimaldi*
**Cop Copine** 9770-8601
*4, rue Princesse Caroline*
**Nicole Shop** 9330-1233
*10, rue Princesse Caroline*
**Sandrine** 9330-1749
*15, rue Princesse Caroline*
**Top Mode** 9315-0278
*22, rue Princesse Caroline*

## LARVOTTO
**Myriam** 9330-9019
*7, av. Princesse Grace*

# EURO TRENDY (MIXED PRICES)

## MONTE CARLO
**Bagherra** 9350-4544
*Métropole Galerie*
**Sara B** 9325-2470
*Métropole Galerie*
**Via Spiga - Max Mara** 9350-4498
*Métropole Galerie*
**Briggy** 9325-3551
*Métropole Galerie*
**Replay** 9325-3040
*Métropole Galerie*
**Events** 9770-6020
*Métropole Galerie*
**Sandra** 9216-0807
*7, bd. des Moulins*
**Benetton** 9330-8256
*21, bd. des Moulins*
**Anemoni** 9325-6644
*31, bd. des Moulins*
**Label Vie** 9350-7779
*41, bd. des Moulins*
**Michéle R** 9350-0675
*2, bd. de France*

## LARVOTTO BEACH
**Byba Boutique** 9350-3699
*39, av. Princesse Grace*
**Chacok** 9350-7445
*39, av. Princesse Grace*

**Lolita**                                        9350-3417
*39, av. Princesse Grace*
**Rive Gauche**                                   9330-7457
*39, av. Princesse Grace*

## LA CONDAMINE
**Il Teatro**                                     9350-9013
*8 bis, rue Grimaldi*
**Il Teatro Classic**                             9350-9012
*9, rue Grimaldi*
**Georges Rech**                                  9225-3949
*15, rue Millo*
**Diesel**                                        9350-3414
*15, rue Grimaldi*
**Gildona**                                       9350-5124
*6, rue Princesse Caroline*
**Dreamland**                                     9325-0539
*7, rue de la Turbie*
**Toi du Monde**                                  9770-5544
*29, rue du Millo*

## FONTVIEILLE COMMERCIAL CENTER
**Camaieu**                                       9205-3995
**Escapade**                                      9205-3999
**Côte Chic**                                     9205-3989

## LINGERIE

## MONTE CARLO
**Balbi**                                         9350-5049
*Park Palace Galerie*
**Alexandre Dubas**                               9350-1725
*Métropole Galerie*
**Elle**                                          9770-8490
*Métropole Galerie*
**Koba**                                          9350-0601
*Métropole Galerie*
**Wolford**                                       9350-8215
*5, av. St. Michel*
**La Ligne Idéale**                               9350-6497
*35, bd. Princesse Charlotte*
**Katy**                                          9350-6622
*10, bd. des Moulins*

## LA CONDAMINE
**Feeling**                                       9350-5093
*7, rue Princesse Caroline*
**Caprice**                                       9205-2412
*3, av. Prince Pierre*

101

## LARVOTTO BEACH
Les Dessous                                             9325-8050
*39, av. Princesse Grace*

## SWEATERS
## (WOMEN, MEN)

## MONTE CARLO
Monesi                                                  9797-3097
*30, bd. des Moulins*

## LA CONDAMINE
Jeanseria                                               9350-2878
*22, rue Grimaldi*
Love 2000                                               9220-1947
*5, rue de la Turbie*
Insolites de Canelle                                    9330-9200
*5, rue de la Turbie*

## MEN'S CLOTHES
## MONTE CARLO
Lanvin                                                  9325-0179
*Place du Casino*
Yves Saint Laurent                                      9350-1020
*Place du Casino*
Hermès                                                  9350-6489
*11-15, av. Monte Carlo*
Gucci                                                   9797-3434
*1-5, av. Monte Carlo*
Louis Sciolla                                           9330-9060
*Park Palace Galerie*
Linea Nuovo                                             9350-2780
*Park Palace Galerie*
Gianfranco Ferre                                        9325-6105
*Park Palace Galerie*
Jean Jacques                                            9350-8785
*Park Palace Galerie*
Jaguy                                                   9330-8456
*17, av. Princesse Charlotte*
Armand Thiery                                           9350-5277
*26, av. Princesse Charlotte*
Alfred Dunhill
*Métropole Galerie*
Oscar Cadence                                           9315-9015
*Métropole Galerie*
Ermenegildo Zegna                                       9216-1322
*Métropole Galerie*

| | |
|---|---|
| **George Miller** | 9770-7808 |
| *Métropole Galerie* | |
| **Gentlemen's d' Oxford** | 9330-0519 |
| *Métropole Galerie* | |
| **Society Club- Hugo Boss** | 9325-2501 |
| *Métropole Galerie* | |
| **Gant USA** | 9350-3030 |
| *Métropole Galerie* | |
| **Brett Merrill** | 9330-3385 |
| *17, bd. des Moulins* | |
| **Façonnable** | 9250-5066 |
| *23, bd. des Moulins* | |
| **Norb-Ferrer** | 9330-8162 |
| *36, bd. des Moulins* | |
| **Hugo Boss** | 9325-2502 |
| *39, bd. des Moulins* | |
| **Ichthy's** | 9330-7515 |
| *43, Place des Moulins* | |

## LA CONDAMINE

| | |
|---|---|
| **Ricry** | |
| *11, rue Grimaldi* | |
| **Attualle** | 9330-3705 |
| *15, rue Millo* | |
| **Top Mode** | 9315-0278 |
| *Rue Princesse Caroline* | |
| **Gian Alberto Caporale** | 9325-0504 |
| *11, rue Princesse Caroline* | |
| **Status** | 9325-7200 |
| *1, rue de la Turbie* | |

## FONTVIEILLE

| | |
|---|---|
| **Camaieu** | 9205-3999 |
| *Commercial Center* | |

# TIES

## MONTE CARLO

| | |
|---|---|
| **Cravatterie Nazionali** | 9350-8880 |
| *Métropole Galerie* | |

## FONTVIEILLE

| | |
|---|---|
| **Erve Jacques** | 9205-9846 |
| *Fontvieille Commercial Center* | |

103

# SHIRTS

Renato Paglia Chemises         9350-2288
*11, av. Princesse Grace (Larvotto)*

## MEN'S AND WOMEN'S SHIRTS

Jaquy         9330-8456
*17, bd. Princesse Charlotte (Monte Carlo)*
Monte Carlo Shirts         9325-0805
*14, rue Grimaldi (La Condamine)*
Erve Jaques         9205-3999
*Fontvieille Commercial Center*

## TEENS AND TWENTIES

### LA CONDAMINE
Il Teatro         9350-9013
*8, rue Grimaldi*
Odeon         9350-9012
*9, rue Grimaldi*

### FONTVIEILLE
Soho Gifts         9205-3938
*Fontvieille Commercial Center*
Camaieu         9205-3999
*Fontvieille Commercial Center*

## CHILDREN'S

### MONTE CARLO
Boutique de Floriane         9216-0916
*Métropole Galerie*
Catimini         9330-0082
*Métropole Galerie*
Chipie Junior         9315-0696
*Métropole Galerie*
Noni         9316-0916
*Métropole Galerie*
Ricriation         9770-8412
*Métropole Galerie*
Baby C         9350-5474
*Monte Carlo Grand Hotel*
Boutique du Rocher         9330-9117
*1, av. de la Madone*
Trottinette         9325-2729
*3, av. St. Charles (off Moulins) Just behind Lloyds Bank*

**Benetton 1-12**                                    9350-5042
*31, bd. des Moulins*
**Jacardi**
*31, bd. des Moulins*
**Baby Boots**                                       9350-8282
*38, bd. des Moulins*
**Malie**                                            9216-1410
*41, bd. des Moulins*

## LA CONDAMINE
**Sandrine**                                         9330-1749
*15, rue Princesse Caroline*

**Gribouille**                                       9330-8081
*11, rue Princesse Caroline*
**Kid Cool**                                         9205-2627
*Fontvieille Commercial Center*

## CHILDREN'S TOYS

## LA CONDAMINE
**Cartoon Joué Club**                                9216-0392
*25, rue de Millo*
**Lollipop**                                         9305-2391
*Fontvieille Commercial Center*

## DISCOUNT USED CLOTHING
## WOMEN'S, MEN'S DESIGNER CLOTHES

## MONTE CARLO
**La Différence**                                    9350-6157
*3, av. St. Charles*
Factory prices for top-line Italian and French fashion.
**Stock Griffe**                                     9350-8606
*5, bis av. St. Michel Park Palace Galerie*
Year-end designer clothes for men and women.
**Mini Maxi Troc**                                   9325-5848
*5, rue des Lilas*
Used women's clothes
**Elégance**                               33 (0) 4 9378-5082
Bd. de la Republique, Beausoleil not far from Monaco Tourist
Office
Here a store where you can buy or sell. A nice selection of some
designer outfits, or if you need a coat the prices are right.

## LARVOTTO
**Zip Retouches**      9770-6920
*31, av. Princesse Grace Estoril Galerie*

# FURS

## MONTE CARLO
**Christian Dior**      9330-7978
*Av. des Beaux Arts*
**Diana Furs**      9330-7377
*31, bd. des Moulins*
**Fourrure Jeunemaitre**      9330-0087
*2, rue Iris*

# CHARMS
(See Jewelry section)

# CHINA AND PORCELAIN

## MONTE CARLO
**Manufacture Porcelain de Monaco**      9350-6463
*Métropole Galerie*
Exquisite designs make these items manufactured in Monaco an original gift idea. Tours of the factory by appointment (see All The Sights chapter)
**Puiforcat**      9350-0110
*2, av. des Spélugues*
**Chinacraft**      9350-7585
*Monte Carlo Grand Hotel*

# CRYSTAL AND GLASS
(Also see Day Trips section, Biot)

## MONTE CARLO
**Lalique**      9325-0502
*Terrasse Hotel de Paris*
**L'Art Vénitien**      9330-4128
*Métropole Galerie*
**Moser**      9770-5445
*Métropole Galerie*
**Zepter**      9310-6470
*5, av. St. Laurent*
(See Gift Shops)

## LA CONDAMINE
**Riccadonna**      9350-8646
*7, rue Grimaldi*
Lots of fun and creative designs.

## COINS

### MONTE CARLO
Wurz — 9325-1040
*Place du Casino*
La Numismatique — 9325-1296
*21, bd. d' Italie*

## GIFT SHOPS

### MONTE CARLO
G.J.3 — 9325-5511
*Sporting d' Hiver*
Czarina — 9216-1989
*Sporting d' Hiver*
Boutique du Rocher — 9330-9117
*1, av. de la Madone*
Items are designed and crafted in Monaco or surrounding areas, and range from knitwear, children's clothing, table mats, enamels and objets d'art. Also located in the Old Town. Run by the Princesse Grace Foundation.
Reverdy — 9350-6375
*2, rue des Iris Place de la Crémaillère*
Geneviève Lethu — 9350-0941
*Métropole Galerie*
Silver House — 9350-1750
*Métropole Galerie*
Zepter — 9310-6470
*5, av. St. Laurent*
La Jolie Boutique — 9330-8210
*15, bd. des Moulins*
Pois de Senteurs — 9330-8884
*25, bd. des Moulins*
G.J.s Decoration — 9330-6033
*29, bd. des Moulins*
De Wan — 9325-8550
*40, bd. des Moulins*

### LA CONDAMINE
Merenda Cadeaux — 9330-2319
*3, rue Grimaldi*
Bahri — 9325-6800
*10, rue Grimaldi*
Arrobbio — 9330-8385
*14, rue Grimaldi*
Formula 1 — 9315-9244
*15, rue Grimaldi*
Antica Decor — 9325-0050
*25, rue Grimaldi*

**Kashmir**     9325-2025
*24, rue Grimaldi*

**Marie Dentelle**     9330-4340
*10, rue Princesse Caroline*

**Etats d' Ame**     9350-1111
*25, rue de Millo*

**Raison d' Etre**     9330-1474
*20, rue de Millo*

**Atelier de Charlotte**     9350-6878
*15, rue Terrazzani*

## MONACO-VILLE (OLD TOWN)

**Boutique du Rocher**     9330-3399
*11, rue Emile Roth*

Features handcrafted gifts designed and crafted by local artists. Part of the Princesse Grace Foundation. There is another location on avenue de la Madone near the Métropole Galerie.

## LARVOTTO BEACH

**Style Harmony**     9350-8733
*5, av. Princesse Grace*

**G.J.'s**     9330-9519
*27, av. Princesse Grace*

## FONTVIEILLE

**Piccolo Punto**     9350-2696
*14, quai Jean-Charles Rey*

**Vérandah Decoration**     9205-2401
*32, quai Jean-Charles Rey*

**Soho**     9205-3938
*Fontvieille Commercial Center*

# GOURMET FOOD AND WINE
# (TAKE OUT-DELIVERY)

## MONTE CARLO

**Boucherie Cachére Sam**     9330-1173
*2, av. Saint Laurent*

Monaco's own kosher butcher, with corned beef and pastrami.

**Mister Brian**     9330-5009
*7, av. du Berçeau*

American and British goodies. (see Les Basics catering)

**Platy Gourmet**     9325-5950
*25, av. de la Costa*

**Maison du Caviar**     9330-8006
*1, av. St. Charles*

Caviar and roasted chickens.

**Au Grand Echanson**     9350-6119
*32, bd. des Moulins*

Fine selection of wine.
**Comtesse du Barry**       9315-9229
*Métropole Galerie*
**Hedilard**
*Métropole Galerie*
Foie gras, wine and gift packages.
**Prichoc-Pizza Phone**       33 (0) 4 9378-1045
*17, bd. de la République*
Best home-delivered pizza.
**French Mikado's**       9216-1718
Take out delivery service for pizza. Chinese and Italian.

### LA CONDAMINE

**Porte d'Or**       9225-1415
*9, rue Grimaldi*
Chinese and Asian specialities
**Caves & Gourmandises**       9770-5494
*23, Albert 1er*
Wine and gourmet goodies.
**La Monégasque**       9330-4214
*57, rue Grimaldi*
Manufacturer of anchovies and seafood.

### FONTVIEILLE

**Dubernet**       9205-3471
*Fontvieille Commercial Center*
Foie gras, sausages and meat specialties.
(See Catering Le Basics for more information)

## CHOCOLATE AND BAKERY GOODS

### MONTE CARLO

**Dragon d'Or**       9350-6716
*35, bd. Princesse Charlotte*
This bakery is just up the street from American Express, and shouldn't be missed by the serious chocoholic!
**Canet Pâtisserie**       9330-8294
*4, bd. de France*
A half a block up from Dragon d' Or, another serious bakery shop.
**Riviera Bakery**       9350-6323
*27, bd. des Moulins*
**Godiva**
*Métropole Galerie*
**Prince's Tea**       9350-6391
*26, av. de la Costa*
**Café Venoise**       9350-6500
*Monte Carlo Grand Hotel*
**Richart Chocolate & Design**       9330-1506
*19, bd. des Moulins*

## LA CONDAMINE

**Chocolaterie de Monaco**         9797-8888
One of the best chocolate makers in Europe. Tours of the factory by appointment.

**Sansano Bakery**         9350-6426
*41, rue Grimaldi*
Light and moist cakes.

## MONACO-VILLE

**Chocolaterie de Monaco**         9797-8888
*Place de la Visitation*

## FONTVIEILLE

**Jeff de Bruges**         9205-3977
*Commercial Center*

# GUNS AND HUNTING SUPPLIES

**Saint Hubert Armurerie**         9330-2357
*8, rue Terrazzani*
Behind the Monte Carlo Condamine Market.

# HEALTH AND DIET FOOD STORES

## MONTE CARLO

**Diététique Gourmande**         9325-2215
*7, av. Saint Laurent*

**Health Store**         9770-8314
*Métropole Galerie*

**Monte Carlo Régime**         9330-7271
*25, bd. Princesse Charlotte*

# HARDWARE-HOUSEHOLD ITEMS

## LA CONDAMINE

**Condamine Bricolage**         9770-8938
*12, rue de Millo*

**Comptoir Monégasque Peinture, et Decoration**     9330-9175
*16, rue Louis Auréglia*

## FONTVIEILLE

**Brico Center**         9798-5151
*13, Prince Héré. Albert*
Located near the Commercial Center

# JEWELRY

## ANTIQUE

### MONTE CARLO

**Renner and Co.**         9325-3439
*La Scala (Main Post Office)*

Templier   9325-0043
*3, av. St. Michel*
Noor Arts   9350-1255
*Métropole Galerie*
SAPJO   9350-5434
*16, bd. des Moulins*
Diana Gem   9325-7191
*26, bd. des Moulins*
David Antique Jewlery   9350-5221
*22, bd. des Moulins*
Passé Actuel   9350-2838
36, bd. des Moulins

## OLD WATCHES

Zebrak   9216-0001
*1, bd. du Jardin Exotique*

## CHARMS

### MONTE CARLO
Fred Joaillerie   9330-7900
*6, av. des Beaux Arts*
Repozzi Joaillerie   9350-8959
*Hotel Hermitage*
Arrobbio   9330-8385
*14, rue Grimaldi (La Condamine)*

## FINE

### MONTE CARLO
Albuquerque   9350-6290
*Place du Casino*
Cartier   9330-8658
*Place du Casino*
Van Cleef & Arpels   9350-5408
*Place du Casino*
Alexandre Reza   9325-3717
*Hotel de Paris*
Wurz   9325-1040
*Place du Casino*
Bulgari   9359-8850
*Avenue des Beaux Arts*
Chaumet   9770-7828
*3, av.des Beaux Arts*
Fred   9330-7900
*6, av. des Beaux Arts*
Gianmaria Buccellati   9350-9010
*Avenue des Beaux Arts*
Piaget   9350-4416
*Avenue des Beaux Arts*

Hermès                                       9350-6489
*11-15, av. Monte Carlo*
Tabbah                                       9350-2202
*Terrasse Hotel de Paris*
Repossi Joaillier                            9350-8959
*Hotel Hermitage*
Zegg & Cerlati                               9770-7480
*2, av. des Spélugues*
Matile                                       9325-2670
*Métropole Galerie*
Au Castel d'Or                               9350-4299
*Métropole Galerie*
Blue Metal                                   9325-2503
*Métropole Galerie*
Van Hubrecht                                 9350-2269
*2, bd. de France*
Ciandano                                     9350-5200
*18, bd. des Moulins*

## COSTUME

### MONTE CARLO
Ciribelli                                    9325-5556
*Place du Casino*
Burma Elégance                               9330-2015
*Métropole Galerie*
Cassio                                       9325-5510
*10, bd. des Moulins*
Cassio d' Or                                 9325-4441
*18, bd. des Moulins*
Le Carat                                     9325-7191
*26, bd. des Moulins*
Divina & Co                                  9350-5247
*36, bd. des Moulins*
Claris A                                     9330-3590
*37, bd. des Moulins*

### LA CONDAMINE
Bahri                                        9325-6800
*10, rue Grimaldi*
Made'Or                                      9330-2870
*18, rue Princesse Caroline*

## MANUFACTURERS

### LA CONDAMINE
Matile                                       9330-1217
*8, rue Aureglia*

### MONTE CARLO
**Didier Joaillerie**       9330-7562
*3, av. Princesse Alice*
**Ciandano**       9350-5200
*18, bd. des Moulins*

### FONTVIEILLE
**Marcel Maechler**       9325-5717
*Stade Louis II Entrée H*

## LEATHER GOODS AND LUGGAGE

### MONTE CARLO
**Louis Vuitton**       9325-1344
*6, av. des Beaux Arts*
**Hermès**       9350-6489
*11-15, av. Monte Carlo*
**Gucci**       9797-3444
*5, av. de Monte Carlo*
**Ichtys**       9330-7515
*Monte Carlo Grand Hotel*
**Scarabeo**       9325-3580
*7, av. Princesse Alice*
**Oliver Jacques**       9330-0381
*Métropole Galerie*
**Remember**       9325-0013
*36, bd, des Moulins*

### LA CONDAMINE
**Mimy Maroquinerie**       9330-0255
*18, rue Princesse Caroline*
**Tosca**       9330-9224
*2, bd, de France*
**Allure**       9330-6899
*14, rue Princesse Caroline*

### FONTVIEILLE
**Bury**       9205-3959
*Fontvieille Commercial Center*
(For Luggage Repairs see Les Basics A-Z)

## LINEN

### MONTE CARLO
**Yves Delorme**       9350-0870
*Métropole Galerie*
**Seasons**       9350-5242
*31, bd. des Moulins*

| | |
|---|---|
| **Dolce Casa** | 9330-1597 |
| *38, bd. des Moulins* | |
| **Aline Boutique** | 9325-0452 |
| *24, bd. d'Italie* | |

## LA CONDAMINE
| | |
|---|---|
| Descamps | 9350-2882 |
| *20, rue Millo* | |

# OPTICAL

## MONTE CARLO
| | |
|---|---|
| **Optique Photo Scala** | 9350-5138 |
| *Across from Hermitage Hotel* | |
| **Grosfillez** | 9350-6248 |
| *8, bd. des Moulins* | |
| **Krys Optique** | 9350-5667 |
| *17, bd. Princesse Charlotte* | |

## LA CONDAMINE
| | |
|---|---|
| **Optique Design** | 9330-8015 |
| *8, rue Princesse Caroline* | |

## FONTVIEILLE
| | |
|---|---|
| **Optique Design** | 9205-9858 |
| *Commercial Center* | |

# PERFUME MANUFACTURERS
(See Day Trip section, Eze and Grasse)

# PERFUME AND COSMETICS

## MONTE CARLO
| | |
|---|---|
| **Parfumerie du Métropole** | 9350-4460 |
| *Métropole Galerie* | |
| **Parfumerie du Helder** | 9330-6510 |
| *6, bd. des Moulins* | |
| **Parfumerie de Paris** | 9350-5271 |
| *20, bd. des Moulins* | |
| **Remember** | 9325-0013 |
| *36. bd. des Moulins* | |

## LA CONDAMINE
| | |
|---|---|
| **Parfumerie du Soleil** | 9330-2375 |
| *1, rue Grimaldi* | |
| **Parfumerie de Paris II** | 9350-1210 |
| *8, rue Princesse Caroline* | |

| | |
|---|---|
| **Marion's Parfumerie** | 9770-7275 |
| *12, rue Princesse Caroline* | |
| **F**ONTVIELLE | |
| **Parfumerie Edith Harley** | 9205-2425 |
| *Commercial Center* | |

## POTTERY

(See Day Trips, Vallauris)

## RUGS

**M**ONTE **C**ARLO

| | |
|---|---|
| Nalbandian | 9350-3030 |
| *Galerie Métropole* | |
| Moghadan | 9325-6768 |
| *23, bd. des Moulins* | |
| Piccolo Punto | 9205-2454 |
| *14, quai Jean-Charles Rey* | |
| *(Fontvieille)* | |
| Beautiful needlepoint works. | |

## SHOES

**M**ONTE **C**ARLO

| | |
|---|---|
| Scarabéo | 9350-4104 |
| *5, av. Princesse Alice* | |
| Atmosphère | 9325-0003 |
| *Park Palace Galerie* | |
| **Chaussures Antoinette** | 9330-7145 |
| *4, bd. de France* | |
| Giovani | 9350-3323 |
| *Métropole Galerie* | |
| Mercedeh | 9550-5770 |
| *Métropole Galerie* | |
| Gabrielli | 9350-1380 |
| *Métropole Galerie* | |
| Jaime Mascaro | 9350-3323 |
| *Métropole Galerie* | |
| Pollini | 9350-6929 |
| *3, bd. des Moulins* | |
| La Botterie | 9325-8055 |
| *14, bd. des Moulins* | |
| **Chaussures Dominique** | 9330-0773 |
| *15, bd. Princesse Charlotte* | |
| Un **Dimanche à Venise** | 9350-8651 |
| *18, bd. des Moulins* | |

## LE CONDAMINE
| | |
|---|---|
| Colette | 9330-1459 |
| *3, rue Grimaldi* | |
| Soft | 9350-5013 |
| *10, rue Grimaldi* | |
| Chausseur aux Capucines | 9330-2832 |
| *13–15, rue Princesse Caroline* | |
| Noel Chausseures | 9330-3490 |
| *13, place d'Armes* | |

## FONTVIEILLE
| | |
|---|---|
| Star Jalima | 9205-3974 |
| *Commercial Center* | |

## SILVER

### MONTE CARLO
| | |
|---|---|
| Silver House | 9350-1750 |
| *Métropole Galerie* | |
| Christofle Pavillon | 9325-2020 |
| *42, bd. des Moulins* | |
| Reverdy | 9350-6375 |
| *2, rue Iris* | |

(Note see gift section for more silver items)

## SPORTING GOODS AND SPORTSWEAR

### LA CONDAMINE
| | |
|---|---|
| Tournier Sports | 9330-3013 |
| *20, rue Grimaldi* | |

### FONTVIEILLE
| | |
|---|---|
| City Sports | 9205-9902 |
| *Commercial Center* | |
| Decathlon | 9205-0150 |
| *2, rue de la Lujerneta* | |

## STAMPS

### MONTE CARLO
| | |
|---|---|
| Brych et Fils | 9350-5262 |
| *31, bd. des Moulins* | |
| Monaco Collections | 9315-0512 |
| *2, av. Henry Dunant* | |
| Monte Carlo Philaterie | 9330-6908 |
| *4, chemin de la Rousse* | |

### LA CONDAMINE
**Timbres de Monaco**           9330-4517
*45, rue Grimaldi*

### FONTVIEILLE
**Office des emissions de Timbres-Poste**      9315-4141
*Fontvieille Commercial Center, 3rd Floor*

## STATIONERY AND BUSINESS SUPPLIES

### MONTE CARLO
**Grande Papeterie**           9350-5443
*14, av. de la Costa*

## TABACS AND NEWSSTANDS

### MONTE CARLO
**Blue Shop**           9350-1504
*Métropole Galerie*
**Café de Paris**           9216-2288
*Place du Casino*
**La Régence**           9350-3109
*28, av. de la Costa*
**Newsstand**           9330-4299
*Monte Carlo Grand Hotel*
**La Maison de la Presse**       9325-3242
*22, bd. Princesse Charlotte*

### LARVOTTO BEACH
**Presse Internationale**        9350-4217
*9, av. Princesse Grace*

### LA CONDAMINE
**Hall de la Presse**          9330-1671
*1, rue Grimaldi*
**La Gitane**           9330-7753
*1, rue Grimaldi*
**Tabacs le Khedive**        9330-2933
*9, bd. Albert 1er*

### FONTVIEILLE
**Le Media**           9205-9855
*Fontvieille Commercial Center*

## TOURIST SOUVENIRS

### MONACO VILLE
The best Monte Carlo souvenirs can be found in the Old Town.

## TUXEDO RENTALS
(see Les Basics A-Z)

## WINE AND LIQUOR
(see Gourmet Food and Wine)

### MONTE CARLO
**L'Oenothèque**                                    9325-8266
*Sporting d' Hiver*
With 120,000 bottles of rare and choice wined to choose from, how can you go wrong. They ship anywhere in the world.
**Au Grand Echanson**                               9350-6121
*32, bd. des Moulins*
Wine, champagnes and spirits at reasonable prices.
**Vino Veritas International**                      9350-1407
*7, av. Grande-Bretagne*

### LA CONDAMINE
**L'Abondance**                                     9330-2584
*11, rue Grimaldi*
Excellent selections of wined of the region, champagne, whisky and liquor.
**Caves & Gourmandises**                            9770-5494
*25, bd. Albert 1er*
**Grand Chais Franco-Monégasques**                  9330-2680
*11, rue Baron de St. Suzanne*
Large selection of wines, and spirits, free tastings by appointment.

# 9
# SAVIOR FAIRE

*Savoir faire* means **"know how"** in French – an idea very important to the Monégasques. In this section I will introduce you to their greetings, customs, and protocol so that as you go about Monaco you will feel less like a tourist and more like a local.

## THE ART OF FRENCH GREETING
The Monégasques and the French are taught at an early age to formally address everyone with whom they are speaking with *Bonjour Madame or Monsieur* without necessarily using a surname. When leaving, it is customary to say good-bye *au revoir*, thanks, *merci*. These expressions are used especially to greet the sales clerk or person in a store and are as natural as a handshake. In the workplace people greet each other with a **handshake** and the expression *salut*, which means "hi".

A handshake is a must especially when meeting someone for the first time. Europeans are more formal than Americans and prefer to be called by their last name until they tell you you may call them by their first name. Some European men make a motion to kiss your hand; this is not sexual harassment but social custom.

## THE ART OF FRENCH KISSING
People who know each other well always kiss on the cheeks. It is easy to learn. You gently touch cheeks and **"kiss air"**! Family members will sometimes kiss three or four times in this manner. This is a charming custom and fun to participate in once you get the hang of it.

## THE ART OF TIME
Military time is used throughout Europe, so 1:00 PM becomes 13:00; 2:00 PM is 14:00; 6:00 PM is 18:00; 11:00 PM is 23:00.

## THE ART OF DRESSING
What to wear and when to wear it is the number one question most travelers face when packing for a trip. Unfortunately most people over-pack and find they don't wear half the things they dragged along. But dressing for Monaco and the Côte d'Azur can be tricky, so I have included a few guidelines to help you decide what to bring. Style here is a combination of laid-back California cool or sport chic, and for evening, it can be sophisticated. For formal occasions, wear jackets and ties at receptions; **black tie** is *de rigueur* **at gala dinners**. It's either short or long evening dresses for women at galas and balls; however, long dresses are more common than short (See Tuxedo rental in Les Basics). At the disco, women can wear anything short, tight and black, either pants or skirts are acceptable - the sexier the better. Men wear jackets, with or with out ties, slacks, and sometimes up-scale blue jeans if they're put together with an Armani jacket, but no athletic shoes. Attention no bare feet,

bare chests, or bathing suit attire is allowed outside beach and pool areas in the Principality. Appropriate dress is compulsory in all public buildings and places of worship.

## THE ART OF DINING

Dinners at home usually start at 8:00 in the evening; most restaurants do not start dinner service until 7:00 or 7:30 at the earliest. Adjusting to the European eating schedules can be difficult for some travellers. Lunch is served between 12:00 and 3:00 PM. Most restaurants stop serving at 2:30-3:00 PM in preparation for the evening meal. If hunger strikes sooner, look for a snack bar, bakery or grocery store to hold you over until dinner. Or if you are a coffee drinker, pop into a café and stand up at the bar for an expresso.

One should arrive promptly for dinner; although being 15 minutes late for a cocktail or buffet is acceptable. Before dinner a light aperitif, cocktail, or champagne is offered. Kir or Kir Royal is white wine and champagne and crème de cassis. Dinner begins with hot or cold appetizers, soup, followed by a fish or meat course; then salad, cheese plate, dessert, fruit and coffee. Various wines are served according to the dish. You may find a block or rack beside your plate, which is a knife or fork rest. It is quite common to keep the same cutlery throughout several courses and when in doubt always use the utensils from the outside first. Bread is plentiful but is not cut with a knife but torn with the hands. Butter is generally not served with bread. A word of advice: Remember to ask what the dress code is. Casual and informal does not always mean jeans, unless specified. A leisurely pace allows one time to savor the food and wine, and experience the famous Monaco *joie de vivre*.

## THE ART OF BEING A GOOD GUEST

Here is what to bring to impress your host or hostess. Social good manners are widely practiced throughout Europe. When responding to an informal invitation to his or her home for a meal, one should bring a small gift. Flowers, chocolates, a plant, or fine soap are appropriate. An even better choice is something from your native country if you happen to have brought it. Bringing a bottle of wine is an American custom that just doesn't translate into good manners unless your host happens to be American; however, champagne is a good alternative.

Now, if you should receive a formal invitation by a public official, foreign consulate or VIP to dinner, then flowers are a safe choice. But never arrive with the flowers in hand. They should be sent before or after the occasion. A florist may ask you *C'est pour offrir?* Say *Oui*, and they will be wrapped with a bow. Sending a mixed flower bouquet is considered bad taste. However, you may send a mixed arrangement as long as it is the same color or the same kind of flower in mixed colors. **Do not send or bring**

**chrysanthemums** because this flower is reserved for funerals and taken to graves on All Saints Day, November first.

## THE ART OF ROYAL PROTOCOL

It's nice to know what to say and do just in case you're lucky enough to be one of those special few who get to meet a member of Monaco's Royal family. When addressing His Serene Highness, Prince Rainier III (pronounced Rain-Yay, Ay as in May, not like Mount Rainier in Washington), you can safely use Sir or Your Highness; the same goes for Prince Albert. Never introduce royalty by using their first name, nor refer to their first name. Everyone knows who 'they' are. Since becoming the husband of The Prince of Hanover, Princess Caroline is addressed as Her Royal Highness, because The Prince of Hanover is directly related to the Queen of England, but Prince Rainier III is a foreign Prince not directly related to any King or Queen. Princess Stephanie is addressed as Your Serene Highness. For both women royals you can safely use Your Highness, Madame, or Ma'am. For example: You might say, "Your Highness, may I introduce or present Mr. and Mrs. Smith." French speakers address the Princes' as *Monseigneur*, and you can too. When writing to the Princes' you use the title **H.S.H. Prince Rainier III**, followed by Your Serene Highness, or Sir. In writing to Princess Caroline it is H.R.H. The Princess of Hanover, followed by Your Royal Highness. Princess Stephanie is H.S.H. Princess Stephanie followed by Your Serene Highness. In the body of the letter you can refer to them as Your Highness, their title, but never by their first name.

The native Monégasques get very upset when they hear foreigners referring to their Royal family disrespectfully by their first names in public. If you want to impress them, be sure to use Prince or Princess. This is particularly important if you want to do business with any Monégasques.

Royalty always enters a room last and are the first to leave the room or party. It is proper etiquette to stand whenever they are entering or leaving the room.

## THE BIG FAUX PAS

Natives of Monaco are **Monégasque** (*pronounced Mon-a-gask*). They have their own language (a dialect derived from Genoa) so please don't make the mistake of calling them French; however, French is the national language. Monaco is not a part of France, but is its own sovereign state within the boundaries of France.

INDUSTRIE MONEGASQUE DU PRÊT-A-PORTER
3.00 MONACO

INDUSTRIE
ELECTRO-MECANIQUE DE LA PRINCIPAUTE
2,50

monaco
1980-1985 CENTRE SCIENTIFIQUE
3.00

MONACO
3,90
INDUSTRIE MONEGASQUE
DE TRANSFORMATION DES
MATIERES PLASTIQUES

MONACO
5,00
ETUDES DE
HAUTE TECHNOLOGIE
PETROLIERE

LABORATOIRE INTERNATIONAL DE RADIOACTIVITE MARINE (A.I.E.A)
MONACO
5,00

MONACO
2,20
INDUSTRIE MONEGASQUE DE
TRANSFORMATION DES PRODUITS
DES PECHES MARITIMES

MONACO
2,40
INDUSTRIE
PHARMACEUTIQUE
ET DE COSMETOLOGIE
DE LA PRINCIPAUTE

# 10
# LIVING AND WORKING IN MONACO

This section is devoted to those who've been bitten by the Monte Carlo bug and are curious to know what it takes to be part of the Monaco life style.

I am asked many times how I came to live here and why I stayed. Well, it's simple. I came as many do, as a tourist. Then, coincidentally, I found some old family friends who lived and worked here and that gave me the idea to try it. I have been here for many years now, and I can honestly say that I have never been sorry I made that decision.

I admit Monaco is not for everyone. However, the negatives - and there are a few - I believe are outweighed by the positives. The biggest advantage is quality of life. You can walk safely anytime, put your kids on the bus unescorted. The crime rate is low because the police are vigilant (they randomly check identification, which offends some people) and streets and elevators are monitored with video cameras. Public transportation is fast and reasonable. I spend no hours on a freeway stuck in traffic, except occasionally during major events like the Grand Prix, when, I admit, it can take 45 minutes to get from the Rock to Fontvieille. I love the air here because there is no major pollution. Not the least of what makes Monaco special is that, although small, it offers excellent cultural events and a wide array of sports activities. (The weather may have something to do with it too). Also, it upholds the French and Italian tradition about food and fortunately, there are restaurants in every price range. When I want to pick up and travel out of Monaco, well, Monaco offers a convenient base. It takes two hours to drive to Genoa, three hours to drive to Milan and under three hours to get to Avignon and the rest of Provence. The biggest drawback to living here is the village mentality and the bureaucracy. (When you read about how to become a resident or how to set up a business here you will see what I mean). Perhaps this is their way of sorting out those who are committed to the Principality from those who are merely indulging a whim. Who knows?

OK, If you've weighed the advantages and disadvantages and given Monaco the thumbs up, here are the things you need to know to settle here.

## LIVING IN MONACO
### RENTING
The first thing to consider is real estate. Current rental prices of apartments are the following: **Studios** (50sqm/500sqft) run between 6,500FF (1000€) to 10,000FF (1538€).

**One bedrooms** called *2 pièces* (60sqm/600sqf) to (100sqm/1000sqft), from 8,000FF (1230€) to 20,000FF (3076€). **Two bedrooms** called *3 pièces* (100sqm/1000sqft) to (200sqm/2000sqft) from 12,000FF(1846€) to 45,000FF (6923€). **Three bedrooms** called *4 pièces* (150sqm/250sqm)-(1500sqf/2500sqft) run between 18,000FF (2769€) and 65,000FF (10,000€).

The amount of rent reflects the surface size, location, view, appointments and newness of the building. This is a plus for those who intend to buy property, but bad news for those who are looking to rent. Studios generally are very over-priced; this is because of Monaco's tax status. You will find the best values in the older buildings with more than three bedrooms. These seem to be priced lower than their counterparts, but may not be the best value for long as an influx of new residents with families are snapping them up. The worst time to look is in April to May just before the busy tourist season begins. The best time is November, December, January and February.

There are two methods for finding an apartment. One is to go through an agency; there are plenty willing to accommodate you and their brokers speak multiple languages. They will charge you a 10 percent commission based on a year's rent. Then be prepared to part with a small fortune because you must pay three months' rent and charges (charges are maintenance fees, which could include heat in some cases), plus a deposit of three months' rent and charges, along with the commission and lease registration fees. This runs about 37,200FF (5723€) for a studio. Rents are payable three months in advance.

Your best chance of finding something reasonable is to have the time to look. Some suggestions: The Monte-Carlo Grand Hotel has re-decorated studios to 3 bedroom apartments, studios start from 10,000FF (1538€) a month, health club membership is included. Call: Cabinet P. Palmero Tel: 9216-7233.

In neighboring France you can try:
**IN BEAUSOLEIL**
**Vacantel Villa Médicis**                    **33 (0) 4 9378-4191**
                                              *Fax: 33 (0) 4 9341-8461*
**Residence Pierre & Vacances**               **33 (0) 4 9241-2000**
*Palais Josephine,*                           *Fax: 33 (0) 4 9241-2001*

**IN CAP D' AIL**
**Residence Pierre & Vacances**               **33 (0) 4 9341-7300**
*Av du General de Gaulle*                      *Fax: 33 (0) 4 9341-7477*
For seasonal rentals
**IN ROQUEBRUNE CAP MATIN**
**Grand Sejours International**                **33 (0) 4 9210-659**
                                              *Fax: 33 (0) 4 9378-6160*
**Résidence Le Golfe Bleu**                    **33 (0) 4 9210-4500**
                                              *Fax: 33 (0) 4 9210-4587*

La Grange Vacances Residence Riviera Beach     33 (0) 4 9328-1981

*Particulier à particulier* want ads in the paper or on the *Havas* board on rue des Iris means **offered directly by the owner.** Renting this way will save money because there is no commission, and you can usually make arrangements to pay monthly. If you're leasing at a slow period you may be able to get a better deal, so try to bargain the price down. The prices of rentals have risen dramatically since mid 90's and rents have more than doubled in some cases. The unfortunate aspect of Monaco is most landlords do not need the rental income and are prepared to wait until the unit is rented at a price they want. Rents also continue to increase according to the cost of living each year unless you negotiate otherwise. You won't receive any interest on your deposit, the landlord retains most of the rights, and you are generally liable for everything that goes wrong.

Hire a *huissier* who will do an *état des lieux* or a complete inventory of things that are wrong (cracks, stains, missing items, all appliances). You might find yourself presented with *frais or honoraires*, which are the costs involved in preparing the rental contract or improvements that the previous tenant made. This process usually separates wanna be renters from the real renters.

# BUYING

If you're planning to buy, here are the rules. Any individual or legal entity, whatever his or her nationality, may become the purchaser of a piece of real estate under the following conditions: proof of national identity, civil status, and marriage contract if one was drawn up. If you are a company you must produce the following: the articles of incorporation, a copy of registration less than three months old, a notarized power of authority to represent the company (if translated into French it must be accompanied by a statement from an authorized translator), a copy of the minutes of the general board meeting authorizing the purchase or sale of the property. When coming from abroad these must be certified as being true copies of the original by the nearest Monégasque consulate. There are separate rules for stock companies who undertake no commercial activities. Your real-estate broker can explain these requirements.

There are laws that forbid the sale or limit the conditions of sale to protect certain pieces of property, such as the ancient buildings on The Rock. Some of these buildings are rent-controlled to provide the Monégasques with affordable housing. A list of available low-rental units is posted at the Minister of Housing office in Fontvieille. But don't hold out much hope because you'll be in a line following the Monégasques and other long-term residents. In addition, these protected properties will be phased out through 2006.

Since 1997 real estate sales prices have been steadily rising and prices for new apartments range from 40,000FF (6097€)-80,000FF (12,195€) a square meter and for apartments in older buildings from 30,000FF (4615€) 50,000FF (7693€) a square meter.

## AGENT FEES

Commission fees generally are between 5 percent to 8 percent of the sales price, but this is negotiable. On residential property, here is the split: 5 percent paid by the vendor and 3 percent by the purchaser. In commercial transactions, the vendor pays 6 percent and the purchaser 3 percent. For exchanges of property or businesses, vendors pay 5 percent and the purchaser pays 5 percent. Most commissions can be negotiated depending on the sales price.

## NOTARY FEES

The person who prepares all the legal documents is a notaire, or notary. They are the legal officials who deal with deeds, registration and the contracts of the parties involved. They also take their share of fees. Fees are set on a percentage of the total sales price before sales tax; from 1 to 10,000FF (1538€) it's 3 percent; from 10,000FF (1538€) to 20,000FF (3076€) it is 2.3 percent, and above this figure the fee is 1.5 percent.

## REGISTRATION FEES

General system fees are calculated on the stated price or the market value, if the latter is higher. The fee is 7.5 percent: 6.5 percent for registration and 1 percent entry fee. The special system fees apply to transactions taking place at the same time as the construction or delivery of buildings and are 1 percent plus VAT. There are some advantages to buying new property; so check with your broker.

## GETTING THE MONACO RESIDENT CARD

Now that you've surmounted finding "a place" you're halfway here. The next thing to do is get the 'alien resident's' card or *carte de séjour*. This is obligatory for all foreigners over 16 years of age staying in Monaco for more than three months. The first step for non-European Union citizens is to visit your nearest French Consulate (**you must apply at your home domicile**) where you must request a *visa of longue durée* from France. This is in accordance with the mutual assistance agreement *"Convention de Voisinage"* signed by France and Monaco in 1963 and modified in December 1997. (Citizens of European Union member countries do not need to apply for a visa from France; they may apply directly to Monaco). To obtain this visa you will need: 1. Proof of means of existence (a work contract or membership of a foreign company.) 2. Bank references or investment income. 3. Proof from your local police department that you have no criminal record. 4. A physical exam by an authorized French doctor in your home area. 5. Nine passport-size photos (2 passport photos for E.U.citizen members) and a photocopy of your passport.

Once you have filled out all the forms and returned them to the French Consulate (non E.U. members only), be prepared to wait for up to three months. You will be contacted and hopefully told that the paperwork has been completed and your visa issued. Once that is done you can start the process all over again in Monaco. In addition you will now have to open up a bank account and deposit the appropriate amount, and show a lease or ownership documents or a lodging certificate (*certificat d'Hébergement*) if you will be living with someone other than yourself. Of course, don't forget a copy of the French visa stamped in your passport. The Monaco visa may be granted after about three months and entitles the holder to an alien resident card or *carte de séjour*. You will be issued a "*temporaire*" card each year for the first three years, then an *ordinaire* card for three years that is renewed three times (9 years). Finally after 12 years you will receive the *privilège* resident card, which is renewable every ten years. For further information contact the Direction Sûreté Public. (Department of Public Safety, Foreign Residents Section) at 9315-3015.

## TAX STATUS

Monaco is a tax haven for most foreigners, and becoming a resident entitles you to its benefits. The sole form of direct tax in the Principality is that imposed on profits generated in industry and commerce. Individual residents of the Principality are exempt from income tax except for French nationals who are taxed in accordance with the bilateral France-Monaco agreement. Companies who are located in Monaco pay a 35 percent rate on their profits. This rate was established following the Franco-Monégasque Convention of May 18, 1963, and has been in effect since 1964. The following are also subject to profit tax: any firm, whatever its legal form, involved in industrial or commercial activities, generating at least 25 percent of its turnover outside Monaco, either directly or through an intermediary. Companies whose work in Monaco consists in generating revenue from the transfer or concession of patents, trademarks, or from literary or artistic rights.

## BANKING AND THE EURO

Banking and financial services are one of Monaco's growth areas, and contributes 18 percent of its economy. The banking system is under the control and conforms to French banking authority rules in accordance with Franco-Monegasque agreements. The Monaco government has been vigilant in exposing money-laundering. In 1993 two new laws were passed, one to make money -laundering a criminal offence under the penal code, and two to create a special unit the SICCFIN (The Financial Information Circuit and Supervision department). This is one of 33 such units operating around the world to counter money-laundering operations.

Since **the beginning of January 1, 1999,** the euro has been legal tender as a currency unit in Monaco. Its value was permanently set at 6.5569 French francs. For conversion purposes the base should be rounded to the nearest franc or euro. Any fraction of a franc or euro equal to 0.5 shall be counted as one whole unit or rounded up. The Monaco government has voted to adopt the continuity of the new currency. Therefore, contracts, debts and value of companies, mutual funds etc. will all be valued in euros. In 2002 Monaco will mint the new Monaco-euro coins.

# WORKING IN MONACO

## HOW TO OPEN A BUSINESS

One must apply to the Sovereign Government for a preliminary authorization to operate any business, craft, industrial activity or service. This authorization is granted on the basis of guarantees offered by the applicant and of the interest that the planned     activity has for the Monégasque economy. In order to apply for authorization, one must do the following: 1) Complete applications from the Direction de l' Expansion Economique (Economic Growth Department) 2) Lease or purchase space     suitable to the operation of your business. Prices for rental property start at 2,000FF (307€) to 5,000FF (770€) per square meter per year; currently there is little space available and office rental prices reflect it. You can contact the Direction de l' Expansion Economique at 9, rue du Gabian, Fontvieille on Tel: 9315-8853 Fax: 9205-7520.

For general information, brochures and a reference library you can walk into the Adminstrative Information Center located in the new Commercial Center in Fontvieille. Call Tel: 9315-4026 Fax: 9315-4086. (Also see business opportunities under Les Basics.) Businesses in Monaco are structured in three primary ways:

**Individual enterprises and collective**
**commercial bodies other than companies**
Guild for mutual economic assistance (GIE)
Joint ventures (rarely used)
Self Employed
**Commercial companies**
General partnerships (SNC)
Limited partnerships (SCS)
Partnership limited by shares (SCA)

Monégasque limited company (SAM) with a minimum capital of 1,000,000 FF –(153,846€)
**Administrative and branch offices**
Administrative office, acting purely on behalf of the group(s) it represents, an agency or branch office of a foreign concern.

Once all the requirements have been satisfied, commercial and industrial companies must register with the Commerce and Industry Register, which will provide a registration number. Your best bet is to contact one of Monaco's English-speaking lawyers, notaires or business consultants who will advise you according to your business requirements.

## PATENT RIGHTS OFFICE

We have been told that it is less expensive to register your worldwide trademarks, patents, designs, models and international patent registration through Monaco than other European countries. Contact the *propriété intellectuelle* division at Tel: 9315-8867 Fax: 9205-7520. Their office is located at 9, rue du Gabian, Fontvieille.

## WANTED: CLEAN, HIGH-TECH, ENVIRONMENTALLY SOUND COMPANIES

Fontvieille at the western edge of The Principality is where 76 acres has been reclaimed from the sea. This has added a fifth to the size of the tiny country and is the model for Monaco's future. Fontvieille has become an export-driven light industrial base, separate from the banks, services and luxury hotels in Monte Carlo, the central sector of the Principality. Here, clean industries and research coexist with a new planned community.

Alone there are 25,500 French and Italian workers that pour into Monaco daily to work in the private sector. Some work for the larger companies like Eaton, the branch of a Cleveland-based multinational that makes parts for washing machines for **Siemens** and automobile parts for manufacturers such as Daimler-Benz, Ford, and PSA. *Mecaplast*, a locally owned multinational with a staff of 500 and over $150 million in sales, specializes in plastic parts for the auto industry. *Silvatrim*, which has $40 million in sales, specializes in hubcaps. *Biotherm*, part of world leader L'Oréal, which produces a wide range of cosmetic products and maintains a research laboratory here. **Asepta**, makers of Akileine creams and **Teramex**, a leader in the gynecology field. **DPS** has carved out a market for cleaning products for the space industry, **IBM** and **General Electric**. Several smaller companies work in the data field and in high-quality printing.

## THE MONACO GOVERNMENT

The Principality of Monaco is a sovereign and independent state in line with the general principles of international law and of particular agreements passed with France. The territory of the Principality is inalienable. The Constitution of December 17, 1962 defines the government as a Constitutional Hereditary Monarchy.

## THE PRINCE IS HEAD OF STATE

H.S.H. Prince Rainier III acceded to the throne in 1949. He is of the House of Grimaldi, which dates from the Middle Ages. Succession to the throne is by direct and legitimate descent and in order of age, males having predominance over females of equal kin. As Head of State, the Prince represents the Principality in relations with foreign powers. He signs and ratifies treaties and reserves unto himself the right to confer citizenship, honors and distinctions.

In certain matters, the Prince is assisted by two purely consultative assemblies: The State Council and the Crown Council. The Crown Council may be consulted by the Prince on matters of foremost interest to the State and by obligation on the following matters: international treaties, dissolution of the National Council, naturalizations, pardons and amnesties. It is composed of seven members appointed by the Prince for three-year terms. The State Council is responsible for pronouncing its opinion on bills and decrees submitted for examination by the Prince. The Prince nominates its members.

## THE LEGISLATIVE POWER

This power is exercised jointly by the Prince and the National Council, composed of eighteen individuals elected by direct universal suffrage by the Monégasques for a period of five years. The Prince proposes laws; the Council of Government tables them on his behalf, and the National Council passes them in public sessions, along with the national budgetary allocations. The National Council shares legislative powers with the Prince in that they debate and pass laws and submit bills. The Prince promulgates them, and they then are published in the *Journal de Monaco* and take effect.

## THE JUDICIARY POWER

Judiciary power is vested in the Prince, who delegates the full exercise to the courts. The courts dispense justice in the Prince's name, but with complete independence. The courts include: the Magistrate for civil cases, Police Court Magistrate for criminal cases, the Court of First Instance for civil and commercial cases or the Criminal Court for criminal cases, the Court of Appeal, the Supreme Court, the Criminal Court (Assise Court) and the Special Jurisdiction Court. The Supreme Court is reserved for constitutional claims falling outside the competence of the administrative courts. They also mediate conflicts of jurisdictional powers.

## THE MUNICIPALITY

The Principality's single municipality is administered by a Municipal Council composed of fifteen members elected for a period of four years and headed by a Mayor and Assistant Mayors.

## MONÉGASQUE NATIONALITY

One may become a citizen of Monaco in **four** ways: **(1)** By birth, by declaration to the Register of Births, Marriages, and Deaths; being born of a Monégasque father or of a Monégasque mother with father unknown, by adoption by a Monégasque subject; residence in Monaco for more than 10 years and renunciation of previous nationality. **(2)** Being born in Monaco of a Monégasque-born father or mother (even if the parent has renounced Monégasque nationality) and having resided in Monaco since minority age (this declaration is possible only in the year following the Monégasque majority of 21); **(3)** By marriage in the case of women who marry a Monégasque subject. **(4)** By naturalization; this is granted at the discretion of the Prince. The applicant must renounce his or her previous nationality, be exempt from liability for military service abroad, and justify residence in Monaco for 10 years after the age of 21. After naturalization, children of minority age ipso jure are Monégasque subjects, but may, if they wish, repudiate Monégasque nationality in the year following their majority.

# 11
# REGIONAL FOOD AND WINE GUIDE

Because Monaco is located between France and Italy, two of the world's best culinary countries, eating here is a special experience. The Italian food is wonderful, and restaurants serve both the light and lean northern Italian and the spicier southern Italian cuisine. The other food choice in Monaco is the area's specialty, French Provençal cooking. There are two distinct regional cooking styles in this cuisine as well. Lavender, rosemary, thyme, winter savory, bay, and juniper are the essence of Provençal flavoring, along with garlic, olives and virgin pressed olive oil. The Nicoise features its own specialties: *pan bagnat, socca, pissaladière,* and *poulpe à la niçoise* (octopus in tomato sauce). Here are some Provençal dishes to look for on the menu:

**Ratatouille** A vegetable stew of tomatoes, onions, garlic, red and green peppers, eggplant and zucchini.

**Bouillabaisse** A famous fish stew from Marseilles, which has many versions, but usually includes Mediterranean white fish, olive oil and saffron.

**Daube** A rustic, slowly cooked beef stew with wine and Provençal spices.

**Farcis** Stuffed peppers, tomatoes, eggplant, artichoke or zucchini with rice, fish and herbs.

**Pistou and Pesto** A paste or sauce of fresh basil, olive oil and garlic. Pesto includes pine nuts. (Used in soup and pasta).

**Soupe de Poisson or Bourrade** An aromatic blend of fish stock, sometimes with tomatoes, served with croutons upon which one spreads *rouille*, a mixture of oil, garlic and *chiles* or *aioli*, a garlic mayonnaise. Topped off with grated Gruyêre cheese. A true Riviera ritual.

**Salade Mesclun** A traditional salad composed of arugula leaves, riquette, oak leaf lettuce, watercress, chicory, dandelion, and sprinkled with fresh herbs.

**Sardines** Seasoned with herbs, stuffed and grilled over fennel twigs.

**Squash Blossoms** Zucchini flowers stuffed with truffles, rice, vegetables dipped in batter and deep fried.

**Tapenade** Puréed olives, herbs, and garlic used to spread on toast or crackers as an appetizer.

**Tians** Baked layers of vegetables and rice, named after the clay dish in which they are baked.

# HERE ARE SOME TYPICAL DISHES
# NATIVE TO MONACO AND NICE

**Barbagiuan Monégasque** 'fried ravioli' is a delicious tidbit of rice, spinach, leek or Swiss chard, eggs, garlic and cheese that is deep fried and served as an appetizer. Those served at the Café de Paris are outstanding.

**Estocaficada** (Fish Stew) Sun-dried salted cod fish pounded and mixed with milk, olive oil, garlic, and lemon to make a delicious stew. This dish originated with early trade between the Scandinavian countries who exchanged salted cod for Mediterranean olive oil.

**Fougasse** A sweet bread flavored with oranges, rum, anis and raisins. Best when still hot from the bakery Ummm!

**La Tourte de Blettes** Two layers of pastry filled with a mixture of (Swiss chard) blette, Parmesan cheese, sugar, rum-soaked currents, raisins, and pine nuts topped with granulated sugar. This is served for dessert.

**Salade Niçoise** A salad that generally consists of tuna, anchovies, peppers, lettuce, tomatoes, hard-boiled eggs and small black olives sprinkled with vinaigrette dressing.

**Soupe au Pistou** A vegetable, tomato, and bean soup flavored with basil and garlic, topped with grated Parmesan cheese.

**Pan Bagnat** A salade Niçoise in a special large, round bread sandwich. Messy but good.

**Pissaladière** A local pizza specialty. Bread dough is spread with onions, anchovies and black olives, then baked in an oven and sold by the slice.

**Socca** A thin pancake made from chickpea flour and olive oil sold hot by street vendors or from Socca shops.

## OLIVE OIL

Many of today's health-conscious people are turning away from animal fats and substituting olive oil, which in this area is especially delicious. Olive oil was nothing new to the Greeks, who introduced it more than 2,500 years ago. In our time, 98 percent of the worlds' olive acreage, which produces over 60 varieties of olive oil, is located in the Mediterranean area.

It is made by pressing the olives without crushing their stones and letting the olive pulp filter through fiber mats. The first pressing is called *vierge* (virgin), then comes the grades of fine, superfine and *vierge* extra. Pure olive oil is a combination of the first and second pressings. Vierge extra is the one to buy since the filtering process has removed any harsh tasting elements. For a Mediterranean treat, use your *baguette* bread to soak the oil off your plate, as good as butter and better for you.

In the markets you will find stands selling a mind-boggling variety of olives. Some are marinated in herbs and olive oil or lots of garlic. Olive lovers should sample several. Well-crafted olive wood items can be found in most souvenir shops. You might look at salt and herb grinders as gifts. Look at *Alziari,* an olive and olive oil merchant off the *Cours Saleya* in Nice, for decorated tins of olive oil marked Nice, easily pretty enough for the table. They also conduct tours of their olive oil mill between November through February. For visits contact the shop M-F Tel: 33 (0) 4 9344-4512. Closer to Monaco is the *Moulin Lottier* in Menton open all year round for sales. Contact Mr. Maurice on Tel: 33 (0) 4 9335-7915

## WINES

The Hotel de Paris in Monaco possesses one of the world's best wine cellars with more than 300,000 bottles of wine. François Blanc's wife, Marie, who discovered that no wine cellar had been included in the original building plans, personally financed this stellar cellar. She set about building the cave in traditional Bordeaux style in 1881 and purchased the best wines, cognacs and champagne money could buy.

During World War II the Hotel de Paris was occupied by the Germans and the hotel manager feared for the loss of his finest wines and cognacs, so he concealed them in a crypt at the bottom of the cellar. Other bottles of lesser vintage were drunk, but fortunately his cache remained intact. Therefore, it is still the deepest wine cellar in the world.

Legend has it that Winston Churchill and Lord Beaverbrook once polished off a bottle of 1815 cognac at the Hotel de Paris before breakfast! Diners at the Grill and the Louis XIV room have a choice of more than 300 different wines from prices ranging between 300FF (46€), for a 1989 Clos des Cordeliers Saumur, to 58,900FF (9061€) for a 1945 Petrus Pomerol. The wine cellar has a champagne alley that boasts bottles dating back to 1805. But don't worry, there is a wine to accommodate everyone's taste and pocketbook.

Wines are classified in four ways. *Appellation Contrôlée, Vin Delimite de Qualité Supérieure VDQS, Vin de Pays* and *Vin de Table*. None of these is a guarantee of quality, the appellation simply mean that each category must conform to certain criteria of origin, quality of grape and grape variety. The criteria for *Appellation Contrôlée* and *VDQS* are stricter, which is reflected in its prices. Another way to choose a wine is by vineyard, but if a name is not familiar, it is better to choose by the year, because a good vintage of *VDSQ* can often be of better quality and value than an average vintage of an *Appellation Contrôlée.*

The original wines of Provence are: *Palette,* a hard resin wine from the pine forests near Aix-en-Provence; *Bandol,* lovely rosés or dark and soft reds and whites from the terraced vineyards above Toulon; *Cassis,* dry-tasting whites and rosés (these should not be confused with the blackcurrant liqueur mixed with white wine to make kir); and *Bellet,* red, white and rosé grown above Nice.

Rosés are the wines most closely associated with the Côte d'Azur. Light and mildly fruity, they are drunk all year round, but are especially wonderful during the summer. Best served well chilled.

While visiting the south of France it might be fun to go to a *dégustation* (**wine tasting**) at a vineyard or wine estate. *Côtes de Bellet* above Nice is the closest wine-growing area to go to, but there are many others further in Provence. To Bellet, take the Route to Digne, turn right just before the Lingostière Carrefour Mall, and follow the signs *Route des Vins Bellet*. It twists and winds around. Eventually you'll come to the *Château Bellet*. For more information you can call *Les Côteaux de Bellet* Tel: 33 (0) 4 9337-8157 or Fax: 33 (0) 4 9337-9383 ask for Mr. or Madame De Charnance. Various tastings, tours and programs can be arranged for a fee. Direct sales of wine open all year, tours by appointment. Two other winery's are: *Château de Cremat*, for tastings, tours and seminars. Contact Madame Christiane Fraiseau Tel: 33 (0) 4 9215-1213 or the winery on Tel: 33 (0) 4 9215-1295 and finally for *Gaec Massa*, contact Mr. Massa on Tel: 33 (0) 4 9337-8020.

You will also see signs posted along the *Route des Vins, Côtes de Provence* that say *Cave* or *Dégustation*. I suggest you follow the sign and drive down that long dirt road until you see the main house. If you don't notice someone around, ring the bell. In most cases, you'll be warmly received and offered several bottles of their harvest to sample. Prices are often surprisingly reasonable. You can buy by the bottle, by the case or *en vrac* (in bulk) if you have *bombonne*, a large wicker-covered bottle holding 10 to 20 liters found in hardware stores. Prices of wine range from 19FF (3€) to 62FF (10€) per bottle and as low as 8FF (1.24€) to 25FF (3.85€) per liter.

For further information about the *Route des Vins des Côtes de Provence,* call the *Syndicat des Vins, Côtes de Provence,* 33 (0) 4 9473-3101, a wine producer's cooperative with more than 400 wines for sale or tasting. Also the *Maison de Vin Côtes* de Provence in *Les Arcs-sur-Agnes* on Tel: 33 (0) 4 9499-5020 has a large display of wine, and provençal food products. If you're short on time, go to the nearest wine purveyor. In La Condamine we like *Grand Chais Franco Monégasques*, 11 rue Baron de Sainte Suzanne, Tel: 9330-2680.

## OTHER LIBATIONS

Other local popular drinks include *Pastis*, an anise-flavored libation that is chilled with ice and diluted with water. *Ricard* and *51* are both dry and their rival *Pernod* is sweeter. It is fashionable to mix this sweeter one with syrups or *sirop*. If you want to drink beer, it is almost always cheaper to drink French brands like Kronenbourg. Monaco has its own beer named in honor of Prince Albert Ier and called Monaco, which at one time was manufactured in the Principality. The least expensive beer is draft beer. Ask for *une pression* or *un demi*, which is a third of a liter.

# TRUFFLE HUNTING

*There was a piglet named Nanette, a truly Provençal coquette*
*She did a little shuffle found us a truffle,*
*and we followed her to the fête.*

November through April is truffle-hunting season and is an experience you might enjoy as a novelty. Truffles, of course, are a mushroom-like food much coveted in France, and are very rare and difficult little things to find.

My truffle hunt started early one sunny crisp Sunday morning in late January. Our four-month piglet Nannette had been trained since she was a month old to sniff out truffles. Truffles are really a fungus that grows along the roots of white oak trees afflicted with a certain tree disease. The trick is to find white oaks with the disease. The ground around the diseased tree is cultivated, making it easier for the truffles to grow and easier for the pigs to unearth them.

Truffle hunters often have business partnerships. Ours was a two-man and one piglet deal: one person trained the pig, the other person owned the field, and the two were to split the proceeds from any truffles found. Tied to a dog lead, Nanette was urged by her owner to *"Allez Allez."* Snout down, she began her search. After a few minutes, eureka, she found a truffle and begins furiously digging with her snout. The trainer kneeled close to her and just before her sharp teeth grabbed the truffle, he gently whacked her snout out of the way. Then he used a two-pronged shovel to unearth the truffle, which was buried quite deep. Once unearthed, I couldn't believe how revolting the newly found truffle was! Moist dirt and bug larva clung to the truffle, which had the consistency of a semi-wet sponge. And the odor was somewhere between a mens' locker room and musky mud. Our star Nanette sniffed out over a kilo and a half (a little over 3 pounds) in just a few hours, fast work considering that truffles go for around 1200FF (185€) a kilo.

To sell, men huddle together in serious negotiation and weigh the truffles in paper sacks, reminiscent of dealers in the diamond market. After the deal, all retire to the bar for a *pastis* (an apertif that tastes like licorice and can leave you legless when you try to stand up after a few). Why all this fuss about a lowly fungus? Well, the Emperor Caligula, Madame Pompadour, Balzac, Kipling, Colette, Dumas, Talleyrand, Baudelaire and Louis XVI ate huge quantities of truffles believing that they have aphrodisiac properties. But the real reason is that once cooked the truffle transforms everything it is cooked with into ambrosia. One should try the squash blossom stuffed with truffle at Roger Vergé in Mougins, an unforgettable taste treat if you have deep pockets. For more information about assisting in a truffle hunt, phone Douglas Gibbons in the Var, Tel: 33 (0) 4 9473-8841.

## CHOCOLATE

Chocolate lovers will be thrilled to learn that Monaco is the home
of one of the best chocolate makers in Europe. The Chocolaterie
de Monaco has been making over 78 kinds of chocolate treats for
more than 80 years. Their standards are high, which means they
don't accept anything less than 60% pure chocolate in their candies.
Their factory is located at 7, rue Biovès, not far from the Princess
Stephanie Youth Center and another boutique the Place de la
Visitation in the Old Town. Open year round. Closed Sunday.
Tours can be arranged by contacting Tel: 9797-8888.

# TWO POPULAR MONÉGASQUE RECIPES

## BARBAGIUAN

Ingredients:
**The ravioli dough:**
250g (1 cup) sifted flour.
1 beaten egg and 5cl of olive oil or half butter half olive oil and salt.
Kneed the dough with the olive oil, beaten egg and salt, form a
ball and let sit for one-hour covered with film wrap.
**The stuffing:**
300g (1-1/4 cup) of cubed veal.
200g (1 cup) of white onions.
2 cloves of garlic.
500g (2 cups) of zucchini.
2 leeks or Swiss chard.
50g (1/4 cup) of cooked rice.
2 eggs, 75g (1/2 cup) of grated Parmesan.
2 tablespoons of fresh basil or to taste.
1 tablespoon fresh parsley, and marjoram to taste.
15 cl olive oil, salt pepper and peanut oil for frying.

1. Chop onions, peel garlic cloves, place in pan with some olive oil.
2. Add the veal, salt and pepper, to taste, and cook over medium
heat for 20 minutes.
3. In a large pot add leeks and zucchini to boiling water. Cook for
15 minutes. Then chop vegetables and add veal. (you may use a
food processor).
4. In a large bowl add cooked rice, fresh herbs, 2 eggs, grated
Parmesan, olive oil, and the vegetable and veal mixture. Mix together.
5. Take half the dough and roll it out in a rectangle (rolled dough
should not be too thick) and cut out rounds, flouring them light-
ly (you can use a drinking glass to cut out the rounds).
6. Then take the filling mixture (about a teaspoon), roll it into a
ball that will fill the center of the ravioli round, fold them in half
and stick the edges with the white of an egg.
7. Drop in heated smoking peanut oil and cook until each side is

golden brown and crisp. Drain on paper towels then and serve as an appetizer or with a mescaline or green salad.

## PAN BAGNAT
Ingredients:
20cm (8 inch) wide x 9cm (3-1/3 inch) high round white crusty bread rolls (one per person).
Sliced or minced raw sweet onions, tomatoes, and green peppers.
Sliced hard boiled eggs, depitted black olives.
Anchovies and or canned tuna.
Lettuce optional.
Any kind of vinegar you prefer like Balsamic, tarragon etc.

1. Cut bread rolls horizontally across and remove part of the bread on the bottom to allow for filling.
2. Pour some olive oil on the bottom and fill it with the above ingredients.
3. Sprinkle the ingredients with vinegar and salt and pepper to taste and cover with the other half of the roll. Cut in half for easier eating.

# METRIC CONVERSION TABLE

## LIQUID MEASURES

| AMERICAN<br>standard cup | BRITISH<br>standard cup | METRIC |
|---|---|---|
| 1 = 1/2 pint = 8 fl. oz. | 1 = 1/2 pint = 8 fl. oz. | 2.37dl. / 2.84dl. |
| 1 Tbl. = 1/2fl. oz. | 1 Tbl. = 0.55 fl. oz. | 1.5 cl. / 1.7 cl. |
| 1 Tbl. = 1/6fl. oz. | 1 tsp. = 1/5 fl. oz. | 0.5 cl. / 0.6 cl. |
| 1 pint = 16 fl. oz. | 1 pint = 20 fl. oz. | 4.73 dl / 5.7 dl. |
| 1 quart* = 32 fl. oz. | 1 quart* = 40 fl.oz. | 9.46 dl. / 1.1 liter |

*1 quart = 2 pints

## SOLID MEASURES

| AMERICAN/BRITISH | METRIC |
|---|---|
| 1lb = 16 oz. | 453 grams |
| 2.2lb | 1kilogram=1000 grams |
| 1oz. | 28 grams |
| 3 1/2 oz. | 100 grams |

## LIQUID MEASURES
1 cup = 16 tablespoons
1 liter =10 deciliter = 100 centiliters
1 tablespoon = 3 teaspoons

Les Basics

## 12
## LES BASICS

Here are practical things any resident should know and every visitor would like to know about living or staying in Monaco. This chapter covers such varied topics as money exchange, computer repair, libraries, lost property, telephones, baby sitters, beauty salons, gyms, medical help and other miscellaneous categories. An effort has been made to list professionals who speak English. Many people in shops, banks, hotels and restaurants speak some English. You will also find that the police as well as taxi and bus drivers speak enough English to help you get around. The other most commonly spoken foreign language is Italian.

## ALCOHOLICS ANONYMOUS
**AA has English-speaking chapters in Monaco**       9330-2927
*Reformed Church (Protestant) 9 rue Louis Notari (Condamine)*
**Al-Anon Côte d'Azur**                     33 (0) 4 9397-3981
*7:30 P.M. Mondays Eglise Sacre Coeur*
*22, rue de France, 06000 Nice*

## ALTERATIONS
**Yves Saint Eugene**                               9315-0828
*Métropole Galerie*

## AUDIO CASSETTES, CDS
(See Shopping)

## BABY SITTING
The standard rate is between 35FF (5.38€) and 60FF (9.20€) per hour. Most good hotels have a list of sitters. Ask for the concierge. The school section is another place to look for sitters or try the **Monte-Carlo Nannies** at 6, rue St. Michel Tel: 9350-2377 or **AFM** baby sitting on Tel: 9350-2505/33, 33 (0) 4 9378-6691.

## BANKS
Monaco is a banker haven and there seems to be one on every street or corner. They are open Monday through Friday beginning 8:30 to 9:00 in the morning until noon or 12:30, and then from 2:00 to 5:00 PM. Some are closed the afternoon before bank holidays. Many banks have a currency exchange and they give the best currency exchange rate.

Twenty-four-hour ATM cash machines are located on the exterior of most banks. They take plastic and some will take foreign currency.

Private banks serve only their clients and not the public. If you want to open a bank account you'll need to deposit six figures in private ones. Other banks will open your account for between four and five figures. There are no residency requirements. Once a check is written, it is almost impossible to stop payment on it, only in cases of loss or theft. **Warning:** No Monaco bank will take large amounts of cash unless you can prove beyond a doubt where it came from.

## BEAUTY SERVICES
## UNI-SEX HAIR SALONS

**Salon Vincent**                                      9330-7001
*Le Meridien Beach Plaza Hotel*
Vincent is the best precision cutter in town. Specify exactly how much hair you want lopped off because he tends to cut quite short.
**Jacques Dessange Monte-Carlo**              9325-0101
*5, bd. des Moulins*
Alix does a good job with color. Geoffery does the cutting. Across the street from the Tourist Office.

## NAIL SALONS

**Margy's**                                            9330-1505
*Métropole Galerie*
**Institut des Ongles**                                9325-7778
*Métropole Galerie*
Cosmetics and Beauty Treatments
**Institut Parfumerie Fragrance**                      9315-9396
Located in Monte-Carlo Grand Hotel. Specializing in the Carita mini-face lift facial which allow you to feel like queen for the day. Full service beauty treatment, nails, products and massage. Ask for multilingual Colette.
**Columbia Tonus Center**                              9325-0327
*7, av. Princesse Grace*
**Margy's**                                            9330-1505
*Métropole Galerie*
**Les Thermes Marin Spa**                              9216-4946
See the sports section for more information regarding this state-of-the art beauty and sports spa. They offer special daily spa programs.
**Zepter**                                             9310-6229
*5, av. St. Laurent*
Noted for their Swissological beauty products that are a fraction of the same famous Swiss La Prarie. www.zepter.com

## BOOK SHOPS (ENGLISH)

**Scruples**                                           9350-4352
*9, rue Princesse Caroline*
A long-established shop and a good selection of English greeting cards and gift-wrap for all occasions.
**British Riviera Film Library**          33 (0) 4 9378-6444
*3 bd. Général Leclerc*
They offer a selection of paperbacks and the best selection of 15,000 English-language videos. (See Video Rentals)

## BORDER CROSSING

There are no custom formalities on border crossings between France and Monaco since a joint agreement in 1865. In fact, it's hard to sort out Monaco's borders. One side of the street can be France, the other side Monaco. A well-traveled American Express executive asked if he needed his passport to enter Monaco. Well, no, but if you want to get your passport stamped you'll have to go to the Mairie (Mayor's Office) in the Old Town or to the main Tourist Office at 2a Bd. des Moulins.

## BUSINESS OPPORTUNITIES

Center of Administrative Information          9315-4026
*22, ave. Prince Héré. Albert*          *Fax: 9315-4086*
*Commercial Center Fontvieille*
One-stop information service in several languages provided by the government to help those seeking to establish their business in Monaco.

Condor          9797-8830
*Le Titien 4, quai Jean-Charles Rey*          *Fax: 9797-8831*
Thinking of establishing your residency and business in Monaco? Swedish Gunnar Everhed and his multi lingual team will handle the details from apartment hunting to business administration and tax planning.
Web site www.condor.mc  E-mail:monaco@condor.mc

## BUSINESS SERVICES

Temporary office facilities, secretarial services, messages, translation, general office services, telex, fax, mail, photocopying, interpreters and meeting rooms are provided by the following:

Business Aides Associates          9797-3484
*13, bd. Princesse Charlotte, Victoria Palace*          *Fax: 9350-7284*
Conveniently located but pricey.

Monaco Business Center          9205-5818
*20, av. de Fontvieille*          *Fax: 9205-5828*
Their professional secretarial services are reasonably priced with quick turn-a-round. Rental offices start from 8,900FF (1356 €), also have fully equipped meeting rooms. They are part of the Global Office Network
Web site: www.monte-carlo.mc/leader/mbc
E-mail: monacobusinesscenter@monte-carlo.mc

## STOLEN CREDIT CARDS AND TRAVELLERS CHECKS

In case of theft, report stolen credit cards at these phone numbers.
American Express          33 (0)1 4777-7200
Diner's Club          33 (0)1 4762-7575
Mastercard-Eurocard          33 (0)1 4567-8484
Visa-Carte Bleu          33 (0)1 4277-1190
Amerian Express Travellers Checks          08-0090-8600

## CURRENCY

FRANCS
The monetary unit in Monaco and France is the franc; French or Monégasque coins are used in denominations of 0.05, 0.10, 0.20,

0.50 centimes and 1-, 2-, 5-, 10-, 20- franc coins. Bills come in 20-, 50-, 100-, 200-, and 500- French franc (FF) denominations.

## EUROS

January 1, 1999 saw the European Union introduce the new euro currency into financial institutions and stock markets. The rate for the French franc was set permanently at (6.5569) or 6.50 French francs to 1 euro. Most goods now reflect prices in French francs and euros. On January 1, 2002 the conversion to the euro will be complete, except in the United Kingdom, Ireland and several other eastern bloc countries that may not choose to join or fail to meet the criteria for the common European currency.

Euro notes or bills will be in denominations of 5, 10, 20, 50, 100, 200 and 500 euros. Coins in denominations of 1 and 2 euros. Then in 0.01, 0.02, 0.05, 0.10, 0.20 and 0.50 cents (representing one hundredth of 1 euro). French euro cents will carry the mark RF to distinguish them as coins issued in France but will be able to be exchanged within the European countries trading in euros. Banks will accept the old currency until 2012. The new symbol for euros is €. Buying things in European countries will be easier because they will be priced in euros. This is extremely good news for people who are accustomed to trading US dollars because the euro has been trading in a range of 1€ (equals) between US $0.96 to $1.10. So looking at the prices of euros is like looking at the price of a dollar plus or minus additional cents.

## CURRENCY EXCHANGE BUREAUS

Many are open every day including Sundays and holidays.

### MONTE CARLO
**American Express**                    9770-7759
*35, bd. Princesse Charlotte*
Open Monday through Friday closed holidays.
**Monafinances**                        9350-0680
*17, av. des Spélugues*

### MONACO-VILLE (OLD TOWN)
**Compagnie Monégasque de Change**      9325-0250
At Parking des Pêcheurs, the car park garage located next to the Monte Carlo Story. Closed Nov. 5 until December 25.

Casinos are almost always open and the exchange rates are favorable, so it's a good place to change money in a pinch. Be prepared to play. Banks may give a better rate of exchange than currency exchange bureaus. If you have the time, it's not a bad idea to check. As of this writing, **ATM machines offer a very good rate of exchange**, but there is no way to know exactly until you receive your statement back home.

# CASH DISPENSING OR ATM MACHINES

## LA CONDAMINE
Société General
*17 bd. Albert 1er*
Barclays Bank
*17 bd Albert 1er*

## MONACO-VILLE (OLD TOWN)
Crédit Foncier
*6, rue Comte Félix Gastaldi*

## FONTVIEILLE
*Commercial Center Complex*

# CAMERA REPAIRS
(See Film Developing)

# CAR WASH
There are indoors inexpensive do-it-yourself car washes at many of the public garages, such as the one next to the Heliport and St. Charles market. There are several car washes on the Basse Corniche, two heading east toward Nice and one heading toward Menton. Located in gas stations.

**Fontvieille Lavage Auto**                    **0607-936090**
*22, Quai Jean-Charles Rey*
They do hand washing interior or exterior for 70FF (11€) or the complete works for 170FF (26€).

# CATERING (TRAITEURS-TAKE OUT)
**Mister Brians**                    **9330-5009**
*7, av. du Berçeau*                    *Fax: 9350-9017*
Carries a full line of American and British food products and specialty items such as premium smoked salmon and caviar. Also offers lunch menu and delivery. Will fax you their daily menu. For lunch orders call 9315-9418. Mister Brian has established a well-respected catering trade for events and boats along the Riviera.

**Platy Gourmet**                    **9325-5950**
*25, av. de la Costa*
Platy has recently hooked up with the new Maxim's across the street to offer their delicacies. Noted for their excellent Italian specialties. Will cater parties for up to 250 people. English speakers should contact the ever delightful Mary Coles.

**Lam Traiteur**                    **9330-8888**
*4, rue de la Turbie*
Chinese and Vietnamese specialties

**A Roca**                    **9225-1595**
*15, rue Louis Notari*                    *Fax: 9205-9995*
They carry Monégasque specialties such as pissaladière, tourte, socca, barbagiuan, fougasse, and pizza with home delivery. Located just around the corner from the police station and in Fontvieille. (See Shopping section Gourmet Food for more information)

## CLIMATE
Monaco justifiably boasts of its 300 days of sunshine a year.
### WINTER
The temperature averages between 40F-5C to 50F-10C degrees in winter months December to March. Because the sea and mountains create temperate weather, the Côte d' Azur winters are mild with warm sunny days and cool nights until the beginning of March. However, at the higher elevations there can be frost and occasional snow.

### SPRING
April showers bring May flowers. Often short rainstorms mark this period. One has to only take to the hills to experience being in a Renoir field of flowers. Temperature average in the 50-60F-10-15C.

### SUMMER
The average temperature in the early summer months is 72F-22C degrees. Most summers are in the 80F-27C with hot spells for a week or so caused by sirocco winds off the desert in July and August. Sea breezes, more often than not, cool down the evenings.

### AUTUMN
One of the loveliest times to be on the Côte d'Azur. With temperatures in the 60F to 70F-15C-21C, people are still sun tanning on the beach until about mid-October. Storm fronts quickly pass leaving a few crisp autumn days. This is the season for mushroom hunting.

## TEMPERATURE CONVERSION
To convert Centigrade to Farenheit multiply by 1.8 and add 32
To convert Farenheit to Centigrade subtract 32 and multiply by .55
Here are a couple of quick reference points:
0°C = 32°F, 5°C = 42°F, 10°C = 50°F, 15°C = 60°F, 21°C = 70°F, 26°C = 80°F, 31°C = 90°F, and 36.9°C = 100°F.

## CLUBS AND ASSOCIATIONS
A list can be found in Bienvenue, a monthly guide obtained at the Tourist Office, as well as shops and hotels.

## COMPUTER PRODUCTS AND REPAIRS
**FNAC** 9310-8181
*Métropole Galerie*
An upscale electronics store well known throughout France.
**Gale Force Computing** 9350-2092
*13, av. St. Michel* *Fax 9350-4526*
The English computer specialists on the Riviera, whether your interest is multi-user accounting network, virtual reality consulting, trouble shooting, software programming or the Internet, call Steve or Penny Gale.
E-mail gfc@monaco.mc  Web site: www.galeforce.com
**Media Computers** 9216-0607
*9, rue Louis Aureglia*
Authorized Apple dealer.

**Microtek**                                        9325-6767
*2, bd. Rainier III*

## CONSULATES
Listed in Bienvenue, the Tourist Office monthly guide, or in the phone book.

## CUSTOMS (DOUANES)
**French Douane**                                   9797-0230
*6, quai Antoine 1er*

## CUSTOM AGENTS
**Office Maritime Monégasque**                      **9205-7615**
*2, rue de la Lujerneta*                          *Fax: 9205-1959*
Fontvieille E-mail: omm@wanadoo.fr
(See Convention section for more information.)

## DISABLED TRAVELERS
Special facilities are common throughout Monaco. When in the Parking des Pêcheurs, simply look for the elevators near the escalators and push the call button. An elevator will be sent to your level. Several escalators have wheelchair lifts. All streets have been modified to accommodate those with physical challenges. Just one note of caution, when it rains, Monaco's hilly sidewalks turn into slippery slides. Be extremely careful.

## DOG STATIONS
Are located throughout the Principality, especially near parks and other green spaces. There are also conveniently located Robo Dog plastic bag stands that one can use to pick up their dog droppings. Unlike France, Monaco is a bit more fastidious about this.

## DRY CLEANERS
(See Self-Serve Laundry section for Laundromats)
### LA CONDAMINE
**Net Express**                                     9330-2668
*7, rue Grimaldi*
Specializes in cleaning costumes, ball gowns and leather.
**Pressing Shangri-La**                             9330-2668
*2, rue Louis Notari*
### FONTVIEILLE
**5 Sec**                                           9205-7030
*Fast Fontvieille Commercial Center*
Lowest prices in town, good for basics but not for eveningwear or anything special.

## ELECTRICITY-VOLTAGE
**Two-hundred-twenty (220)** volts is the standard current used throughout Europe. Wall sockets are the two-prong (*prise de courant*) kind. Don't forget a plug adaptor for your hair dryer or electric shaver and a 1000-watt transformer in case yours isn't dual voltage. You'll need a heavy-duty 50-watt 50-60Hz. transformer

*(transformateurs)* for motorized electrical appliances. Many answering machines, fax machines, and portable phones can easily be adapted by replacing the 110V transformer with 220V transformer. These can usually be bought or ordered at an electronics store. The electrical appliances are the same; it's only the transformer that needs to be changed. Don't bother to bring your television or video if you're planning a Trans-Atlantic move from the US. The American system is **NTSC** and is not compatible with the European **PAL** or **SECAM** system.

## EMERGENCY SERVICES

| | |
|---|---|
| Fire Department | Press 18 (or 9330-1945) |

In case of fire or accident (or heart attack), it's good to know that it is the firemen (pompiers) who are the fastest in case of an emergency, and that they are also trained paramedics. Their vehicles always have the right of way.

| | |
|---|---|
| Police Department | 17 or 9315-3015 |
| Ambulance Service | 9330-1945 |
| Poison Control Center in Marseille | 00 33 (0) 4 9175-2525 |
| Youth Hot Line E-mail: jjecoute@webstore.mc | 9350-0909 |
| SOS Drug Hot Line | 9350-0808 |
| Alcoholics Anonymous | 9388-3716 |
| Radio Taxis | 9315-0101 |

**Bloc Notes** - A daily list of doctors on call *(médecin de garde)* and pharmacies open for emergencies *(pharmacie de garde)*. This can be found on Channel 1 on the TV as well as in the Nice Matin daily newspaper.

**SAMU** In France, emergency medical service with trained doctors who respond to calls but not as fast as pompiers.
Call **Tel: 33 04 9392-5555. Or dial 15.**

## FAX SERVICES
Offered at the main post office, secretarial services and hotels. (See business services)

## COMMERCIAL FILM AUTHORIZATION
Television and film crews are free to film just about everywhere and everyone in most other places in the world, but not so in Monaco. If you are thinking about filming a television program, a movie or commercial, make careful notes. To get authorization to film **Societe Bains des Mer (SBM) properties**, for example everything in the Place du Casino, you must contact Mme.Rebaudo-Martini on Tel: 9216-6210 or Fax: 9216-2001 or E-mail presse@sbm.mc.

To receive authorization to film in the streets and general views in Monaco you must apply to the *Centre de Presse*, Tel: 9315-2222, Fax: 9315-2215 or E-mail: presse@monaco.mc. Filming the **Palace**, the **Place du Palais** or **Palace Square** is restricted, and all authorization for these requests should be directed to Mr. Armond Deus, Palace press officer, Fax: 9330-2626 or E-mail presse@palais.mc. Be sure to state exactly everything you want to shoot, the time and date and the purpose of your film. The *Centre de Presse* will give confirmation of **all authorizations to you**. If you want to film the *Jardin Exotique* you must apply to the *Mairie*, **Town Hall** Tel: 9315-2863. Last, but not least, is the important *Sûreté Publique*, 3 rue Louis Notari. Introduce yourself and give them a copy of your proposed shooting schedule so they can alert the ever-watchful police to your whereabouts. This will save you some of the hassle of being asked for your filming authorization by dozens of officers. Always keep several copies at the ready.

## FILM DEVELOPING
### MONTE CARLO
| | |
|---|---|
| **K. Photographie** | 9330-8808 |
| *Park Palace Galerie* | |

Fast service, repairs and color photo copying. Multi-lingual.

| | |
|---|---|
| **Foto Quick** | 9350-4110 |
| *Métropole Galerie* | |
| **R.A.P.P.O.** | 9330-1113 |
| *32, bd. des Moulins* | |

Speaks English and does camera repairs.

### LA CONDAMINE
| | |
|---|---|
| **Daniel Mille** | 9797-1310 |
| *17, rue de la Turbie* | |

Does the best developing of black and white film.

| | |
|---|---|
| **Riviera Photo** | 9330-1261 |
| 22, rue Grimaldi | |

### FONTIVIELLE
| | |
|---|---|
| **Studio Phénix** | 9205-3650 |
| *9, av. Héré. Albert* | |

Professional developing for color film.

| | |
|---|---|
| **Photo Team** | 9330-1261 |
| *Fontvieille Commercial Center* | |
| **Carrefour** | 9205-5700 |
| *Fontvieille Commercial Center* | |

They have the lowest film developing prices: 1.50FF (0.23€) each print with 48-hour service; 1.80FF (0.27€) with 24-hour service.

## FLORISTS
### LA CONDAMINE
| | |
|---|---|
| **Allione Fleurs** | 9330-2549 |
| *1, rue Grimaldi* | *Fax: 9325-1826* |

This shop is owned by Narmino.

| | |
|---|---|
| **Bouquets** | 9325-4104 |
| *40, rue Grimaldi* | *Fax: 9330-6014* |

## MONTE CARLO
**Sorasio**                                        **9330-7101**
*Place du Casino*                              *Fax: 9325-0496*
A long time favorite, but pricey.
**Narmino**                                        **9359-5405**
*27, av. de La Costa*                          *Fax: 9350-8965*
Ask for Nicolas Matile, you won't be disappointed in their prices
or their stunning arrangements.
**Fleurisia**                                      **9350-0562**
*10, bd. d' Italie*

## GROCERY STORES AND HYPERMARCHÉS
### FONTVIEILLE
**Carrefour**                                      **9205-5700**
*Fontvieille Commercial Center*
Medium-size hypermarché, a modern grocery that has a little bit
of everything. **Please note: always weigh your produce before you
go to the checkout counter.**

## MONTE CARLO
**Marche U**                                       **9350-6860**
*30, bd. Princesse Charlotte*
They have a gourmet food section.
**Marche Royal**                                   **9216-1631**
*Métropole Galerie*
Have excellent gourmet foods and Middle Eastern specialties.
**Codec Top**                                      **9330-0554**
*1, rue des Genêtes* located in the Millefleuri Apt. complex

## LA CONDAMINE
**Casino**                                         **9350-5678**
*17, av. Albert 1er* (has underground parking)

## TAKE-OUT FOOD
(See Catering and Shopping chapter Gourment Food)

## INSURANCE AGENTS
In French known as *Assurance*, here is a list of insurance agents
who handle car, house and personal property.

## LA CONDAMINE
**Dorfmann Assurance**                             **9330-8600**
*3, rue Princesse Caroline*                    *Fax: 9350-8254*
Has a very competitive rate for car insurance, and prompt service.

## MONTE CARLO
**Eric Blair**                                     **9350-9966**
*33, bd. Princesse Charlotte*                  *Fax: 9770-7200*
Comprehensive insurance packages. E-mail: insure@monaco.mc

**Pierre Aoun**       **9797-3939**
*3, av. St. Charles*       *Fax: 9325-7437*
Web site: www.cybermonaco.mc/passur  E-mail: mat@monaco.net
**Swisscourtage Assurances**       **9330-4243**
*27, av. Princesse Grace*       *Fax 9330-1223*
This company carries special car insurance that provides you with
a rental car in case you have a breakdown or your car is stolen.
Usually there is little provision for this in standard car insurance
policies.

## INTERNET ADDRESS
For current information on activities in Monaco and Grand Prix
results.
http://www.monaco.mc
http://www.monte-carlo.mc
The official Monaco Government site.
http://www.monaco.gouv.mc

## INTERNET CAFÉS
### MONTE CARLO
**FNAC**       **9320-8181**
*Métropole Galerie*
Has free Internet access and lessons.
### FONTVIEILLE
**Dito Document Center**       **9310-1160**
*Le Coronado, 20, av. de Fontvieille*       *Fax: 9310-1161*
Open daily M-Sa from 8:00 AM to 8:00 PM  E-mail: dito@imcn.mc
Has quick print capabilities, PC and Macintosh rentals and access
to the internet.

### LA CONDAMINE
**Stars & Bars**       **9350-8575**
*6, quai Antoine 1er*

## LANGUAGE
The official language in Monaco is French, but English and
Italian are widely spoken and understood. The traditional
language, Monégasque, is a dialect that derives from Genoa and
can be heard spoken by some of the older Monégasques. It is
taught in the school systems.

## LANGUAGE SCHOOLS
## (FRENCH AND ENGLISH)
### LA CONDAMINE
**The Regency School**       **9205-2121**
*7, av. Prince Pierre*
**Busy Bee Work Shop**       **9770-5049**
*Av. La Turbie*
Here is the place to improve English through play activities for
ages 4-12. Also adult conversation groups.

## IN FRANCE
**Institute de Français**                    **33 (0) 4 9301-8844**
*23, av. Général Leclerc, Villefranche-Sur-Mer,  Fax: 33 (0) 4 9376-9217*
*06230 France*
Web site: www.institutdefrancais.com  E-mail: instfran@aol.com
The Institute offers 8-hour-a-day; 2 , 4 , and 8-week total immersion French classes. The emphasis is on speaking. There's always an interesting group of people who take these courses, including diplomats and business executives. Lower rates from December through March.
**Centre Mediterranée**                      **33 (0) 4 9378-2159**
*Chemin des Oliviers Cap d'Ail*              *Fax: 33 (0) 4 9341-8396*
Web site: www.monte-carlo.mc/centremed
E-mail: centremed@monte-carlo.mc
This school is close to Monaco on the bus route and reasonably priced.  Usually language classes are held in the morning with extra curricular activities in the afternoon. Programs for teens as well as adults in the summer.

## LAUNDROMATS OR LAUNDRY
## SELF-SERVICE
Bring lots of 10, 5,and 2FF coins or € coins. The 2000 cost for doing 5 Kg (11 lbs.) 30FF (5€), 7 Kg (15 lbs) (6€) and 16kg (35 lbs) (11€). Drying 2FF for 3 mins.( 0.30€).
**Self Laverie 7/7**
*Escalier (Stairs) du Riviera, Beausoleil, France*
Located off boulevard de la République just behind the Monte Carlo St. Charles Market, only three blocks north of the Tourist Office.
**Self Laverie**                             **33 (0) 4 9378-7477**
*1, rue Jean Jaurès Beausoleil, France*
Take Bus #2 Jardin Exotique and get off at Moneghetti stop.
**Self Laverie**                             **33 (0) 4 9378-6744**
*103, av. 3rd du Septembre, Cap d'Ail, France*

## LEGAL SERVICES
## MONTE CARLO
**Mr. Jean Billon**                           **9325-0888**
*Billion Conseil & Services*                 *Fax: 9350-0640*
22, bd. Princesse Charlotte
E:mail: billonics@imcn.com
Mr. Billon is Monaco's leading lawyer on labor issues.
**Mr. Donald Manasse**                        **9350-2921**
*4, bd. des Moulins*                          *Fax: 9350-8208*
E-mail dmanasse@moncao.mc
An American Mr. Manasse is a long established lawyer who practices general law.
**Mr. William Easun**                         **9310-5510**
*Eversheds*                                   *Fax: 9310-5511*
*24, bd  Princess Charlotte*
This is a branch of the large British firm that offers multiple legal

services. Web site: www.Eversheds.com
E-mail: eversheds@monaco.mc

## FONTVIEILLE
**Mr. James Duffy III**                                    9205-7999
*7, rue du Gabian*                              *Fax: 9305-7722*
Another long established lawyer who practices between here and
the US.

## LIBRARIES
### LA CONDAMINE
**Bibliothèque Louis Notari**                             9330-9509
*8, rue Louis Notari*
They have an English book section, but you must ask for it. Open
9:00 to 12:00 and 2:30 to 6:30 PM. Monday through Friday.
**Bibliothèque Princesse Caroline**                       9315-8001
*1, bd. Albert 1er*
For children

### MONACO-VILLE
**Princesse Grace Irish Library**                         9350-1225
*9, rue Princesse Marie de Lorraine*            *Fax: 9350-6665*
Located in Monaco-Ville, this is a small research library speciali-
zing in Irish Literature. Open 2:00 to 6:00 PM. Monday through
Friday. Web site: www.monaco.mc/pglib
E-mail pglib@monaco.mc

### MONTE CARLO
**St. Paul's Church Library**                             9330-7106
*22, avenue de Grande Bretagne*
Open Wednesday 10:00 to 11:00 AM, 5:00 to 6:30 PM, and
Saturday 10-11:30 AM.

## LOST AND FOUND
### LA CONDAMINE
**Sûreté Publique**                                       9315-3018
(Public Safety Administration)
*3, rue Louis Notari*

## LUGGAGE REPAIRS
(See Shoe Repair)

## MASSAGE
### MONTE CARLO
**Institut Parfumerie Fragrance**                         9315-9396
Home of the Carita mini-lift facial, massage and manicure and
pedicure service.
**Monte-Carlo Grand Health Club**                         9350-6500
**Thermes de Marins Spa**                                 9216-4040
(See Sports chapter Health Spas for more information)

## MARKETS OUTDOORS

The best two markets are: *La Condamine*, Place d'Armes (bottom of Monaco-Ville) and the **Monte Carlo St. Charles Market**, which is located one block up from the Hotel Alexandra and borders on the Beausoleil market. Open between 7:00 AM and 12:00. A trip to one of these markets is a must do. Locals gather for coffee and conversation while doing their daily shopping at the Condamine market. Take in the colors of the wide variety of fruits and vegetables and the aromas of roasting herbed chicken, fresh-baked bread and croissants. Plenty of parking in the convenient underground garages or on nearby streets.

## MARRIAGE

Only residents are allowed legally to be married in Monaco, and one of the persons who is getting married must be domiciled in Monaco at least one month from the public notices *(banns)* posted on the Mairie or Town Hall. The notices must be posted for a duration of at least ten days and include two Sundays. The couple must produce birth certificates and proof that public notice banns have been posted. All foreign documents must be accompanied by translations into French by the appropriate consulates. There is *non-caveat* that one of the couple to be married does not live in the Principality or does not have residence of six consecutive months.

## METRIC CONVERSIONS
### To Convert

Multiply By

| | |
|---|---|
| Inches to centimeters | 2.54 |
| Centimeters to inches | 0.39 |
| Feet to meters | 0.30 |
| Meters to feet | 3.28 |
| Miles to kilometers | 1.61 |
| Kilometers to miles | 0.62 |
| Square meters to sq. feet | 10.76 |
| Square feet to sq. meters | 0.091 |
| Hectares to acres | 2.47 |
| Acres to hectares | 0.40 |
| *Imperial Gallons to liters | 4.546 |
| Liters to Imperial gallons | 0.22 |
| US gallons to liters | 3.79 |
| Liters to US gallons | 0.26 |
| Kilograms to pounds | 2.205 |
| Pounds to kilograms | 0.4536 |

*5 (UK) imperial gallons = 6 US gallons

## MEDICAL HELP

Monaco has endeavored to upgrade and maintain its medical facilities and to utilize the newest medical techniques. The Government has just appropriated funds to completely renovate the whole facility. Unlike the United States, most medical tests are not done in the doctor's office. Doctors will recommend a medical laboratory that carries out the prescribed tests.

Pharmacists are licensed to provide first aid, recommend nonprescription medications and advise on combating poisonous mushrooms.( Mushroom hunting is quite popular in the fall season). Some pharmacists are herbalists, specializing in herbal treatments, and carry homeopathic products. Oh, don't be surprised if you are prescribed a suppository to administer certain medications. They are widely used here and in France. Also, you might be asked to give yourself your own injections, which can be purchased at the pharmacy. Sometimes an equivalent of a medication your home doctor prescribed can be found by asking the pharmacist, who will look it up. But don't count on it. Bring medicines from home.

Emergency and hospital facilities are generally good in Monaco and France. But if you experience a major medical problem you might consider flying directly to your home domicile for treatment. Many U.S. health insurance companies will cover you in Europe, but you will have to pay out of your pocket first and get reimbursed later. Best to check with your particular insurer or take out an additional travel health insurance policy. **Canadian Visa Gold** cardholders are covered for 30 days hospitalization outside Canada.

## HOSPITALS

**Princesse Grace Hospital**                                   **9325-9900**
E-mail: corresp@chpg.mc

The hospital has a general emergency service, specialized surgery departments, maternity wing, modern diagnostic scanners, an oncology department with the latest equipment, and lithotriptor that destroys kidney stones without surgery. It is also a center for the treatment of drug abuse and offers anonymous AIDS screening. The nursing school prepares students for the official French state nurse diploma.

Office hours are open from 8:30 AM to 6:30 PM. Monday through Friday. Visiting hours are: Medical clinic and surgery service 11:00 AM to 8:30 PM. Intensive cardiology care units from 1:00 PM to 3:00 PM. Other services from 1:00 PM to 3:00 PM. and 6:30 to 8:00 PM.

**Cardio-Thoracique Center**                                  **9216-8000**
*11, av. d'Ostende*                                       *Fax: 9216-8299*
Web site: www.ccm.mc   E-mail:info@ccm.mc

Operating since 1987, this is one of the best heart centers in Europe, devoted to advanced research in thoracic and cardiovascular pathology. There is an expert residential staff who works with creator and director world-renowned cardio surgeon Dr. Vincent D'Or and his surgical team. They offer patients package prices depending on the type of care and hospitalization needed.

Hospital rooms are more like designer suites in five-star hotels with beautiful port views and soundproofed for Grand Prix watching. Evening meals are served with choice of wine, and restricted diet menus are tasty. Patients not covered under the French or Monaco social security system must pay all their own expenses

and ask reimbursement from their own insurance plan or country.
The center honors Blue Cross/Blue Shield insurance.

**Hemodialysis Center of Monaco**                    9205-6800
*32, quai Jean-Charles Rey* Located in the port of Fontvieille, this
modern center is equipped with fourteen dialysis machines fitted
with ultra filtration command to supply kidney patients with secu-
re and comfortable dialysis. The center is staffed with expert dialysis nurses and supervised by a resident specialist. It is connected
to all other medical facilities, including the nephrology services at
the Pasteur Hospital in Nice.

## DOCTORS
Here is a list of multi-lingual doctors who speak or understand
English. Residents who seem satisfied with their quality and service have recommended them. However, we do not claim to be experts
on medical qualification and we offer these names on that basis.

## GENERAL PRACTITIONERS
**Dr. Guy Millou**                         33 (0) 4 9378-7111
*Residence Tenao Palace 230, av. Delphine, Beausoleil, France*
Well thought of by many of his patients.

**Dr. Nabil Sharara**                      33 (0) 4 9378-4862
*3, bd. Général Leclerc Alcazar Building*
Located in Beausoleil, the other side of the street is Monaco,
about a block and half up the hill from the Office of Tourism.

**Dr. Michel Péroti**                              9315-0303
*19, bd.des Moulins*

**Dr. Michel Pantaléo**                    33 (0) 4 9341-4646
*Residence St. Martin*
43, av. Paul Douimer, Roquebrune Cap Matin, France
A Homeopathic general practitioner who treats children and
adults.

**Dr. Eva Bare**                           33 (0) 4 9301-5379
*32, av. de la Liberté, Eze, France*
Located in the Hotel Cap Roux building Basse Corniche. She speaks
English, German and French; studied in the United States.

## GENERAL SURGEON
**Dr. Claude Huguet**                              9325-6254
*Europa Residence Place des Moulins*

## CANCER, ONCOLOGY
**Dr. Michel Hery**                                9325-9900
*Chief of Oncology, Princesse Grace Hospital*
Has the most advanced equipment in the market.

## CARDIOLOGY
**Dr. Vincent D'Or**
**Dr. François Burlon**                            9216-8000
*Cardio-Thoracique Center*                     *Fax: 9216-8299*
E-mail: info@ccm.mc

## DERMATOLOGY
Dr. Christine Choquenet-Chabrier          33 (0) 4 9378-4565
21, bd du Général Leclerc, Beausoleil, France

## EAR, NOSE, AND THROAT
Dr. Pierre Lavagna                        9205-7601
*2, rue de la Lujerneta*
Fontvieille

## GASTRO-ENTEROLOGY
Dr. Daniel Rouison                        33 (0) 4 9378-3300
*11, bd. du Général Leclerc, Beausoleil, France*
Excellent English and credentials.

## GYNECOLOGY
Dr. Paule Verdino                         33 (0) 4 9378-6746
*5, av. Alsace, Beausoleil, France*
She speaks good English, specializes in infertility. Sometimes hard
to get an appointment
Dr. Anne Marie Cheutet                    33 (0) 4 9341-8085
*1, bd. Général Leclerc, Beausoleil, France*
Located in the Banque Populaire building just across from the
Place de la Crèmaillére north of the Tourist Office.
Dr. Françoise Ragazzoni                   33 (0) 4 9378-6681
*Palais Gallia, Place Crèmaillére, Beausoleil*
Located behind the Crèmaillére Restaurant.
Dr. Didier Joly                           33 (0) 4 9378-5848
*11, bd. Monéghetti, Beausoleil, France*
He specializes in pregnancy and delivery, and according to his
patients has a reassuring bedside manner.

## PEDIATRICIANS
Dr. Marie-Gabrielle Notari                9350-0987
*10 bd. d' Italie*
Dr. François Remediani                    33 (0) 4 9378-0124
*2, av. Camille Blanc, Beausoleil, France*

## PLASTIC SURGEON
Dr. Yves Trémolet de Villers              9325-5500
*5, av. St. Michel*
E-mail: yvestdveillers@compuserve.com
Besides his work here in Monaco, he is a professor and practices
at the University of California in Los Angeles. Be mindful: he is
hard to reach because of his transatlantic travels.

## RADIOLOGY
Dr. Michael MacNamera                     9325-9880
Chief of Radiology, Princesse Grace Hospital
American born and trained, tops in his field, does advanced heart
research with Cardio-Thoracique Center. Handles Magnetic
Resonance Imaging (MRI).

Dr. Alina Greco                                            9325-8980
*Princesse Grace Hospital*
Tri-lingual, Italian, English, French with training in Italy and
London.

## UROLOGY
Dr. Christian Choquenet                                    9325-7660
*8, bd. des Moulins*
Chief of Urology Princesse Grace Hospital

## DENTISTS
### MONTE CARLO
Dr. Claude Pallanca                                        9350-5591
Dr. Arthur Goldstein
*2, av. St. Charles*
Dr. Pallanca is a professor at the University of Nice Dental School.
His associate, Dr. Arthur Goldstein, is an American dentist who
also specializes in gum disease.
Dr. Bruno Fissore                                          9325-6666
Dr. Amelia Fissore                                         9350-4345
*3, av. St. Michel*
This husband and wife dental team have trained in the United
States.

### LA CONDAMINE
Dr. Thierry Giorno                                         9330-1057
*7, rue Suffren-Reymond*
Just across the street from the Ferrari dealer, Dr. Giorno also spe-
cializes in tooth implants and restorative dentistry.
E-mail: Giorno@monaco.mc
Dr. Chavet                                          33 (0) 4 9378-4953
*15, bd. de la République, Beausoleil, France*

## ORTHODONTIST
Dr. Michel Ballerio                                        9330-0236
*38, bd.des Moulins, Monte Carlo*
E-mail:balleriomichel@csl.com
American trained.

## PHARMACIES
### MONTE CARLO
Pharmacie Campora                                          9330-8310
*4, bd. des Moulins*
Pharmacie de la Costa                                      9350-5234
*26, av. de la Costa*

### LA CONDAMINE
Pharmacie Médecin                                          9330-1706
*19, bd. Albert ler*
Pharmacie Centrale                                         9330-2101
*Place d' Armes*

| | |
|---|---|
| **Pharmacie Internationale** | 9330-3599 |
| *22, rue Grimaldi* | |
| Multi-lingual staff | |

**FONTVIEILLE**
| | |
|---|---|
| **Pharmacie de Fontvieille** | 9205-7648 |
| *Commercial Center* | |
| Open until 9 PM. | |

## MOVERS

| | |
|---|---|
| **Cursi V.F.** | 9205-7628 |
| *1, av. Prince Pierre* | |
| **Société Monégasque de Transports** | 9330-6442 |
| *2, rue Iris* | |

## NEWSPAPERS-MAGAZINES-CIGARETTES

Monaco newsstands carry a variety of international newspapers and magazines from around the world. You can find in English the following American papers: USA Today, The International Herald Tribune, The Wall Street Journal, Barrons and The New York Times. (It can only be found at the Monte Carlo Grand news shop). The Sunday N.Y. Times edition usually comes in on Monday. The major British papers: The Guardian, The Times, Daily Express, The Daily Mail, The Mirror, The Telegraph and Financial Times. The Sunday editions of the British papers can be found at the Café de Paris, the Blue Shop in the Métropole Galerie and the Khedive on bd. Albert 1er. Between 3:30 and 4:00 PM on Sunday. (It's a good idea to call ahead as wild cat strikes by various unions sometimes impede the Sunday deliveries). At other newspaper agencies on Monday morning.

## NEWS STANDS

**MONTE CARLO**
| | |
|---|---|
| **Café de Paris** | 9216-2288 |
| *Place du Casino* | |
| **La Régence** | 9350-3109 |
| *28, av. de la Costa* | |
| **Newsstand** | 9330-4295 |
| *Monte Carlo Grand Hotel* | |

**LA CONDAMINE**
| | |
|---|---|
| **La Gitane** | 9330-7753 |
| *1, rue Grimaldi* | |
| **La Maison de la Presse** | 9325-3242 |
| *22, bd. Princesse Charlotte* | |
| **Tabacs le Khedive** | 9330-2933 |
| *9, bd. Albert I* | |
| **Le Media** | 9205-9855 |
| *Fontvieille Commercial Ctr.* | |
| **Presse Internationale** | 9350-4317 |
| *9, av. Princesse Grace* | |

## PETS

SPA                                                        9330-2020
*12, av. d'Ostende  (in France)*          *33 (0) 4 9341-0362*
Provides shelter for run away animals

## DOG GROOMER

Aristochiens                                    33 (0) 4 9378-5000
*19, bd. République Beausoleil*
Pet Ambulence                                              9325-4220

## VETERINARIANS

Dr. Isabelle Basson-Blanchi                                9205-7477
*Quai Jean-Charles Rey. Fontvieille*
English speaking, she also makes referrals to kennels, and dog sitters.

## PHONE CARDS

(See Telephone Services)

## POLICE-SECURITY

Sûreté Publique                                            9315-3018
*3, rue Louis Notari*

Emergency Number is **17** Firemen **18**

There are not many places left in the world where a woman can walk all over town at any time of night wearing her jewels, or park her car in a public garage after 8:00 PM with a feeling of safety and security. All this can be credited to the Sûreté Publique's 500 officers and inspectors, who are conspicuous and courteous. They are assisted by more than 60 high-tech surveillance video cameras, some with infrared night vision. These are installed throughout the Principality on major streets, intersections, public elevators, parking facilities and walkways. Although it looks a little like "big brother," this surveillance actually acts as a deterrent to crime in Monaco, and in other cities around the world.

The Maritime division is responsible for port and helipad duty along with ensuring the security of Monaco's offshore underwater coral reef preserve established by Prince Rainier III. Criminals who are caught are quickly dealt with in a matter of days, those found guilty can expect to receive stringent penalties. The slammer is first-class but only short-term; prisoners are quickly transferred to lesser accommodations in France. Monaco maintains around a 1:67 police-to-resident ratio and yes, it means you will see a lot of police around, but we residents appreciate it. It makes us feel very safe.

## PORT INFORMATION

Monaco Harbor Master                                       9315-3700
V.H.F. Channel 12                              *Fax: 9315-3715*
Fontvieille Harbor Master                        Tel: 9315-8569
V.H.F. Channel 9                               *Fax: 9315-3712*

# POST OFFICE

**Main Post Office**                                           9797-2525
*La Scala Palace*
Beaumarchais Square across from the Hotel Hermitage. They
have a full range of services: telephones, telegrams, fax and phone
cards. Open Monday to Friday 8:00 AM to 7:00 PM, Saturday
8:00 to 12:00 PM. Telephone service open every day from 8:00
AM to 9:00 PM.

# BRANCH OFFICES

| | |
|---|---|
| **La Condamine** | 9305-7348 |
| *Next to the old train station* | |
| **Fontvieille** | 9205-6477 |
| *Next to the fire station* | |
| **Larvotto Beach** | 9350-8122 |
| *Behind Larvotto Beach* | |
| **Monaco-Ville** | 9330-3410 |
| *Across from the Mairie* | |
| **Avenue des Moulins** | 9330-7899 |
| *Place des Moulins* | |

International packages weighing more than 1 kilogram (2.2 lbs.)
must carry a customs declaration. When receiving items from
other countries, you may be liable for a duty tax and handling fees
for packages over 1 kilogram or 2.2 lbs.

# PUBLIC PARKING

Over 15,000 spaces are available in the various covered garages all
with closed video surveillance and attendant. See map and
Getting There, Getting Around section for more information on
"Monaco Parking" cards. Most garages have a free 60-minute
grace period.

# RADIO STATIONS (ENGLISH)

Riviera Radio on Channel 106.3FM in Monaco or 106.5 FM in
France. This long-established English language station airs the
BBC news, financial news, sport reports, maritime and land weather bulletins, information about regional activities, films and
music programs. Features a Job File and Community Chest where
you can advertise items for sale or wanted to buy. Phone Tel: 9797-
9494 or Fax: 9797-9495.

# RELIGION

Monaco is a Catholic state, but its constitution guarantees full
religious freedom.

**ANGLICAN**
**St. Paul's Church**                                         9330-7106
22, av. de Grande-Bretagne

**BAHA'I**                                                    9350-9495
Feasts and welcoming

## CATHOLIC

### MONTE CARLO
Eglise St. Charles                          9330-7490

### MONACO-VILLE
Cathedral                                   9350-8770
Chapelle de la Miséricorde                  9330-8770

### LA CONDAMINE
Eglise St. Martin                           9330-1780
Eglise St. Dévote                           9350-5260
Eglise du Sacré Coeur                       9330-7526

### FONTVIEILLE
Eglise St. Nicolas                          9205-2329
Chapelle des Carmes                         9330-8640
Chapelle des Franciscains                   9330-8693

### JEWISH
Synagogue, Community Center                 9330-1646
*15, av. de la Costa*

### CHRISTIAN
Monaco Christian Fellowship                 9330-2927
*9, rue Louis Notari Condamine*

## SCHOOLS

College Charles III                         9315-8675
*Av. de l'Annonciade*

The school provides an international section and receives foreign pupils at all levels primary, junior, middle and senior schools. This section offers the French Baccalaureate International Option. The OIB students follow a French syllabus with the following subjects: history, geography, English language and literature. The program prepares students for admission to anglophone universities worldwide and French Universities and les Grandes Ecoles.

The staff consists of qualified professional teachers with years of experience. The student body is approximately 20 percent Anglophone (British, American, Canadian) the remainder are Francophone. In the primary and junior schools the children have 4 hours of English a week. In the middle and senior schools the pupils have 6 hours of English plus 2 hours of history and geography in English a week. Extracurricular activities include magazine club, theater and singing.

Admission procedures require that students be nationals or residents of the Principality, Carte de Séjour holders. This school, like all the public schools in Monaco, is free. Criteria for admission into the international section are based on academic ability, review of school reports and tests in English.

Lycée Albert Ier                                      9315-8000
Place de la Visitation
Web site: www.meditnet.com E-mail: albert1er@medinet.com
Lycée Technique de Monte-Carlo              9315-8672
*Av.de l'Annonciade*
A secondary technical school providing programs in commercial
services, hotel services and mechanical and electrical services.

There are also several private fee-paying schools in Monaco.

## ECOLE, COLLEGE, LYCÉE FRANCOIS D'ASSISE-NICOLAS BARRE

This is a non-denominational school from primary to secondary
school
**Primary and college**                          9797-1050
*11, rue Princesse Marie de Lorraine*
**Lycée**                                                 9030-8693
*11, av. Roqueville*
**The International School of Monaco**    9325-6820
*12, quai Antoine 1er*                          *Fax: 9325-6830*
Offering primary bilingual education. For more information
contact
Headmistress Diana Smith. E-mail: intlschl@monaco.mc

## SHOE REPAIR
### MONTE CARLO
**Rambaldi**                                           9330-7846
*1, av. St. Laurent*

### LA CONDAMINE
**Clef Express**                                       9350-6423
*1, av. de la Madone*
Also makes keys, rubber stamps and plaques.

### FONTVIEILLE COMMERCIAL CENTER
**Clef Express**                                       9205-2526
Also makes keys, rubber stamps, and plaques.

## SKATE BOARDS, ROLLER BLADES AND IN LINE SKATES
Using any of the above apparatus for transportation is prohibited
on sidewalks and streets. You may use them along the boardwalk
area at Larvotto Beach and Port areas only.

## STAMPS
Office des Emissions de Timbres-Poste
**New Issue Office and Exhibition**          9315-4141
*Fontvieille Commercial Center 3rd floor.*
In 1885 Prince Charles III decided to create Monaco's own pos-
tage stamps, highlighting the independence of the Principality.

Indeed, an accurate history of Monaco and world events can be seen through these stamps. In this era, the Prince continues the tradition of his ancestors with a hands-on approach in the selection of subjects for the stamps and the artists to create them. These famous, beautiful stamps are much sought after by stamp collectors around the world. A favorite of collectors is a portrait of Princess Grace created by master engraver Czeslaw Slania; a dual issue between Monaco and the United States

New issues are sold at special booths in the main post office, the new issue office and in the Monaco-Ville branch. You can become a subscriber to the semi-annual first issue mailing list at the Office des Emissions, or by requesting a subscription form by mail or Fax 377 9315-4142. The forms are available in four different languages. The cost is 50FF or (7.50€).

Remember, letters sent from the Principality must have Monégasque stamps, not French stamps. Letters sent from France must have French stamps! **Orange mailboxes are Monaco, Yellow ones are French.**

## TELEVISION STATIONS

Channel surfing the world best sums up Monaco's excellent cable television. There are 32 channels broadcasting in French, Italian, German, Spanish, and English. English-speaking channels are: CNBC 13, Sky News 20, BBC Prime 24, BBC news 31 and CNN 26. Some American series programs like Friends, Seinfeld and New York Police Blues can be found in English versions on Channel Jimmy'z (21). There are even more possibilities with the new digital system viewed through new digital boxes. All can be purchased through Monaco's Teledistribution at 29, av. Princesse Grace Tel: 9350-3838. Discreet is the word if you want to opt for English Sky satellite television. Many private companies can hook you up and there seems to be no specific law against it; however, some apartment buildings outlaw satellite dishes.

European broadcasting standards are not as puritan as American, so be prepared to see R-rated movies and Italian topless dancers during prime time, and hard core X-rated pornography from 12:00 onwards. You might want to check the scheduling before allowing your children to have carte blanche with the set while you are out.

## TELEPHONE SERVICES

**Office de Telephones**                                    **9966-3300**
*14, av. de Fontvieille*
Web site: www.monaco-telecom.mc
E-mail: monaco-telecom@monaco-telecom.mc
Open M-F 9:00-1:00 PM and 2:00-5:00 PM, Monaco will be one of the first, to offer broadband ADSL lines in Europe.

## PHONE CARDS

Phone cards are the most popular method of phoning all over Europe. These cards can be bought at the post office and tobacco shops. They come in units of 50 to 120 units. A 120-unit card is good for a 20-minute call to the United States between 8:00 PM through 2:00 PM. Phone booths abound everywhere and are found in every post office. Phone numbers are listed in the booths if you wish to receive calls. Rates and charges are listed in the green pages of the phone directory.

The cheapest time to call the United States and Canada is from 8:00 PM through 2:00 PM the next day. At 2.76FF (0.42€) per minute, except to Alaska and Hawaii, which is 7.54 FF (1.16€) per minute off peak time or 9.47FF (1.45€) during peak time, which is 2:00 PM through 8:00 PM. Please note that using a phone card is more cost- effective than using AT&T. Currently, the best value on American phone cards is MCI during the 12:00 PM to 8:00 PM time slot, followed by Sprint. However, international phone service is changing daily and it is probably wise to find out what is the latest "cheap" call. (See Below) Generally, the most inexpensive times to call throughout France are between 7:00 PM and 8:00 AM. Peak times are between 8:00 AM through 7:00 PM.

## CALL BACK SERVICE

To save money and TVA (VAT) on your long-distance calls, especially to the United States, join one of the call back services. You can be hooked into a computerized dedicated line in the United States, which calls you back without charge and lets you make your long-distance calls at a substantial savings over French rates. You also have access to 800 numbers.

**Riviera Communications Telegroup**          33 (0) 4 9203-0856
*17, rue Albany, 06160 Juan Les Pins France*
Customer service Tel: 33 (0) 1 4143-9640 or
E-mail: service-client@global-access.fr

## LOCAL CALLS

Monaco now has its own country code and telephone company, separate from France. The new country code as of June 1996 is 377. To call from anywhere outside the Principality you must dial 377 then the Monaco number. The country code for France remains the same 33, however they have added new regional codes that follow the country code. **Paris is 01**, the **northwest is 02**, the **northeast 03**, the **southeast 04** (that's us the Alpes Maritimes), and the **southwest is 05**. When in France dial the 10 digit number.

## INTERNATIONAL CALLS

When calling from Monaco or France, you must dial **00**. For **example,** to call the United States, dial 00 1 which is the country code for the U.S., or dial 00 44 for England, or 00 39 for Italy.

## MOBIL TELEPHONE CALLS

Throughout Monaco and France you just dial 06 and the 8-digit number. You do not have to dial 00 or a country code while in France or Monaco. To call a Monaco or French mobile phone number from other countries you must include the country code 377 or 33. However you drop the 0 in the (0) 6 prefix. So to call a mobile phone here from the United States you would dial 011 377 607XXXXX.

## TOLL FREE NUMBERS OR NUMERO VERT
00 800 replaced the old 05 prefix for these numbers. From some phones you can begin by dialing 8.

## INTERNATIONAL DIRECTORY ASSISTANCE
00 377 12 (+) country code)  Example:  00 377 12 (1) for the US or (44) for the UK.

## FREQUENTLY CALLED NUMBERS

| | |
|---|---|
| Local Directory Assistance | 12 |
| AT&T | 08 0099 0011 |
| MCI | 08 0099 0019 |
| Sprint | 08 0099 0087 |
| Canadian Bell Card | 08 0099 0016 |
| DHL | 01 5535.3030 |
| Federal Express | 08 0012 3800 |
| Chronopost | 04 9321 3311 |
| Jet Services | 04 9374 1515 |
| UPS | 08 0087 7877 |
| AOL Internet Access In Nice | 33 (0) 4 9321-4098 |
| Toll Free | 08 3606-1310 |
| Correct Time | 3699 |
| Tourist Information | 159 |
| Repairs-Complaints | 13 |
| Local Weather-Sea and Navigation Reports | 9330-1313 |
| Weather:        in France | 08 3668 0101 |
| Cote d'Azur | 08 3668 0206 |
| Harbor Master | 9315-3700 |
| English Message Service Nice Airport | 33 (0) 4 9321-3012 |
| Information Nice Airport | 33 (0) 4 9321-3030 |
| Aerodrome Cannes-Mandelieu | 33 (0) 4 9390 4040 |
| Roissy-Charles DeGaulle (Paris) | 33 (0) 1 4862 2280 |

### AIRLINES

| | |
|---|---|
| Air France | 33 (0) 4 9318 8989 |
| American Airlines | (0) 8 0187 2672 |
| British Airways | 33 (0) 8 825 825 400 |
| British Midlands | (0) 8 0005 0142 |
| Delta Airlines | (0) 8 0035 4080 |
| Easy Jet | 00 44 870 6000 00 |
| Heli-Air Monaco | (377) 9205 0050 |
| Iberia | 33 (0) 4 9321 4848 |
| K.L.M. | 33 (0) 1 4456 1818 |
| Lufthansa | (0) 8 0163 3838 |
| Sabena | 33 (0) 4 9321 7460 |
| SAS | 33 (0) 4 9321 3455 |
| United Airlines | 33 (0) 4 4897 8282 |

# WAKE UP CALL

*55* followed by 4 digits corresponding to wake up time
ex:*55* 0830 = (8 hours 30 minutes AM) then # symbol.
To cancel hit # 55* symbol. To verify correct number dial*55*
Cost per call is 3.71FF (0.57€). * is called *etoile* # is called *diese*

# MINITEL

An innovative computer supplied by the phone company and
stationed in every post office that provides instant access to
directory assistance without calling the operator. Available to
homeowners who are charged by the minute for access to a
variety of services such as banking, weather, news, trains, airplane
schedules, sports entertainment and general information. To use
this service turn the unit on. Pick up the telephone receiver and
dial the service code (3611 for directory service 3615 for
information). When you hear the tone, then press the
connection/fin key, and hang up the receiver. Some post office
models are automatic and require no physical telephone.

## RENTAL CELLULAR PHONES

The standard for cell telephones in Europe is GSM, however, more
countries are subscribing to the standard that allows the caller to use his
or her mobile phone just about anywhere in the world.

### MONTE CARLO
**Dancom**                                              9330-6666
*6, av. Saint Michel*
Sells or rents cell phones, walkie-talkies and phone accessories by
day or month. E-mail: dancom@monaco.mc

### PARIS
**Call'Phone**                                   33 (0) 1 4071-7254
Web site: www.groupett@planete.net
E-mail:groupette@planete.net
This company distributes cell phones at all the major Paris airports.

### US, FRANCE, UNITED KINGDOM, ITALY
**Omni Point**                    Toll Free US 1-877-OMNI-2-GO
This company rents or sells GSM cell phones to be used world-
wide. Or if you are from Europe you can use your own GSM com-
puter chip in a rented American phone with GSM capabilities.
For more information www.omnipoint.com

## PUBLIC ELEVATORS
(See Transportation and Map.)

## TRAFFIC INFORMATION
107.7 FM for all traffic conditions, updates every 30 minutes in
English during the summer, or on Riviera Radio 106.3 & 106.5 FM

# TIPPING

## RESTAURANTS

Prices shown include VAT and service. Service is 15 percent (usually included in the price of the food), but if you've received excellent attention you might leave another 5 to 10 percent. It's customary to leave some kind of a tip. You may leave coins, but please don't leave the little gold centimes. It's considered an insult.

## CAFÉS AND BARS

Café drink prices are steep. Don't feel obliged to consume them quickly and give up your table. Tip around 5 percent of the bill or less depending on the service. Three to five francs is often enough. This is one of the qualities of life here that everyone enjoys!

## TAXIS

Usually you tip 5 to 10 percent of the fare. Chauffeured car drivers could get 10 percent of the total bill, more if you've received great service, but 12 percent is the maximum.

## CONCERTS, PLAYS AND MOVIES

Five francs per person to the usher who seats you. This is especially the case at concerts, plays, and sometime movies.

## MISCELLANEOUS TIPPING

One should tip hairdressers 5 to 10 percent of the bill, the shampoo girl should get 10 FF (1.53€), as should hotel services, porters and gas station attendants if they do more than just pump gas.

Any home-delivery person should be tipped 5-10FF (1.53 - 2€). Parking attendants should be tipped 10FF(1.53€). Public bathroom attendants must be tipped at least 1FF (0.15€) and more like 2 to 3 francs, or (0.30€ to 0.45€). You'll find the bathrooms with attendants to be the cleanest. Monaco gets high ratings in cleanliness, availability, and handicapped-friendly access to its public bathroom facilities. Not always true in France and Italy where one must often politely ask and offer to pay to use the toilettes even in emergency situations! This holds true for bars and restaurants; one must order something before one can 'go', so plan ahead.

Everyone remarks how expensive food is compared to the U.S. But keep in mind that the VAT (Value Added Tax) ranges from 19.6 percent on all goods and services, and 5 percent on food items. See VAT section for more information. Europeans often complain when they receive their bills in the United States that local and state taxes are tacked onto the bill, increasing the cost. No matter where you seem to be the tax man gets his due. So just be aware of the different systems between the US and Europe and you will have a better understanding of the bill and the cost.

# TOURIST OFFICES

Information on Monaco can be obtained from these local and international tourists' offices:

Direction du Tourisme et des
Congrès de la Principauté de Monaco
Administration:               **+377 9216-6116**
*2a, bd des Moulins*      *Fax: +377 9216-6000*
E-mail: dtc@monaco-congres.com
Information: +377 9216-6166
Web site: www.monaco-congres.com
**Monaco Government Tourist and Convention Office**
**New York**                **(212) 286-3330**
*565 Fifth Avenue 23rd Fl.*    *Fax: (212) 286-9890*
New York, NY 10022 (U.S.A.)   **Toll Free: 1-800-753-9696**
E:mail: mgto@monaco1.org
Web site: www.monaco.mc/usa
**Monaco Government Tourist and Convention Office**
**London, England**         **44 207 352-9962**
*3/18 Chelsea Garden Market*   *Fax 44 207 352-2103*
*Chelsea Harbour, London SW10 OXE*  **Toll-Free: 0500-006114**
E-mail: monaco@monaco.co.uk
**Office du Tourisme et des Congrès de la Principauté de Monaco**
**Paris**               **33 (0) 1 4296-1223**
*9, rue de la Paix*      *Fax: 33 (0) 1 4261-3152*
*75002, Paris, France*
**Monaco Government Tourist and Convention Office**
**Milan, Italy**          **39 (0) 2 8645-8480**
*Via Dante, 12*      *Fax: 39 (0) 2864-8469*
*20121 Milan, Italy*
**Monaco Government Tourist and Convention Office**
**Dusseldorf, Germany**     **49 211 323-7844**
*WZ Center*       *Fax: 49 211 323-7846*
*Konigsallee 27-31*
**Monaco Government Tourist and Convention Office**
**Tokyo, Japan**        **81 (0) 3 5798-7403**
*Uhnex Twaindle 101*    *Fax: 81 (0) 3 3280-2655*
*Shirogane-dai 5-15-5, Minato-Ku*
*108 Toyko, Japan*

## TVA AND VAT (VALUE ADDED TAX)
### SHOPPING REFUNDS

This consumer tax is added onto most products and services, including gasoline. The current rate as of April 1, 2000 is 19.6 percent, which can rise to more than 50 percent on luxury items. It is 5.5 percent on food items, medications, books and utilities. The French government is planning to drop the tax back to its original 1995 level of 18.6 percent as soon as 2002.

You can get reimbursed for your purchases if you are (1) A visitor to Monaco or France, (2) you purchase more than 1200FF- (185€) from one store, or (3) if you're doing business such as exhibiting at a convention. Certain companies will assist in getting your VAT reimbursement. To receive reimbursement on purchases, ask the store to provide you with a detaxe form, It will give you the details of your purchase. You pay the full amount of your purchases.

When you leave France, take your detaxe form and the purchase item to the customs at the border point. The form will be stamped and an addressed envelope provided for you to post the completed document. You will receive your reimbursement by mail. You have six months to make your claim and foreign residents can claim refunds on purchases made six months prior to their leaving. Allow adequate time at airports for custom points as lines can be long during peak travel seasons, especially in Paris. This may sound complicated, but it is quite easy and can save you quite a bit of money especially if you made purchases that were on sale. So do it!

## TABACS

Tabacs are found in every village, often combined with a bar. They sell tobacco, cigarettes, smokers' items, cigars, newspapers, magazines, stationary, postage stamps, lotto tickets and racing forms. In France they are authorized to sell all varieties of car registration stickers, parking fine stamps and other official documents. In Monaco you can find forms to use when amending leases or writing to the minister of state.

Cigar aficionados may buy Cuban cigars in the Blue Shop in the Metropole Galerie and the Café de Paris news shop.

## TRANSLATION SERVICES

**Communication Multilingue Organization**      33 (0) 4 9209-9092
*420, av. de Pessicart 06100 Nice France*      *Fax: 33 (0) 4 9209-9272*
Operating for the past ten years, this is the premier company that specializes in simultaneous and technical translations.

## TUXEDO RENTAL

**LA CONDAMINE**
**Jacques Bourdin**                                    9330-4922
*5, rue Princesse Caroline*                          *Fax: 9330-8469*
The owners don't speak much English but luckily you don't need much talking to fit a Tux (or as it is called here *"Le Smoking"*) for *"tenue de soiree"* or black-tie events.

## VETERINARIANS

(See Pets)

## VIDEO RENTALS

**British Riviera Film Library**          33 (0) 4 9341-8571
L'Alcazar Galerie, 3 bd Général Leclerc in Beausoleil
More than 15,000 English language videos in Pal, Secam, and NTSC. Also carries DVDs and will install satellite systems, rent video players and DVD players. Open M-Sa 10:00 - Noon and 4:00 PM until 8:00 PM. Closed all day Sunday, Tuesday and Wednesday mornings.

# VIDEO CAMERA RENTALS
Lemoine                                    9330-7397
*15, bd. des Moulins*

# YACHT CLUB
Yacht Club of Monaco
16, Quai Antoine 1er                       9310-6300
*Fax: 9350-8088*

Web site: www.yacht-club-monaco.mc
E-mail at: ycm@yacht-club-monaco.mc
Under the direction of Bernard d'Alessandri, this top-notch facility started out as a venerable regatta society in 1904. The club is private; however they hold many races and events during the year, which are exciting to watch. (See Events Calendar). Every 2 years in September they host the Monaco Classic Week that brings the best old boats to the sparkling port. There are also reciprocating agreements with many other yacht clubs, so check your listings. They have a noted sailing school that can be reached on Tel: 9330-6363.

# 13
# ACTIVITIES FOR CHILDREN AND TEENS

Contrary to what most visitors think, Monaco has a growing community of young professionals with families. The government and the schools provide incredible services for Monaco's youth, starting with the crèche, daycare for three-month-olds, which allows mothers to return to work. Top-rated schools provide a strong academic program through high school. There are extracurricular classes in music, art and sports.

## FOR CHILDREN
## A LIST OF PLAY AREAS AND THINGS TO DO

(Please refer to All the Sights to See and Shoestring chapter Freebies for further information).

- Oceanographic Museum
- National Doll Museum
- Changing of the Guard 11:55 every day in the Place du Palais. Get there early for a good viewing position.
- A ride on the Monte Carlo Aquavision Catamaran
- Exploring Fort Antoine*
- The Jardin Exotique and Anthropological Museum
- Naval Museum
- Lollipop Video Arcade level 2 in Fontvieille Commercial Center
- Checking out the fabulous yachts and boats in the Port*
- Seeing the Fireworks Displays in July and August*
- The International Circus the last week of January and/or the first week in February
- Watching a Go Karting Race held in October*
- The November Fair, an old fashion carnival set up throughout the port area with space rides, fun houses, shooting galleries, super slides, candy apples and cotton candy.
- The Grand Prix of Remote Control Miniature Cars *
- The Zoo, children under 7 free*
- A ride on the Azur Express
- Watching the fishermen fish along Quai Président J.F. Kennedy just before the tunnel in the Port, or in the Fontvieille Port. Another fishing spot is just around the bend before the Parking des Pêcheurs*
- International Dog and Cat Shows
- Free concerts on the port during the summer*
- Beach Volley Ball Larvotto Plage*

* Free Activities

# PLAY AREAS

## LARVOTTO BEACH

For kids looking for other kids to play with this is the best congregating place from toddlers to teens. Marcel Pagnol Parc offers regular playground equipment. The boardwalk along the beach has a small merry-go-round and is the only place in Monaco where children are allowed to roller-skate, skateboard or roller blade. At the east end of the beach one can find pick- up volleyball games. A new gathering spot is La Spiaggia next to the nets.

## LA CONDAMINE

The boardwalk along the port is another spot where children can run freely. There is a carousel and motorized robots near the swimming pool. Teens will find video games and foosball (table soccer-football) at one of the open-air cafes. This is also a spot where you can do in line skating. After the success of a small ice skating rink in December 99, the government is thinking of converting the Olympic swimming pool into a rink for a few months during winter.

## MONACO-VILLE

Tucked just below the Place du Palais, on the Fontvieille side with the entrance in the Saint Martin Garden, is a wonderful playground for toddlers to age 6.

## FONTVIEILLE

Located between the Princess Grace Rose Garden and the Espace Fontvieille, children will be enchanted by a marvelous park with a lake featuring ducks, swans and turtles. There is also a playground with high quality equipment. McDonalds has a play pit on its second level that is a good place for 2-6 year olds.

## JARDIN EXOTIQUE

Between Boulevard de Belgique and Boulevard du Jardin Exotique is the Princesse Antoinette Park. Equipped with a playground and a party room available by reservation for children's parties, the park also contains a **Miniature Golf Course** and a **mini soccer field.** (Party Room Tel: 9330-6382)
(See Les Sports section)

# TEENS

Since I know when to bow to the higher authority, I went directly to a group of Monaco teen-agers for this information. This is what they told me. In the summer, the beach is the place for pick-up games of volley ball, meeting friends and working on a tan. In Cap d'Ail, they congregate at Plage Mala. "In" sports: biking, soccer and hiking.

The **Princess Stephanie Youth Center** is a favorite meeting place (membership costs 90FF (14€ ). It has organized activities such as ping pong, dances, dance lessons (Hip Hop, Rap, etc), cooking, craft workshops, board games, table soccer and movies. The Center also offers excursions for skiing, canyoning, canoeing, rafting and other seasonal planned trips. For information: Tel: 9350-7505, 24, av. Prince Pierre.

According to my teen sources, the top spot for 17-year-olds and up is the Sparco Cafe. This Formula 1 designed restaurant, bar and disco is where the well-heeled line up for an evening's entertainment, or, in the daytime, play video games.

**The Fontvieille Commercial Center** (it's a mall) is another draw for this age group, who go there to check out the shops and buy a burger at McDonald's. In **Monte Carlo,** the Métropole Galerie FNAC is where kids like to listen to CDs, read books, use free Internet access or play computer video games.

Last but not least, for the movies they go to the Sporting d' Hiver year-round, and to the open-air cinema in summer.

## 14
# CONVENTION INFORMATION

Monaco is one of the worlds most sought after venues for meetings and conferences. The reasons are obvious. First of all, the setting is beautiful; the accommodations are luxurious and its well-trained staffs make any meeting, regardless of size, run efficiently and professionally.

## THE GRIMALDI FORUM

Located between Avenue Princesse Grace and the sea, Monaco's latest convention and cultural arts center. Its design has been dynamically executed to meet the demands of high level conferences, conventions, product launches, trade fairs, exhibitions and cultural events. One of its main features is a space allocation system flexible enough to suit any client needs. The multi-use building also provides a number of complementary meeting spaces. For more information contact the Grimaldi Forum 10, av. Princesse Grace MC 98001 Monaco.
Tel: 9999-2000 Fax: 9999-2001 E-mail: gf@grimaldiforum.com.

### THE AUDITORIUMS

**Salle des Princes** seats up to 1900 people or can be downsized to accommodate 1300 people. It has a 700 sq.meter (7,000 sq.ft) stage and all the technical, acoustic and visual aspects of any large metropolitan Opera house.
**Salle Prince Pierre** seats up to 800 people and the **Salle Camille Blanc** can seat up to 400 people. Both halls offer state of the art audio-visual equipment for even the most sophisticated events.

### THE EXHIBITION HALLS

**Espace Ravel** offers a floor area of 4,300 sq. meters (43,000 sq. ft) that includes a 2,500 sq. meter (25,000 sq.ft) open space unencumbered by pillars, and a 7 meter high ceiling, creating a vast unbroken vista that will facilitate the staging of a variety of events. This exhibition area can accommodate a trade fair, a cocktail party for 3,500 people or a gala dinner for 2,500 guests.
**Espace Diaghilev** is a 3,900 sq.meter (39,000 sq.ft) space featuring a special air treatment system designed to protect delicate works of art. It can hold up to 400 people using a system of retractable seats.

### THE BREAKOUT ROOMS

The number of these rooms can be increased from 13 to 24 according to the client's needs, with seating from between 20 to 400 and a total capacity of 2,075 seats. These breakout rooms are perfect for smaller seminars or workshops.

## AUDIOVISUALS

The new facility provides the latest in sound systems, communications and projection systems, including front and back projection screening, mobile control rooms, mobile translation booths, and infrared translation systems. ISDN lines, closed circuit television, conference calling facilities, video and sound recording, video and slide projection, television and radio studios, recording studio, external networking though relay satellite and Internet access and interactive terminals.

## FOOD SERVICES

Two restaurants, **The Guelfe** (500 seats) and **The Genois** (500 seats) operate during conferences and exhibitions for a total of 1000 seats. A lobby bar with terrace will provide another 500 seats. Open year round, **A la Carte will** accommodate 180 people with terrace dining.

## EASY ACCESS

Access to the exhibition Salles des Princes space will be by a direct link from Avenue Princesse Grace, where a hoist will lift the semi-trailers to the unloading platform. Lighter vehicles can be driven into the Ravel and Diaghilev exhibition space through specially built access ramps. There is access to the internal loading zones on five different levels of the building. Visitors will have a number of independent entrances to each of the venues, making various functions completely independent and allowing them to take place simultaneously.

## ADDITIONAL SERVICES

Located within the Grimaldi Forum: a multimedia center, a business center, a pressroom, newsagent, and on the spot automated banking/money exchange and post office facilities.

The following is a list of other excellent venues for meetings and conventions in Monaco:

### THE MONTE CARLO CONVENTION CENTRE AND AUDITORIUM (C.C.A.M.).

Suspended over the Mediterranean like a ship moored at the foot of the Casino's beautiful gardens, it has three levels. The Rainier III auditorium seats 1,100 people and the stage is convertible from 110-220 sq. meters (1,100-2,200 sq. ft.). This facility has a wide range of audiovisual capabilities, including translation booths that can be used to translate up to 11 languages simultaneously. Projection from 8mm up to 70mm films, video projection, slides projection of VHS etc. and closed circuit television.
Web site: www.monaco-congrès.com
E-mail: ccam@monaco-congrès.com

## BREAKOUT ROOMS
There are four breakout rooms that can hold between 35 to 180 people, with a surface area between 131 sq. meters (1,310 sq. ft.) and 284 sq.meters (2,840 sq. ft.)

## THE LOBBY
Has a floor surface of 197 sq. meters (1,970 sq.ft.) that can house up to 100 stands with possibility of an additional 120 set up in the Monte Carlo Grand attached foyer.

## ADDITIONAL SERVICES
There is a business center, snack bar for coffee breaks and areas that can be designated for press, travel or currency.

## THE MONTE CARLO GRAND HOTEL
Has some of the finest conference facilities and services to satisfy the needs of meeting planners Connected to the C.C.A.M., it can service a small group of 10 or as many as 2000.

## THE MEETING ROOMS
**Salle d'Or is** 1,406 sq. meters (15,135 sq. ft.) of floor space and can be divided into two separate rooms (I, II) that can seat up to 1800 for a cocktails or 1420 for a banquet.
**Grand Prix A** has 140 sq. meters (1507 sq. ft.) of floor space and seating for 130 people.
**Grand Prix B** has 156 sq.meters (1,776 sq. ft) of floor space and can seat up to 150 people.
**Lacoste** has 82 sq. meters (883 sq. ft.) of floor space and can seat up to 65 people.
**Petit Salon** has 74 sq. meters (797 sq. ft.) of floor space and can seat up to 50 people.
**Naiade A, B, C, D** are four breakout rooms that run between 65 sq. meters (700 sq. ft.) to 46 sq. meters (495 sq. ft.) and can seat between 65 to 43 people.

## THE LOBBY
Facing the sea, the lobby **Salon Foyer** has 642 sq meters (6,911 sq. ft) of floor space, is easily accessible to the Salle d'Or.

## FOOD SERVICES
The hotel is known for its capability to handle large groups efficiently. We've seen a group of 1500 sail through several buffet lines in about 20 minutes. They offer a wide variety of foods and are willing to create special menus. They are also noted for their outside catering.

## AUDIOVISUAL
The basic equipment with capabilities for internal television broadcast.

## ADDITIONAL SERVICES
Business center, dance floors and stage units available.

## THE INTERNATIONAL CONFERENCE CENTER
(C.R.I.) is located at the site of the Princesse Grace Theater.
**The Salle Ponant** has seating for between 210-400 people with a surface area of 334 sq.meters (3,334 sq.ft.) while the **Salle Spélugues** has a seating capacity of 48-80 people, floor space of 180 sq. meters (1,800 sq. ft.).

## AUDIOVISUAL
Both rooms have simultaneous translation, film, (8mm, 16mm, 35mm), slide and video projection capabilities.

## ADDITIONAL SERVICES
There is a pressroom, business center and lobby bar.

## THE MONTE CARLO SPORTING D' ETÉ
There are two rooms: **Salle des Etoiles**, home of top-notch entertainment in the summer; the roof and windows slide open to reveal Monte Carlo under the stars. The seating capacity for the room is 1,200 people but can be reduced to 500 people. The floor space is 1,122 sq. meters (11,220-sq. ft.) the stage is 225 sq. meters (2,225sq.ft.) The lighting effects include a 90-track organ, and a 4kw Pani projector. There are 11 removable windows.
**The Salle Mediterranean**, has 827 sq. meters (8,270 sq. ft.) of floor space. The room seats 500 people and has a 151 sq. meter (1,510 sq. ft. bar area).

## THE SPORTING D' HIVER
Has six conference rooms that seat between 30 to 40 people. There is floor space of between 141 sq. meters 1,410 sq. ft. and 420 sq. meters (4,200 sq. ft.) The Sporting d' Hiver is located in the heart of Monte Carlo, across the street from the Hotel de Paris.

### ESPACE FONTVIEILLE (CHAPITEAU)
In Fontvieille is a big top circus tent made of thick canvas, which offers a unique convention possibility. White on the outside, blue on the inside, the floor space measures 4,212 sq. meters (42,120 sq.- ft.) 58 meters (190 ft.) in diameter. Four pillars support the tent itself. The canvas filters the daylight, allowing for all types of projections and interior lighting effects. It seats a maximum of

4,230 people with 3000 bucket-style seats, 1,505 benches, and 200 raised box seats. The central platform is 312 sq. meters (3,120-sq. ft.), with the first 3 rows of seats stored. The area can be increased to 2,087 sq. meters (20,870-sq. ft.). There is plenty of flexibility to accommodate many different size exhibitions. The open space around the outside of the tent can also be utilized in creative ways. For more information contact Mr. Neu 9205-2345.

## THE SEA CLUB

Another recent addition to the Principality, this convention complex is directly connected to Le Meridien Beach Plaza Hotel. It has four levels and can accommodate up to 700 people in the two main rooms. There are 14 breakout rooms for committee meetings and three panoramic terraces.

### LOBBY LEVEL
230 sq. meter (2,300 sq. ft.) area with elegant staircase leading to the upper floors and terrace.

### SALON MEDITERRANEAN
1 large 549 sq. meter (5,490 sq. ft.) room that can be divided into 2 rooms of equal size. It has sliding glass windows that open onto a 900 sq. meter (9,000sq. ft.) terrace overlooking the seawater swimming pools and leading to a private beach.

### LEVEL 1
Lobby of 90 sq. meters (900 sq. ft.)
Four Breakout rooms: **Salon Pacific** 88sq.meters (880 sq.ft) with 40 sq.meter (400 sq. ft.) terrace overlooking the sea. **Salon Adriatique** 54 sq. meters (540 sq. ft.). **Salon Baltique** 18 sq. meters (180 sq. ft.). **Salon Egee** 45 sq, meters (450 sq. ft.)

### LEVEL 2
Lobby area 180 sq. meters ( 1,800 sq. ft.) with equal terrace space. **Salon Atlantique** 579 sq. meters (5,790 sq. ft.) that can be divided into 3 separate meeting rooms.

### LEVEL 3
Business Center

### LEVEL 4
Lobby of 180 sq. meters (1,800 sq. ft.)
Six Breakout rooms: **Salon Mistral** 35 sq. meters (350 sq. ft.). **Salon Tramontane** 26 sq. meters (260 sq. ft.) **Salon Alizee** 68 sq. meters (680 sq. ft.) that can be divided into two. **Salon Foehn** 26 sq. meters (260 sq. ft.). **Salon Sirocco** 56 sq. meters (560 sq. ft.) can be divided into two. And **Salon Zephyr** 128 sq. meters (1,280 sq. ft.)

## LEVEL 5
A garden roof top terrace with 330 sq. meters (3,300 sq. ft. of space) with a pergola and exterior lighting.

## THE CAFÉ DE PARIS
**Salon Bellevue**, which sits on top of the Café de Paris, offers a meeting room with terrace that over looks the Casino Square. The terrace can accommodate up to 250 people for cocktails. The panoramic views of the Casino and west toward Italy will delight guests in the main room. The food is catered from the Café de Paris kitchens.

## HOTELS AT A GLANCE
Hotel de Paris (SBM)    4 Stars +
11 meeting rooms, 25-300 seats
135 rooms, 19 junior suites and 43 suites.
Hermitage Hotel (SBM)    4 Stars +
10 meeting rooms, 30-110 seats
196 rooms, 17 junior suites and 18 suites
Mirabeau Hotel (SBM)    4 Stars
3 meeting rooms, 30-120 seats
89 rooms and 14 junior suites.
Monte Carlo Grand Hotel    4 Stars +
12 meeting rooms, 20-1,450 seats
619 rooms and suites.
Métropole Palace Hotel    4 Stars +
8 meeting rooms, 20-300 seats
170 rooms, 45 junior suites and 12 suites
Le Meridien Beach Plaza Hotel    4 Stars
6 meeting rooms, 125-370 seats
332 rooms, 8 suites and 24 VIP roof top suites.
Abela Hotel    3 Stars
2 meeting rooms, 35-200 seats
192 rooms, 18 suites, 10 business woman rooms,
and 9 rooms adapted for disabled persons.
Marriott Hotel Cap d'Ail    3 Stars
9 meeting rooms, 18-360 seats
183 rooms and suites.

(See hotel section for contact numbers)

## FREIGHT , CUSTOM BROKERS, SET-UP INSTALLERS
Each hotel my have contracts with individual brokers but here are some that are commonly used:

**L' Office Maritime Monégasque**                    **9205-7615**
*Congress Service*                                   *Fax: 9205-1959*
*2, rue de la Lujerneta E-Mail: omm@wanadoo.fr*
*MC 98000 Monaco*
**Mathez Monaco International**                       **9310-1330**
*Congress Service*                                   *Fax:9310-1331*
*19, av. des Castelans*
*MC 98000 Monaco*
**Société Curti**                                    **9315-0002**
*3, rue Plati*                                       *Fax: 9350-0951*
*MC 98000 Monaco*

## BUSINESS MACHINE RENTALS
**Burmatec**                                         **9325-2121**
*7, rue Orchidees*                                   *Fax: 9325-4471*
**Euro-Document**                               **33 (0) 4 9394-5422**
*76, av. Mar. Juin, Cannes*                 *Fax: 33 (0) 4 9394-5465*

## COMPUTER RENTALS
**Eurolocation Informatique**                   **33 (0) 4 9392-4127**
*Montee Barelli, Nice*

## TRANSLATION SERVICES
**Communication Multilingue Organization**   **33 (0) 4 9209-9092**
*420, av. de Pessicart, 06100 Nice*       *Fax: 33 (0) 4 9209-9272*

## AUDIO VISUAL SPECIALISTS
Action International                                  **9777-7879**
*7, rue du Gabian, Gildo Pastor Center*             *Fax: 9777-7878*
Internet site: www. meditnet.com/action
                              E-mail: action@medinet.com

# 15
# MONACO ON A SHOESTRING

Contrary to the myth that only millionaires can afford to stay in Monaco, we will show you that the Principality is easily accessible to the visitor without a big budget. Don't believe it? Read on.

## MODERATE PRICED ACCOMMODATIONS
These hotels start at 500FF (77€) for a single and 650FF (100€) for a double in low season; and 650FF (100€) for a single to 800FF (123€) for a double in high season. All take credit cards.

Our personal choice is the **Abela** in Fontvieille, or the **Marriott** in Cap d'Ail, because they are the newest and have air conditioning and a pool. They are the popular choices of businessmen and traveling families consequently they are often fully booked so plan ahead.

### MONTE CARLO
**Hotel Alexandra**                                            **9350-6313**
*35, bd. Princesse Charlotte*                         *Fax: 9350-4712*
Situated in the heart of Monte Carlo, good for shopping along the boulevard des Moulins, this restored turn-of-the-century hotel is a find. All 56 rooms soundproofed and with air-conditioning.

**Hotel Balmoral**                                            **9350-6237**
*12, av. de la Costa*                                      *Fax: 9315-0869*
Older hotel with superb port views situated next to the Hotel Hermitage. Very centrally located. Some rooms have a balcony and others have air conditioning. 54 rooms 7 junior suites and 5 apartments. Web site: www.hotel-balmoral.mc
E-mail: balmoral@cyber-monaco.mc
**Hotel du Louvre**                                           **9350-6525**
*16, bd. des Moulins*                                      *Fax: 9330-2368*
Centrally located with easy access to buses, this traditional small hotel will make your stay pleasurable. Some rooms have sea views. Thirty-three soundproofed rooms, most with AC. Sorry, no pets allowed.   Web site: www.monte-carlo.mc/louvre E-mail: hotel-louvre@monte-carlo.mc
**La Masion d'Or**                                            **9350-6666**
*21, rue du Portier*                                       *Fax: 9330-7600*
This small charming hotel is decorated in the style of a 19th century palace. Located on Italian restaurant row, close to sea and Casino. There are eight rooms and suites all nicely decorated in a different color. AC.   Web site: www.hotelmaisondor.com
E-mail:monica@hotelmaisondor.com

### LA CONDAMINE
**Hotel Miramar**                                             **9330-8648**
*1, av. Président J.F. Kennedy*                        *Fax: 9330-2633*
The only hotel right on the port. Twelve modern rooms with showers, 8 with AC. Panoramic bar and terrace. Racing fans take

note; it is directly on the Grand Prix track!

**Hotel Ambassador-Monaco**       9330-2556
*10, av. Prince Pierre*       *Fax 9330-03*
Located conveniently in the Condamine and close to parking, bus service, shopping and sightseeing. It has 35 comfortable rooms that have been soundproofed and air-conditioned.
Web site: www.monte-carlo.mc/ambassador
E-mail ambassador@monte-carlo.mc

**Tulip Inn Monaco Terminus**       9205-6300
*9, av. Prince Pierre*       *Fax: 9205-2010*
The rooms were refurbished in 1999 in bright and cheerful modern provençal style and are good value. La Sariette serves provencal dishes, and Le Corail offers seafood and tapas. 54 soundproofed rooms, 12 with sea view.
Web site: www.terminus.monte-carlo.mc
E-mail: tupipinn-terminus@monte-carlo.mc

### FONTVIEILLE
**Abela Hotel**       9205-9000
*23, av. des Paplins*       *Fax 9205-9167*
This hotel built in 1989 is an excellent value. As a consequence, it appeals to the business traveler and is usually booked in advance. The 192 contemporary California-style rooms are soundproofed and air-conditioned with sea, port and mountain views. There are 9 rooms adapted for handicapped persons, 18 suites, 10 businesswomen rooms and one whole floor dedicated to non-smokers. Most rooms have terraces. Outside pool.
E-mail abela-hotel@monte-carlo.mc.

## BUDGET LODGING
Room prices are 310FF (48€) for a single to 400FF (62€) for a double in low season and 500FF (76€) for a single and 700FF (107€) for a double during high season.

### LA CONDAMINE
**Hotel de France**       9330-2464
*6, rue de la Turbie*       *Fax: 9216-1334*
A clean modern hotel of 26 rooms, each with shower, TV and direct telephone lines. An excellent location for the port and old town. Parking and transportation are close by.
Web site: www.monte-carlo.mc/france
E-mail: hotel-france@monte-carlo.mc

**Hotel Helvetia**       9330-2171
*1, bis rue Grimaldi*       *Fax: 9216-7051*
The Helvetia has 25 rooms, 21 of which come with bath or shower. Perfect for the no-frills traveler.
Web site: www.monte-carlo.mc/helvetia.
E-mail: hotel-helvetia@monaco.mc

**Hotel le Versailles**                          **9350-7934**
*4, av. Prince Pierre*                          *Fax: 9325-5364*
A moderate priced hotel with 15 rooms, all with bath or shower, TV and direct dial phones. Well placed for sight seeing, transportation and parking. A popular French-Italian restaurant next door.
Web site: www.monte-carlo.mc/versailles
E-mail: hotel-versailles@monte-carlo.mc

**Hotel Cosmopolite**                          **9330-1695**
*4, rue de la Turbie*                          *Fax: 9330-2305*
The only one-star hotel in the Principality is naturally the least expensive. It has 24 rooms, 5 with shower. Good location.
E-mail: hotel-cosmopolite@monte-carlo.mc

**Princesse Stephanie Youth Hostel**                          **9350-8320**
*24, av. Prince Pierre*
Basic youth hostel accommodation catering to travelers between 16 and 31 years old. Stays are limited to 3 nights during the summer and beds are given out each morning on a first come first serve basis.

## HOTELS IN THE NEIGHBORHOOD

Hotels in France, right outside of Monaco, are sometimes less expensive because the price of land is cheaper. Rates for a double room in a two ★★ hotel run between 120FF (18€) to 720FF (110€), three ★★★ double rooms 230FF (35€) to 2,000FF (308€) and 4 ★★★★ 450FF (69€) to 6,500FF (1000€). Bordering Monaco is **BEAUSOLEIL**, which is a five-minute walk to the Casino, shopping and convenient parking at several new garages. The following offers a list of good budget hotels in Beausoleil that are always in demand.

**Hotel Olympia**                          **33 (0) 4 9378-1270**
*17, bd. Général Leclerc*                          *Fax: 33 (0) 4 9341-8504*
Money saver hotel with 32 rooms. AC, TV and mini bar.
E-Mail: olympia06@aol.com

**Hotel Diana**                          **33 (0) 4 9378-4758**
*17, bd Général Leclerc*                          *Fax: 33 (0) 4 9341-8894*
35 agreeable rooms with TV.

**Hotel Cosmopolite**                          **33 (0) 4 9378-3600**
*19, bd. Général Leclerc*                          *Fax: 33 (0) 4 9341-8422*
23 rooms with shower and T.V.

**CAP D'AIL** is on the western border of Monaco, adjacent to Monaco's Football stadium, Stade Louis II in Fontvieille. There is frequent bus service between Monaco, Nice and the airport.

**Marriott Cap d'Ail**                          **33 (0) 4 9210-6767**
                          *Fax: 33 (0) 4 9210-6700*
Rooms have splendid views either facing the yacht harbor or the mountains. The hotel has174 tastefully appointed guestrooms and 12 suites all with AC. There is an outdoor pool. It's a short walk to the beach and tennis courts, but it has an in-house fitness center. US and Canada   the toll free number is 1-800-228-9290, U.K.0800-221-222, and in France the toll free number is 0800-908-333  Web site: www.marriott.com

In the town of **CAP D'AIL**, here are two budget priced hotels:

**Edmonds Hotel**                              33 (0) 4 9378-0855
*87, av. 3rd du September*
Run by a British-French couple, it has a well-attended restaurant.
10 rooms.

**Hotel Normandy**                             33 (0) 4 9378-7777
*6, allée des Oranger*              *Fax: 33 (0) 4 9378-4826*
21 rooms, some with sea views.

**International Youth Hostel**                 33 (0) 493781858
*Villa Thalassa*
A student favorite.

To the east is **ROQUEBRUNE CAP MARTIN** where there are
several smaller hotels and restaurants. (See day trips). Frequent
bus service to and from Monaco, Nice and airport.

**Hotel Westmins.ter**                         33 (0) 4 9335 0068
*14, av. Louis Laurens-Cabbee*      *Fax : 33 (0) 4 9328-8850*
Small hotel not far from Monaco and Roquebrune Cap Matin
beach. This is a favorite of tennis journalists and photographers
during the tennis tournament. 31 rooms.

**Alexandra**                                  33 (0) 4 9335-6545
*93, av. Winston Churchill Cap Martin*   *Fax: 33 (0) 4 9357-9651*
40 rooms with AC, parking and allows dogs.

**Victoria**                                   33 (0) 4 9336-6590
*7, Promenade du Cap Martin*        *Fax: 33 (0) 4 9328-7202*
30 rooms with AC, parking and allows dogs.

## RESTAURANTS

Here is a list of ($) 60-120FF (9-18€) places to get a reasonable
meal.

## MONTE CARLO

**Borsalino**                                  9350-6692
*4, bd. des Moulins*
Not far from the Tourist Office. This is a good spot to get a pizza
or plate of spaghetti.

**Capocaccia**                                 9325-5952
*6, impasse de la Fontaine* (Park Palace Galerie complex)
Italian panini and sandwiches during lunch.

**Flashman's**                                 9330-0903
*7, av. Princesse Alice*
English pub fare.

**L'Ascot**                                    9770-6406
*1, av. des Citronniers*
You can watch horse racing while enjoying an open faced "bru-
schetta" sandwich. Open for dinner and live music.

**Lina's Sandwiches**                          9325-8610
*Métropole Galerie*
Made to order and take-a-way sandwiches for picnics.

**Sam's Place**                                9350-8933
*1, av. Henry Dunant*
Your basic no-thrills steak place. Reliable food at moderate prices.
Good chili.

**Tip Top**                                                    9350-6913
*1, av. des Spélugues*
A late-night spot.


## LARVOTTO BEACH
**Baobab**                                                     9350-8690
*Larvotto Beach*
A boardwalk favorite offering a diverse menu, pasta and salads
**La Spiaggia**                                                9350-5080
*Larvotto Beach next to the Sea Club*
This snack bar is the latest contender for the 'in' spot on the beach.
Best place to get into a pick-up game of volleyball or badminton.
**Festival**                                                   9350-4570
*Avenue Princesse Grace-Larvotto Boardwalk*
Salads, sandwiches, pizzas and ice cream.


## LA CONDAMINE

**A Roca**                                                     9325-1595
*15, rue Louis Notari*
Features regional and Monégasque specialties such as pissaladiére,
torte, socca, barbagiuan and fougasse and pizza with home delivery.
Located just around the corner from the Casino market and down
the street from the police station.
**Bambi**                                                      9330-3506
*23, rue Princesse Antoinette*
The secretary's special spot with lots of locals residents.  An out-
side terrace.
**Chez Egar Tea for Two**                                      9350-1010
*11, bd. Albert 1er*
Good pizza, other light food fare.
**Huit et Demi**                                               9350-9702
*4, rue Langle*
Pizza and pasta.
**Le Caravelle**                                               9350-7728
*On the Port*
On the port next to the underground passageway, a sunny place for
people watching and a sandwich.
**Le Dauphin Vert**                                            9330-8630
*20, rue Princesse Caroline*
This recently redone snack bar has always been frequented by
locals and visitors.
**Le Royalty**                                                 9350-4202
*21, rue Princesse Caroline*
Snack bar with 'para mutual' betting.
**Le Shangri-La**                                              9350-7452
*17, rue Princesse Caroline*
Snack bar with pizza, crêpes and ice cream.
**Le Touareg**                                                 9330-1935
*13, rue de la Turbie*
Coucous specialities and low prices.

**Pattaya**                                          9325-3900
*On the Port, near the Jetty*
Excellent salade niçoise and ice cream delights.
**Pizzeria Monégasque**                              9330-1638
*4, rue Terrazzani*
Wood-burning ovens and cauda bagna and a Monégasque vege-
table crudité are notable in this cozy setting.
**Stella-Polaris**                                   9330-8863
*3, av. Président J.F. Kennedy*
Good for lunch and portside action. Mixed menu with exotic
South Pacific specialties
**Warm Up**                                          9330-5230
*Rue Suffren Reymond*
Lower level, locals' hangout.

## MONACO-VILLE (THE OLD TOWN)
**Bar Félix**                                        9330-3415
*22, rue Basse*
The place for a sandwich and a drink.
**L'Express**                                        9330-4394
*22, rue Comte Félix Gastaldi*
Locals' and tourists' pick, daily specials and outside dining behind
the Cathedral.
**Confetti**                                         9325-1717
*2, rue Emile de Loth*
A hole-in-the-wall where local football fans congregate for espres-
so, quiche and tarts. Only a few tables but the take-out is quick.
**Da Sergio**                                        9330-3415
*22, rue Basse*
Whitewashed cellar walls, good daily specials, and pizza.
**D'Avuta**                                          9330-7199
*1, rue Bellando de Castro*
Mixed menu, charming courtyard dining.
**La Pampa**                                         9330-3375
*8, place du Palais*
Snack bar on a sunny terrace. Great place for people watching in
front of the Palace.
**Pasta Roca**                                       9330-4422
*23, rue Comte Félix Gastal*di
Good value for money.

## FONTVIEILLE
**La Bodega**                                        9205-2618
Situated next to the Commercial Center, this is a busy steak and
pizza place. Open from 7:00 AM til 11:00 PM.
**Gerhard's Café**                                   9205-2579
*42, quai Jean-Charles Rey*
Snack bar and tea room.
**Hip-Hop Café**                                     9205-2860
*16, quai Jean-Charles Rey*
Salads and sandwiches.

**McDonalds**                              9205-3990
*Fontvieille Commercial Center*
Undoubtedly one of Mc'D's best views, situated on a spot overlooking the harbor. Pirate playship for kids. Will satisfy any cra-
ving for American junk food. Credit cards accepted

**Pizza du Stade**                          9205-2253
*11, av. des Castelans*
Located in the stadium, overlooking indoor pool and basketball
courts, also terrace. Here is where the sporting meet.

**Poisson d' Or**                            9205-9799
*16, quai Charles Rey*
Snack bar food.

**Ship & Castle**                          9205-7672
*42, quai Jean-Charles Rey*
Your Olyde English pub fare and ale.

# WHO SAYS MONACO IS TOO EXPENSIVE?
## ...THE FREEBIES

Here is a list of free things to see and do in Monaco, including fun
things for children.

**The Changing of the Guard** takes place at precisely 11:55 AM
every day in front of the main entrance to the Palace. The ceremony is performed in full dress uniform (black in winter, white in
summer) and has not changed for more than 100 years. Note to
get a good viewpoint get there at least 20 minutes before especially in the summer months.

      **Fanfare de la Compagnie des Carabiniers.** Monaco's
regimental band. The Fanfare recruits young carabiniers (French
military men) with solid musical training. Within the company
there is a small orchestra that has an extensive repertoire playing
popular, jazz, and religious music. Also a brass ensemble. They
perform June through August. Check Bienvenue.

      **Stroll Around the Old Town** (*See All the Sights to See
section*) Don't miss the *Monaco Cathedral, Chapel of Mercy,* or the
*Princesse Grace Irish Library.* Explore the ruins of *Fort Antoine.*
Make an appointment to see the *Museum of Old Monaco* and
meander through the *St. Martin Garden.* If you're in the
Condamine, check out the yachts in the harbor and visit the
*Church of St. Dévote* then walk toward Larvotto beach and take
moment to go through the **Japanese Garden.** In Fontvieille take
a tour of Stade (Stadium) Louis II, or take a moment to sit and
smell the roses in the fragrant and beautiful **Princesse Grace Rose
Garden.**

## SPORTS ACTIVITIES
Free sports activities include snorkeling, volleyball at Larvotto
Beach, or jogging along the new cushioned running path
alongside boulevard du Larvotto or hiking along the sea.
(Also see Sports section for more information.)

# SPECTATOR ACTIVITIES

## JANUARY

Watch the Monte Carlo Rallye drivers arrive and depart from the harbor. Celebrate the traditional burning of the boat on St. Dévote.

Check out the circus animals in town for the Monte Carlo Circus Festival, around the big top tent in Fontvieille.

## FEBRUARY

Watch the best television programming from around the world at the International Television Festival at the C.C.A.M. Screenings are open to the public in all categories.

Take a look at the Imagina Innovative Village for the latest in multi-media special effects and computer graphics.

## MARCH

Good Friday Procession through the Old Town.

## APRIL

See the Interior Design Home and Garden exhibit and special events during the Spring Arts Festival.

ATP Tour sponsors children's tennis clinics with top men players on Larvotto Beach.

The Pro-Celebrity Pentathlon in the Espace Fontvieille.

## MAY

See the World Music Awards broadcast live on a big screen on Larvotto Beach.

## JUNE

Check out free concerts for the Fête de la Musique on June 21. Join in the dancing on the Palace Square for the Fête St. John in the Old Town. Or watch the procession on the Fête Dieu (Pentecost Monday)

Midsummer Night Festivals are held in Monaco-Ville and Monte Carlo with magicians, fire-eaters, music and folk crafts and groups.

## JULY

Make dinner plans followed by watching the International Fireworks Festival. Catch some of the biggest private yachts in the world docked near the Monaco Yacht Club during the ShowBoats Rendezvous.

## SEPTEMBER

The International Bob-Sleigh Push Competitions, Pro-Beach Volleyball followed by the fast moving Pro-Beach Soccer.

Pro-Celebrity Golf Tournament at the Monte Carlo Golf Club.

Monaco Classic Week (Bi-annual) with old classic boats.

Monaco Classic Car Rallye.

## OCTOBER
Monaco Heritage Day with free admission to most museums.
Admission is free during the weekdays to the International Fair
held in the Espace Fontvieille.
Monco Kart Racing Cup held on the port.
Monaco Children's Exhibition in Espace Fontvieille
Radio Controlled Yachts are raced in the harbor.

## NOVEMBER
Participate in the flag waving on the Palace Square and cheer for the
Royal family and watch the fireworks the evening before.

## DECEMBER
A new International Dance Forum and exhibition will be held at
the new Grimaldi Forum. Also the new Monaco World Dance
Awards.
For more information see the Big Event Calendar section.

## CHILDREN'S ACTIVITIES
See Children's Activities.

## FREE TOURS
**Chocolaterie de Monaco**
Chocolate lovers will be thrilled to learn that Monaco is the
home of one of the best chocolate makers in Europe. It has been
making over 78 kinds of chocolate treats for more than 80 years.
Their factory is located at 7, rue Biovès, with an additional boutique
in the Place de la Visitation in the Old Town. Tours by appointment can be arranged by calling 9797-8888 Open year round.
Closed on Sunday.

## THE MONACO PORCELAIN MANUFACTURING COMPANY
(Manufacture de Porcelaine de Monaco)
Yes, Monaco has its own high quality porcelain manufacturer.
Their factory is located in Fontvieille at 5, rue Gabian while their
boutique is located in the Métropole shopping Galerie. Free gui-
ded tours are given by appointment. Call Mr. Joram Rozewicz at
9205-7755. Open year round M-F 9:00 AM to 4:00 PM.
Web site: www.mdpm.com E-mail: info@mdpm.com

## MISCELLANEOUS BEST VALUES
**CAR RENTAL**

| | |
|---|---|
| Century Car Rental | 33 (0) 4 9227-0510 |
| ML Rent A Car | 33 (0) 4 9334-4800 |

## TRANSPORT VIA THE NICE AIRPORT
RCA Bus ( Rapides Côte d' Azur)   33-(0) 4 9321-3080
Round trip tickets 80FF (12€) or 6 card trips for 390FF (60€)

## DISCOUNT AND USED DESIGNER CLOTHES

**La Difference**                                         9350-6157
*3, av. St. Charles*
Designer women's and men's clothing. Mainly Italian designers.

**Stock Griffe**                                          9350-8606
*5, bis av. St. Michel*
Located in the upper level of the Park Palace Galerie
Carries year end men's and women's French and Italian designer
labels at a discount.

**Elégance**                                      33 (0) 4 9378-5082
*Bd. de la République, Beausoleil*
Located near the laundromat and St. Charles Market in
Beausoleil, and not far from the Monaco Tourist Office. This
shop carries used clothing.

## DRY CLEANING

5 Sec                                                     9205-7030
*Fontvieille Commercial Center*

## FILM DEVELOPING

**Carrefour Supermarche**                                 9205-5700
*Fontvieille Commercial Center*

## GROCERIES AND HOUSEHOLD PRODUCTS

**Carrefour Supermarche**                                 9305-5700
*Fontvieille Commercial Center*

## LAUNDROMAT

**Self-Laverie 7/7**
*Escalier (Stairs) du Riviera, in Beausoleil.*
Located off boulevard de la République behind the Monte Carlo
St. Charles market. Three blocks from the Monaco Tourist Office.

## RESTAURANT

Louis VX                                                  9216-3001
*Hotel de Paris*
Their lunch only "tasting menu" for 500FF (77€) includes wine,
a splurge but well worth the price.

## BUDGET GRAND PRIX WATCHING

Bring your picnic basket, blanket and grab a spot on the lawn on
the Palace hillside to get a birds eye view of the Grand Prix. (See
Big Events section for more details)

We hope you will agree after reading this section you too can have
fun in Monaco without being a millionaire.

# YOUR FAVOURITE BUDGET FINDS

# 16
# DAY TRIPS

One of Monaco's great advantages is its proximity to other parts of the French and Italian Riviers.. Whether you have an hour, one-half day or an entire day, you can go in either direction – toward Nice or toward Italy – and find a host of things to see. Easy access to the autoroute with the new tunnel, or to the more leisurely coast road. You can do these day trips by car or train on your own, or with a bus tour. Here are some favorites.

## IN ITALY
### SAN REMO

A quaint, seaside Italian town with a ritzy casino and fashionable shops. Outside of Milan, this is the closest you will come to designer shopping for high end Italian clothing and good design items for the home. It also has an impressive outdoor market on Saturday and Tuesday mornings. Some prefer it to the Ventimiglia market, which is on Friday, because the San Remo market is smaller and there isn't as much junk to wade through to get to the good stuff, such as leather goods and silk scarves. The market is open early in the morning and promptly closes for lunch at noon. Take lunch in one of the local eateries, then hit designer stores like Armani Emporium, Annamoda, Fendi, Gucci, Sisely, Max Mara and Boggi when they open at 3:30 PM. San Remo is sixteen miles from the border and about a half an hour from Monaco. Parking along the seaside. Turn right and cross the train tracks to get to it.

Here are some recommended restaurants.
**Trattoria de Porto da Nico**          00 39 184-501988
*9, Piazza Bresca*
Best seafood restaurant in town. A locals' favorite.
**Remo and Lucia**                      00 39 184-533862
*13, via Gioberti*
**Piccolo Mondo**                       00 39 184-509012
*Via Piave, 7*
Popular with French visitors in for the day, so get there close to 1 PM or you won't get in. Be sure to order the minestrone, the best.

### VENTIMIGLIA

Just to the east of Menton is Ventimiglia, which has a huge, open-air market every Friday. Unlike most markets that close at 12:30 or 1:00 PM, this one is open all day. It's a good shopping possibility for those people who are attending conferences and whose time is limited. Just follow the line of cars to the parking lot. The market is at least twice the size of the one in San Remo. Don't be afraid to bargain; walk away when you don't get the price you

want. Start at 20 to 30 percent off and try different stands. You'll
be surprised how one guy is willing to cut his price while another
vender won't. Most salespeople speak a little English because this
is a main tourist market. You may use your francs, Euros or credit
card to pay. By the way, if you like gold jewelry, the jewelry stores
in Ventimiglia are the places to get the best prices.

**Balzi Rossi**                                          00 39 184-38132
*Frontier San Ludovico*
Located just across the border and facing the sea. Closed M-Tu. lunch.
Expensive. Reservations suggested.

**If**                                                   00 39 184-26909
236, Via Vitt Emanuele
Centrally located in picturesque Bordighera. Closed Monday.

**Degli Amici**                                          00 39 184-253526
*Piazza della Liberta, 25*
*Vallebona*
In a tiny picturesque village just above Bordighera You can't miss
the restaurant because it is just to the side of the square. Mama is
in the kitchen, so rest assured the dishes are very fresh and deli-
ciously original. Reasonable prices closed Monday.

# IN FRANCE

## MENTON
On the French side of the Italian border, Menton is a pretty reti-
rement town on the sea that backs up to the mountains. During
the 1800s many British expatriates brought their gardening exper-
tise to the Côte d'Azur so that today Menton has some of the
most beautiful and authentic English gardens outside of England.
Private visits to some of these gardens may be arranged through
the Tourist Office. There has always been a strong British community in Menton, and some of their illustrious have breathed
their last here, namely, the inventor of rugby William Willis, illus-
trator Aubrey Beardsley and writer Katherine Mansfield.

The main walking street is filled with shops, flower
stalls and an open market. There is a brocante (antique bric-a-
brac) fair on Fridays. A Renaissance Fair is held biannually with
crafts, jousting contests and shopkeepers dressed in medieval costumes. Every February, Menton, known as the Lemon Capital of
the World, holds a Lemon Festival featuring floats and sculptures
created with lemons. Fun parades. For information call the Tourist
Office on Tel: 33 (04) 9357-5700 or Fax 33 (0) 4 9357-5100.

**Au Pistou**                                            33 (0) 4 9357-3489
*2, rue du Fassan*
On a small street near Nouvelles Galleries just behind the walking
street. Offers Menton specialities, pasta and seafood. A locals
favorite, reasonable.

**Le Nautic**                                    33 (0) 4 9335-7874
*27, quai Mauléon*
Great seafood on the main street kitty corner from the Cocteau
Museum and near the old town. Expensive.

## ROQUEBRUNE-CAP MARTIN

Roquebrune is a small hilltown close to Monaco. Its chief attraction is the 10th century castle, one of France's oldest and a
Grimaldi possession from 1350 to 1848. It is largely unfurnished,
but well worth a visit. Be prepared for a steep climb on medieval
stone streets. The shops in the village are built into the sides of
rocks and they feature first-rate olive wood items, such as cheese
trays and salad bowls. Roquebune, which means 'Brown Rock,'
was associated with Winston Churchill, Dutch art forger Hans
van Meegeren and the renowned French architect le Corbusier,
who drowned at Cap Martin in 1965. Cap Martin is another of
the spectacular peninsulas marked with sumptuous villas along the
Côte d'Azur. Empress Eugenie of Napoleon II fame wintered here
as did Empress Elizabeth of Austria. The poet William B. Yeats
died in Cap Martin in 1939.

## ROQUEBRUNE VILLAGE
**Les Deux Frères**                              33 (0) 4 9328-9900
*Center of the Village*
Hotel and restaurant owned by a Dutch father and son. Nouvelle
French cuisine and dreamy view of Monaco. Expensive.
**La Dame Jeanne**                               33 (0) 4 9335-1020
*1, chem. St. Lucie*
Rustic, quaint and country describes this traditional exceptional
French restaurant. Romantic nooks and dramatic views.
Expensive.
**Au Grand Inquisiteur**                         33 (0) 4 9335-0537
*15, rue du Château*
Situated in an Old World wine cellar, moderately priced menu.
**Piccolo Mondo**                                33 (0) 4 9335-1993
*15, rue Grimaldi*
Italian cuisine, beware of off-the-menu items as your bill will escalate. Good food and ambiance. Expensive.
**Vista Palace Hotel**                           33 (0) 4 9335-0150
*1551, Grande Corniche*
A four-star hotel with killer panoramic views and excellent restaurants. Have lunch or a drink on the terrace overlooking the
coast from Italy to Cannes while parapenters sail by. High on the
hill between Roquebrune Village and La Turbie. You can't miss
the building with the large blue V.

## LA TURBIE

Reached from the Grande Corniche above Monaco, La Turbie lies along the Aurelian way, a Roman road that ran from Italy to Gaul (modern day France). The town rises high above the mountain bluff that overhangs Monaco. It is home to an interesting site, the Trophée des Alpes, built in Roman times and since renovated, to celebrate their conquest 2000 years ago of the non-Roman-speaking peoples of the region. Delightful little restaurants redolent with smells of Provençal cooking and Italian wood-burning stove pizza. Views are magnificent by day or night.

## EZE VILLAGE

Seen from far off, the magical village of Eze resembles something out of a fairy tale. It clings to the side of a pinnacle rising 1,200 feet above the sea and is spectacularly lit up at night. If you are driving on the Moyenne Corniche you can't miss it. During the day, you must park your car (or get out of the bus) in the Car Park and walk up hill to the village. It is well worth the trip to visit the exotic garden atop the ruins of a castle destroyed in 1706. Views are extraordinary on a clear day. Eze village is home to the famous hotel and restaurant Chévre d'Or and Château Eza. Cool off with a drink on the terrace of either; you won't be disappointed. At the base of the village you will find the Fragonard Perfume Factory, where you can take a tour and see how perfume is made. Afterward they will sell you your favorite perfume at a fraction of the cost you'd find at home. Just across the street is Gallimard perfume showroom and glassblowers from Biot, displaying their wares and the art of glassblowing. If you don't have time to visit Grasse and Biot, this is a good alternative.

**Château Eza**                                    33 (0) 4 9341-1224

Breathtaking views, very expensive, but you can sit on the terrace and sip tea or spoon an ice cream for less. Very Expensive

**Château la Chévre d'Or**                         33 (0) 4 9341-1212

This is four-star dining at its best, more breathtaking views, a good recommendation for lunch if you want to treat yourself. Very expensive.

## CAP D'AIL

Take the coast road east heading for Cap d'Ail just outside Monaco. You will be on the Basse Corniche, take a left turn just before the Casino Supermarket, and follow the signs toward Plage Mala. The road twists and turns until you reach a dead end. Park wherever you can and walk the rest of the way straight down. This is where the discreet meet to lunch and swim, a beautiful little inlet of crystal clear water surrounded by cliffs. Call to reserve your beach mats ahead on the weekends and for lunch reservations.

| | |
|---|---|
| La Réserve | 33 (0) 4 9378-2156 |
| Eden Plage | 33 (0) 4 9378-1706 |
| Edmond's Hotel | 33 (0) 4 9378-0855 |
| La Pinède | 33 (0) 4 9376-3710 |

Select your own catch of the day on a terrace overlooking the sea.

## BEAULIEU-SUR-MER

Famous for its casino, wedding cake conference center and Greek-imitation Villa Kerylos, this seaside resort is the perfect theatrical setting, which may be the reason so many films have been shot here. The road off to the side of Beaulieu will take you to Cap Ferrat.

**Chez Marrone**                    33 (0) 4 9301-0455
*81, bd. Edouard VII*
A locals favorite restaurant; reliable food at reasonable prices.

**African Queen**                    33 (0) 4 9301-1085
*Located in the Harbor*
Long-established restaurant, good salads, pasta and barbecued meat served until midnight. A celebrity watching spot.

**Les Agaves**                    33 (0) 4 9301-1312
*4, av. Marechal Foch*
Excellent chef. Ask for their specialties; the terrine and fish soup are tops. Moderately priced.

## ST. JEAN CAP FERRAT

One of the four prestigious peninsulas along the coast, this being perhaps the most expensive and the most prestigious. It extends about two miles into the sea with an arm off to the east on which the little port and town of St. Jean is located. To the west the Cap makes a six-mile loop where luxurious villas are set behind flowered-covered walls. You can't see much of the huge homes, but take a moment and visit the Rothschild Villa Museum, now under the auspices of the French government, for a taste of the life behind the hedges. The gardens behind the villa are famous. Speaking of famous, Jack Nicholson, Warren Beatty, Ivana Trump and many other celebrities have been spotted strolling the shaded lanes around the Cap. Starting points for your walks can be Beaulieu beach or at the south end of town where the Cap splits in two. Stop off at one of the port-side cafés for a crêpe and cool beer or a good fish repas.

**Les Hirondelles**                    33 (0) 4 9376-0404
*36, av. Jean Mermoz*
A romantic terrace opposite the yacht harbor. Fish is the main attraction with good pastries for desert. Since dining la carte is more expensive, lunchtime menus are the best value.

**Le Sloop**                                    33 (0) 4 9301-4863
*Port de Plaisance*

The menu offers the best value at this popular open-air fresh sea-food restaurant overlooking the port. Closed Wednesday and Sunday evenings except July and August.

## VILLEFRANCHE

This natural deep-water port just to the east of Cap Ferrat is a quaint, almost mythic village, one of everyone's favorites on the Riviera. Because Villefranche's harbor is so deep, it has been home to both the Russian and American navies (at different times of course). Nowadays the big boats in the harbor are cruise ships or private yachts that anchor here for a day. Most visitors from the ships take the time to go up to the 17th century fortress, still in use as a town hall, just on the top of the hill. Or on Sundays, stop at the lively antique market. There is also a small beach and lots of café life along the port. In 1925, Jean Cocteau came to Villefranche where he collected an artistic circle around him in the Hotel Welcome. As a souvenir of his affection, directly across from the hotel, he decorated the little chapel of St. Pierre and dedicated it to the fishermen of Villefranche, Saint-Jean, Cap Ferrat and Beaulieu. Open mornings until noon; closed for lunch, then from 2:00PM-6PM. Summers until 8:30PM.

**Carpaccio**                                   33 (0) 4 9301-7297
*Promenade des Marinières*

Wonderful fresh seafood with a view over the bay. Expensive but worth the splurge.

**Le Dauphin**                                  33 (0) 4 9301-7513
*3, quai Courbet*

Excellent seafood at reasonable prices. On the waterfront.

**Le Frégate**                                  33 (0) 4 9301-7131
*Quai Courbet*

A busy and popular seafood-only restaurant on the waterfront. Pleasing atmosphere. Moderately expensive.

**Don Camillo**                                 33 (0) 4 9376-7647
*Place du Marché*

Busy café restaurant on the square as you approach the waterfront. Good place for light appetites. Prices for half bottles of wine are a bargain. A value spot.

**Le Versailles**                               33 (0) 4 9301-8956

Located a mile east on the Basse Corniche, you can't beat the panoramic view and excellent food. Many movies have been shot from the terrace. Moderately expensive.

**La Trinquette**                               33 (0) 4 9301-7141
*Avenue Général de Gaulle*

Situated on the other side of the old Port. Known for its bouilla-baisse, bourride, and grilled sardines. Be sure to book in advance. A locals' favorite.

# WEST OF MONACO

## JUAN LES PINS AND ANTIBES

Pronounced **G-j-wan-lay-Pan** and **On-tee-b,** these two towns are on the east side of Nice. Juan les Pins is a little slip of a beach town, next to Cap d'Antibes, with great boutique shopping open from morning until late night. A carnival atmosphere reigns during the summer and especially during its great jazz festival. Most of the beaches are private and it may be wise to pay the fee to stretch out on a chaise and watch the ceaseless activity. (Also a crowded public beach available). Throngs of young and old jam the intersection of the main streets to listen to the competition between the two live bands emanating from the cafes. A street away is restaurant row, a pedestrian street, and two good choices for food:

**Le Pousse Pousse**                              33 (0) 4 9361-4199
*12, rue D. Dautheville*
Chinese, Vietnamese, wonderful nem (Spring rolls). Delicately flavored dishes make this a top choice. Moderately expensive.

**Mezza Rock Cafe**                              33 (0) 4 9361-6070
*16, rue D. Dautheville*
Italian cuisine. As always a good choice in this area. Reasonable.

## ANTIBES

Founded by the Greeks, Antinopolis, the city opposite Nice, was once a Grimaldi stronghold. After World War II, the Grimaldi castle was transformed into a museum and offered to Pablo Picasso as a studio. In gratitude, Piccasso left a collection of his works, including 181 paintings and 76 ceramics created while he was there, on permanent loan to the museum. For Picasso fans, this little castle- museum overlooking the sea is a joy. It displays some very interesting art, his original ceramics and his Joy of Life painting series, and is a small enough museum to keep the interest of museum-weary children.

Afterwards walk through the enchanting old town with its arches, ancient wood doors, and windows overflowing with colorful flowers. There is a good produce market everyday and on Thursdays the old town accommodates a larger one with clothes. At the port, boat lovers can walk all the way to your right and look at the boat of their dreams. For here is where many of the biggest, most expensive, most lavish yachts in the world winter and/or dock in the summer.

**Le Clos des Moines**                              33 (0) 4 9334-4610
*8, rue Arazy*
Located on the zone piétonne in front of the post office, it has your basic Italian and fish specialties at reasonable prices.

**Restaurant du Bastion**                    33 (0) 4 9334-1388
*1, av. Général Maiziers*
On the old ramparts, traditional Provençal cooking. The menus are moderately priced.

**La Marmite**                               33 (0) 4 9334-5679
*Rue James Close*
A cozy place on a pedestrian street in the old town.

**Les Vieux Murs**                           33 (0) 4 9334-0673
Rustic interior and terrace with a view. Long-time favorite with the locals.

## BIOT

Pronounced **Bee-ott**, the town is about 10 kilometers north of Antibes and sits on a high hilltop. It's the Provençal town known for its famous glassblowing. The main glassblower is *Verrerie de Biot,* just by the southeast exit from the town, open daily except holidays, Tel: 33 (0) 4 9365-0300.

This is a fine place to see how glass is blown and shaped into everyday objects of quality or into art glass. In the building adjacent to the glass blowing, you may purchase the famous bubbled Biot tableware. Across from the Verrerie is a wonderful Art Glass Gallery where glass artists from Europe and America sell their work.

You can't miss the ultramodern **Fernand Léger Museum** even if it is off the road. Just follow the sign a short way to a gigantic wall of mosaic, which constitutes the front of the museum, dedicated to one of the masters of modern art. The museum is open all year, closed on Tuesdays, Tel: 33 (0) 4 9365-6361.

**Galerie Des Arcades**                      33 (0) 4 9365-0104
*Located in the village*
A 16th-century inn on the old village square with a character all of its own. Run by the same family since the 50s, they offer Provençal food such as garlic-flavored soup, ravioli, Daube, and fresh pasta. Original Vasarely's hang on the walls and an art gallery downstairs. Closed Sunday evenings and all day on Monday. Reasonable.

**Le Plat d'Estain**                         33 (0) 4 9365-0937
*20, rue St. Sébastien*
On the main street in the old village, this has always been a favorite low-budget eatery with the locals. Provençal specialties.

**L'Auberge Du Jarrier**                     33 (0) 4 9365-1168
*30, passage de la Bourgade*
This is not a budget restaurant, but it serves up some memorable meals. The loup and other fish are special, and their delicious chocolate dessert will give you your chocolate quota for a year.

## VALLAURIS

If your interest in crafts has been sparked in Biot, we suggest a trip to Vallauris as well. Here is the town made famous by Picasso when he decided to experiment with ceramic in the 40's. He met potters Suzanne and Georges Ramie in their Madoura workshop and was inspired to make his own ceramics by redesigning pots and amphorae into women, roosters, other shapes and painting abstracts on large ceramic plates. Today, you may see the fruits of this production at the museum in Antibes and at the **Musée National Picasso** at the Place de la Liberation in Vallauris. A great museum for pottery lovers, every other year it hosts a huge exhibition of potters from all over the world. Next door, in the vestibule of the chapel, Picasso frescoed the walls with his versions of war and peace, reminiscent of his famous "Guernica." Vallauris has many pottery shops up and down its main streets, and although most of it is not very original, look closely. Now and then there are pieces in stores and galleries that are well worthwhile to take home.

**Le Manuscript**                                    33 (0) 4 9364-5656
*Chemin Liniter*
Known to its local customers for authentic French country cooking. Setting is charming with rough stone walls and a lovely tiled floor.

**La Gousee d'Ail**                                   33 (0) 4 9364-1071
*11b, av. de Grasse*
Another long-time country-style cooking spot that is a favorite with locals.

## ST PAUL DE VENCE

This is a hilltown that everyone who comes to the Riviera wants to see. It is a medieval village, famous for its famous celebs and artists, and it epitomizes the word "quaint." Just 20 kilometers (32 miles) from Nice, you park your car and walk through the narrow winding streets and shop. The shops on either side of the pebble path are mostly souvenir stuff, perfect for south of France gifts and remembrances. However, among these emporiums are art galleries, some quite good. For local color, do as people have done for ages, sit in the café at the beginning of the village and watch the men play boules. Before you know it, you'll want to join in. On the road to St. Paul is one of the best private modern art museums in the world, The **Maeght Foundation**. If you like modern art, don't miss it, especially the sculpture garden where you walk among the Miros, Calders, Arps and Giacomettis. Inside, the foundation displays – in addition to special exhibits – such artists as Chagall, Dubuffet, Braque, Bonnard and Matisse. Open 10AM every day.

Colombe d'Or                                 33 (0) 4 9332-8002
*Place du Gen. De Gaulle*

Relaxed atmosphere in one of the most frequented restaurants on the Riviera. Known for its collection of modern art, acquired over the years from celebrated artists, then unknown, who traded meals for paintings.

Restaurant Henry                             33 (0) 4 9332-8275
*La Petite Chapelle*

A tiny chapel with delightful shady garden just beneath the main gate to the village. Simple grilled fare, sardines, trout, steak or roast chicken. Reasonable.

La Brouette                                  33 (0) 4 9358-6716
*830 Route de Cagnes*

Easy to miss on the road from Cagnes to Vence, but worth seeking out for Baltic specialties. Rustic dining room setting with view of St. Paul.

# CANNES

## THE LERINS ISLANDS
## SAINT HONORAT

Off the beaten tourist tracks and lying just a few miles off the coast of Cannes, the Lerins have a long and rather unusual history. Settled by Greeks, then inhabited by Romans, their monastic heritage began toward the end of the 4th century when St. Honorat founded one of the first French monasteries which bears his name. By the end of the 1700s more than 4,000 monks lived on the island. Six hundred became bishops and 20 actually achieved sainthood. It is here that St. Patrick underwent his training. The old monastery is open to the public from 10 AM to noon and 2:00 PM to 6:00 PM from June to September.

## SAINT MARGUERITE

The larger of the two islands, covered in pine trees and boasting a beautiful beach. This island was named after the sister of St. Honorat. You can visit a fortress built by Richelieu in the 17th century and used for many years as a prison. Its most famous inmate was The Man in the Iron mask whose real identity has never been discovered although rumored to be the illegitimate brother of Louis XIV. If you choose to spend the day on the island swimming, bring a picnic lunch or eat at one of the three restaurants. Ferryboats leave Cannes at regular intervals from the Gare Maritime just next to the port.

## GRASSE

Principally known as the Perfume Capital. The industry was launched when Catherine de Medici set a fashion for perfumed gloves.

Actually it was a perfume maker from Florence, named Tombarelli, who set up the town's first distillery and convinced many other merchants to abandon the tanning of leather for the lucrative business of perfume making. The demand became so great that Grasse's own flower production had to be supplemented by supplies from surrounding areas: roses from St. Paul, jasmine from Mougins, Opio, Vallauris and Plascassier, violets from Tourrettes, lavender from the alpine regions of Provence, and orange-blossom, narcissi, and carnations. It's interesting to take the tour of the perfume factories and find out what it takes to be a 'nose'. Open all year round. **Parfumerie Fragonard**, bd. Fragonard, Tel: 33 (0) 4 9336-4465; **Parfumerie Galimard,** Route de Cannes, Tel: 33 (0) 4 9336-0810; and **Parfumerie Molinard,** 60, bd. Victor Hugo, Tel: 33 (0) 4 9336-0162. As a bonus, you'll also be able to buy the essence of your favorite fragrance at a fraction of the cost.

**Ma'tre Boscq**                           **33 (0) 4 9336-4576**
*13, rue de la Fontette*
The best restaurant in the old town with Provençal cuisine; moderately priced menus.

## St. Tropez

Located 75 kilometers (113 miles) west of Cannes or about an hour and forty-minute drive from Monaco. Check the train station to go by rail to St. Raphael then via bus to St. Trop. Summer is packed with semi-nude bathers, whereas the fall and spring (before Easter) is a bit less hectic.

Of course, we all know Brigitte Bardot made it famous in the 50s and before then it was just another sleepy fishing village. During the off season it reverts to that village atmosphere, with only a few cafés and restaurants open to accommodate fishermen, local tradesmen and a few eccentric and celebrity residents. As in the summer, you'll find them at *Sénéquier's* or *Le Gorille* sipping pastis and playing boules on the Place des Lices. Join the throng of shoppers during the morning market. The big market day is Saturday wonderful smells of fresh roasting chicken, pizza, 20 kinds of olives fill the air next to stalls of lace, brocante, antiques, posters, and traditional provençal yard goods. The beaches are located about three miles east of town. Drive out for a leisurely stroll or head up to Ramateuelle or Cogolin, the later known for its hand-carved pipes and carpets.

**La Table du Marché**                    **33 (0) 4 9497-8520**
*38, rue G. Clémenceau*
Popular since the day it opened the doors, call ahead for a table. Located just off the Place des Lices. Not-quite-nouvelle cuisine, light fish, pasta and excellent local wine from Minuty vineyard. Expensive.

**La Frégate**                           33 (0) 4 9497-0708
Just one street in from the port and a handy place to get a satis-
fying three-course meal at a resonable price.
**Les Oliviers**                         33 (0) 4 9497-2013
Take the street next to the Tourist Bureau until it runs into the
restaurant. Popular with the locals.
**La Ferme du Magnan**                   33 (0) 4 9449-5754
RN 98 between Cogolin and La Mole. Wood-grilled specialties,
free-range chicken, rabbit and fresh fish. Call ahead.

# OTHER DAY TRIPS

# NOT QUITE IN THE NEIGHBORHOOD, BUT CLOSE...

## AIX-EN-PROVENCE
An old Roman town about two hours' drive via the autoroute.

## CASSIS
A small fishing village pre-St.Tropez between Toulon and Marseille.

## BANDOL
A beach town noted for its rosé wine.

## POQUERROLLES ISLANDS
A good place to unwind and scuba dive, no cars allowed. West of Toulon and south of Hyères, then take the ferry at Giens.

## THE MERCANTOUR PARK
Get back to nature, glorious hiking trails, mountain lakes.

## AUPS
Land of truffles (See regional food and wine section)

## MOUSTIER ST. MARIE
In June and July purple Provence lavender fields are at their peak. The City is noted for its pottery.

## OTHER DAY TRIPS

# 17
# A PETITE HISTORY

## THE BEGINNING

During the last Ice Age, prehistoric man migrated south to the more temperate regions and sought refuge along the Mediterranean coast. Remains of those first dwellers were found in a cavern in the Saint Martin gardens. From about 1000 BC the region between Provence and Genoa was inhabited by the Ligurians. They imposed their language and customs on the indigenous peoples. Between 5-4 BC the Celts invaded the area, pushing the Ligurians farther up into the mountains. The Celts were a collective group of tribes that extended from Ireland in the north, the Balkans in the east, to Gaul (modern-day France) and Italy in the south. They were remarkable for their height, masculinity and blue eyes and blonde hair. They were a people who loved war, adventure, pleasure and feasts.

During the same period, the Greek colonists in Marseilles set up trading posts in Hyères, St. Tropez, Antibes and Nice. Greek history tells us that Hercules, returning from Spain after killing the tyrant Geryon, landed in Monaco harbor. It is said that a small temple was built in Hercules' honor on the promontory jutting out to the sea, which was commonly referred to by Greek and Roman sailors as "The Rock." Henceforth the land was called Portus Herculis Monoeci.

Between 58-51 BC the region came under the influence of the Roman Empire and Julius Caesar. If you take a short trip straight up from Monaco, you'll find the town of La Turbie and the "Trophée des Alpes," (6 BC) a monument of the Roman Empire's conquest of the Ligurian tribes. La Turbie has celebrated it's 2,000-year anniversary. After the fall of Rome, from the 5-6 centuries AD, the region was plundered and invaded by the barbarian Vandals, Visigoths, Burgundians, Ostrogoths and Franks. In 800's, the Saracens passing to and from Italy, Spain and Gaul sacked the coastal areas.

During the Middle Ages, the Genoese, Monaco's nearest large neighbor considered Monaco to be a part of their domain and obtained formal ownership from German Emperor Henry VI in 1191. The Genoese then built a fortress in Monaco and sent a small garrison of soldiers to protect their interests. (This building would later become the Palace of Monaco).

Attracted by its location, land concession and tax exemption, many shopkeepers, craftsmen and farmers joined the sailors and soldiers living in Monaco. In 1247 Pope Innocent granted the Monégasques the right to build their own church, which is when the Eglise St. Nicolas was built, today the Cathedral of Monaco stands on the original building site.

## THE GRIMALDIS

One of the aristocratic families of Genoa, the Grimaldis belonged to the Guelphs, who were considered the defenders of the Pope's

authority. The Guelphs were in constant conflict with the
Ghibellines, the supporters of the German Emperor. At the end
of the 13th century the Ghibellines tossed out François and
Rainier Grimaldi, a wealthy sea trader who commanded ships in
the service of Charles II, the king of Naples. His nephew François,
nicknamed the "Maliza" (the crafty one), hoping to gain promi-
nence in his eyes, decided to roust the Ghibellines from the fortress of Monaco.

So on the evening of January 8th, 1297, disguised as a
monk, François sought shelter for the night. Because the Genoese
fortress was guarded by only a small garrison, he was able to pull
his sword and kill enough of them to open the gate and seize the
fortress for himself. Note: the family coat of arms displays two
monks holding a drawn sword. The seizure of the fortress enabled
Rainier to wage war on Genoa with France, who had made him a
French Admiral. It was Charles I, the son of Rainier, who founded the house of Grimaldi.

## 1300 TO 1600S
The Grimaldis have always fought to keep their land, which
extended from Roquebrune to Menton. Through this period, they
waged wars against Genoa, Pisa, Venice, Naples, France, the Earls
of Provence, Spain, Germany and England. The support of such
efforts took its toll and the local population lived in poverty. In
1480 Lucien Grimaldi persuaded King Charles VII of France and
the Duke of Savoy to recognize Monaco's independence.

In 1525 Augustin Grimaldi signed the treaty of Burgos
with Spain and for the next 116 years Monaco was under Spanish
influence. Monaco's fortress was slowly transformed into a Palace,
fortification was increased (an example seen when one walks up
the Rampe Major to the port of Augustin before reaching the
Palace square), along with a huge water tank built under the main
courtyard. In 1633 the Spanish King permanently recognized the
title of "Prince of Monaco" to replace the Lord of Monaco.
Honoré II became the first Prince of Monaco.

Honoré II began secret negotiations with Cardinal
Richelieu of France, which resulted in the treaty of Péronne 1641,
signed by King Louis XIII. This treaty protected the sovereignty
of the country and all privileges and rights on sea and land. King
Louis XIII bestowed upon Honoré II the Duchy of Valentinois,
the Earldom of Carladès, the Marquisate of Les Baux and the
Seigneurie of Saint-Remy in Provence. Honoré grew up in Milan
and was influenced by the intellectual salons in Paris. Like his
16th-century ancestors, he had a love of the arts and became a
great collector of tapestries, silverware, furniture and paintings.
His collection of 700 pictures included works by Raphael, Durer,
Titian, Michaelangelo, Rubens and local artists.

## 1700S THE REVOLUTION
Honoré II of Monaco, recognized by the French King as a
foreign prince with a title of "ducs et pairs étrangers," deemed to

owe a special loyalty to France. Benefits held by foreign princes included position in all processions behind royal blood princes and their wives privileged to bring two carriages into the royal courtyard and seat themselves on tabourets (Stools) in the presence of the Queen. Other rights accorded to nobility included the right to be heard in a high court of law, exemption from corporal punishment, the choice to be beheaded rather than hanged if found guilty of a capital offense and total immunity from direct taxation. However, the drawback was that they could not increase their wealth from manufacturing or business.

Noblemen paid huge dowries so that their daughters could be married into royalty. The rank of nobility is as follows: the King, the Queen, the heir apparent Crown Prince; legitimate descendants in the male line of the present or former kings, princes of royal blood (all those who descend from former kings other than those of the present line) and finally foreign princes. In Monaco, women have always had the right to reign.

Prince Honoré II's only son died in 1651, making his grandson Prince Louis I his heir at the age of nine. Determined to strengthen the ties to French nobility, he arranged a marriage to Charlotte-Catherine de Gramont, daughter of the influential Duke de Gramont. Both Prince Louis and Princess Charlotte became closely associated with the French King Louis XIV. Prince Louis I died in Rome in 1701, where his godfather, King Louis XIV, had appointed him French ambassador. Prince Louis I was well known in Rome for his 300-coach entourage.

Prince Antoine I followed in line. Having grown up at the court of Versailles, he was a great music lover and kept an orchestra and opera company. He married Marie of Lorraine, the daughter of the Count d'Armagnac. Princess Marie produced three daughters and the male line of the Grimaldis came to an end. A search began to find Princess Louise-Hippolyte a suitable husband who would be willing to take the name of Grimaldi. For two years neither grandfather d'Armagnac nor Prince Antoine could come to agreement. Finally Princess Marie took matters into her own hands and had Prince Antoine's great-uncle suggest Jacques de Goyon-Matignon, the twenty-six-year-old son of Count de Matignon. Princess Louise-Hippolyte succeeded her father but died from small pox less than a year into her reign. In a formal portrait she poses with a black mask, perhaps suggesting her real self would emerge as the reigning Princess of Monaco.

Prince Jacques I, who briefly succeeded her, was forced to abdicate in favor of their son Prince Honoré III and become his legal guardian. Prince Jacques and Prince Honoré returned to Paris and lived in what is now the Hotel de Matignon or residence of the French Prime Minister. Prince Jacques continued to acquire a fabulous collection of furniture and art. Prince Honoré III embarked on a French army military career. During most of his life, Prince Antoine I's favorite illegitimate son, Chevalier de Monaco, ruled Monaco.

The French Revolution significantly impacted the rein

of Prince Honoré III. In January 1793 a convention elected by the three communes of Monaco, Menton, and Roquebrune depossed the Grimaldis and confiscated their property. Monaco was annexed to France and renamed Fort d'Hercule. All the Grimaldis' objects of wealth were sold at auction. The grand apartments were turned into a military hospital, the throne room was turned into a kitchen, the palace turned into a poorhouse. Prince Honoré III was thrown into prison. His daughter-in-law was one of the very last people guillotined before Robespierre was defeated. She could have saved her life if she had agreed to say that even though separated from her husband, she was pregnant.

In the age of Napoleon after the French Revolution, Honoré III had two sons, the oldest Honoré, duke of Valentinois and Prince Joseph. It was his brother Prince Joseph who distinguished himself when he joined the Emperial Army in 1807. He was nominated as an Officer d'Ordonnance of Napoléon I and became a chamberlain to the Empress Josephine. The son of Honoré IV, Honoré -Gabriel received honors during the campaigns of 1800 and 1806 and became an aide de camp to the King of Naples. Honoré IV delegated most of the authority to his brother Prince Joseph and then to his oldest son Honoré -Gabriel, who was to become the future Prince Honoré V. It was the friendship with Talleyrand that secured the restitution of the position of Prince and the independence of the Principality during the Vienna Congress.

In 1815, Monaco was handed over to Sardinia as its protectorate. The Principality had been fighting this for centuries. The Sardinian government imposed various rules prohibiting manufacture of tobacco and other constraints. To affirm the Principality's independence, the Prince created the Corps of Carabiniers (the Palace Guards), began a trade in citrus fruits and encouraged the development of small businesses. Prince Honoré V died in 1841 without heirs, and was succeeded by his brother Prince Florestan. During his reign, the towns of Menton and Roquerbrune declared their independence in 1848 because of the severe taxes levied on them by Prince Honoré IV.

## 1800s MONTE CARLO
Prince Charles III succeeded his father Prince Florestan. Many upheavals continued in Europe that changed the boundaries, territories and alliances of its neighbors. Monaco formally sold Menton and Roquebrune to France in 1861 for 4 million francs. Thus ended the imposed and unwanted Sardinian Protectorate. Monaco regained its full sovereign state and made agreements with France to maintain roads, customs, postal, and telegraph services.

But now reduced to one-sixteenth of its area and one-seventh of its population, the Principality resembled just another run-down medieval town, isolated from its neighbors with a population of just 1200. In the Condamine there were a few orchards and flowerbeds, and on the Spélugues plateau just a few scrubby trees. In 1850, one would hardly believe the fate that awaited this destitute 'rock' thirty-three years later.

The Principality was extremely isolated, easy land routes were nonexistent and letters were carried by the pedon, who delivered the mail on foot from either Nice in the direction of France or to Ventimiglia in the direction of Italy or by sea. A good picture of life in Monaco in the early 19th century is depicted in these lines taken from Philibert Florence's Sketches and Souvenirs:

"The great attraction of the evening was the nightly apparition of the mail lantern on its way from Genoa to Nice. When it appeared at the forked road at Cap Martin, its progress was followed. When hidden by the mountain and lost from view for a while, its reappearance was awaited, and the evening ended when the lantern had disappeared behind La Turbie. This mail coach, its lanterns lit, was a piercing sight to the Monégasques. Surrounded by their ramparts and closed doors, it represented the coveted object of all their desires."

In the meanwhile, to escape the harsh European winters, tourists from England, Germany, and Russia were flocking to the neighboring towns of Beaulieu, Nice and Cannes. But not to Monaco. Finally however, the right for the railway to pass through Monaco and a new road built along the coast to Nice ended the Principality's isolation and paved the way for the tourist trade it enjoys today.

Prince Charles III, who had inherited his mother Princess Caroline's sharp business acumen, saw the advantages of having a gaming casino in Monaco because gambling in France was not yet legal. His mother's private secretary, Mr. Eynaud, went on a fact-finding tour to Baden Baden, then the model for spa-gambling success in Germany. Realizing the excellent potential of revenue for Monaco, Prince Charles authorized the creation of the thermal and gambling company "Société des Bains de Monaco" in November of 1856. Two Frenchmen were granted the right to build a hotel, villas, spa, casino and steamboat services between Monaco and Nice. They were to provide games and distractions of all types. The only house in the Condamine was home to Monaco's first and only roulette table. Unfortunately, this first attempt at attracting tourists ended in failure.

Seven years later in 1863, François Blanc came from Hamburg at the request of Prince Charles III and was given a fifty-year concession to run the Société des Bains de Monaco et Cercle des Etrangers, (a club for foreigners). Access to the Casino was and still is forbidden to Monégasques. Now called Société des Bains de Mer (S.B.M.), it was capitalized with 15 million francs (2,287,000€) and had 30,000 shares.

Mr. Blanc is credited for creating Monaco's gold rush. He built nineteen hotels, over a hundred villas, streets, squares, and a park on the Spélugues hill. In 1866, Prince Charles decided to name this new city Monte-Carlo (Italian for Mount Charles) after himself. Train service was inaugurated in October 1868, which took only fifteen minutes from Nice. Monaco experienced its first real estate boom. For example, a building site purchased for 1200 francs (185€) sold a year later for 625,000 francs (96,000€). Not much has changed. Monaco is one of the world's most expensive real estate markets because of its limited supply of land. In 1869, Prince Charles abolished all direct taxation, so the wealthy were not only coming for pleasure but also to avoid heavy taxation at home. Prince Charles founded the Order of Saint Charles, bestowed titles of nobility, minted money, created the national red and white flag and issued postage stamps.

Monaco became fashionable to the rich and famous, and it welcomed Emperor Franz-Joseph, Russian aristocrats, the Prince of Wales and American millionaires. The Hotel de Paris was inaugurated in January 1864. Its model was the sumptuous Grand Hotel in Paris. No expense was spared to make it one of the leading hotels of the world, a fact that remains true more than one hundred years later. Mr. Blanc brought in top landscape designers to lay out the gardens and a very important architect to plan the Casino and Opera House. Blanc got Charles Garnier by a stroke of luck. The famous architect was in the process of completing the Paris Opera when the sponsors ran out of money. Mr. Blanc bailed them out in return for a smaller version to be built in Monaco. The Opera is formally called the Théatre de Monte-Carlo, but commonly referred to as the Salle Garnier. The first performance in the theater was given by Sarah Bernhardt in January 1879 and was François Blanc's last hurrah; he died within the year. His son Camille inherited controlling interest in S.B.M., which at the time was valued at more than 72 million francs (11,000,000€).

## 1900S PROSPERITY ARRIVES

Prince Charles III, suffering from blindness, died at Château Marchais in l'Aisne in 1889. His son Prince Albert I, succeeded him. Since boyhood Prince Albert I had a keen interest in the sea, a trait he inherited from his ancestors. Influenced by Professor Milne Edwards, he set out on his ship Hirondelle I to study and research the seven seas. To house his numerous finds, he began construction on the Oceanographic Museum, which was completed in 1910. In Paris four years later, he established the Oceanographic Institute, which published scientific papers relating to oceanography. Before that time, while evacuating an area of the Jardin Exotique Prince Albert I found the remains of Cro-Magnon man. In 1902 he founded an Anthropological Museum; and the Institute of Human Paleontology in Paris in 1910. The Exotique Garden he founded in Monaco contains cactus and succulents from more than a hundred countries and is a favorite attraction in Monaco. Prince Albert I also modernized Monaco's harbor and built a tunnel under the rock, connecting the new area Fontvieille to the port. He rebuilt the Place de la Visitation, and restored the Palace. He was passionately interested in all the sciences and became known as the "Scientific Prince."

During the Second Empire rule of Emperor Louis Napoléon and Empress Eugénie, France tried to emulate the lifestyle of Louis XV with outrageously extravagant balls and salons. During this era, a marriage was arranged between Prince Albert and Lady Mary Victoria Douglas Hamilton, the daughter of the 11th Duke of Hamilton and Princess Marie of Baden. Lady Mary's spoiled nature and love of the Paris social life conflicted with Prince Albert's intellectual and scientific nature and the marriage lasted less than a year. Lady Mary bore him a son, Prince Louis II, in July of 1870 and he lived with her in Baden Baden. When war broke out between France and Prussia, the royal couple divorced.

By the end of the war the restless aristocracy sought out the salons of the literary, artistic and philosophical intelligentsia. This suited Prince Albert very well and soon he was frequenting the salon of the young, attractive, and brilliant Duchess de Richelieu, who at seventeen had married into one of France's most aristocratic families. The Duchess was the former Alice Heine from a wealthy Jewish American New Orleans family. She was a woman who not only spoke several languages, but one who could converse about many serious subjects. Prince Albert had met his match and quickly fell in love.

This was an era when Monaco became a leader in many diverse fields. The first Monte Carlo Rallye was run in 1911 under the direction of Monégasque Alexandre Noghès. This was just 13 years after the first "horseless carriage" competition in 1898. In 1929, Monaco put on its first Grand Prix with sixteen cars racing around the streets of the Principality at 80 kilometers per hour (46 mph). Team Bugatti was the first winner.

Henri Rougier made European aviation history in Monaco when he flew his biplane solo nonstop over water from Monaco to Cap Martin and back in March of 1910. In 1913 at Camille Blanc's urging, Monaco hosted a large air show with three different competitions. Monaco also took the first steps in the development of the first helicopter. Engineer Maurice Léger, with the support of Prince Albert I, realized the first vertical flight on May 4, 1905. Monaco was now a leading point for air connections between Europe and Africa.

Under Camille Blanc and Princess Alice's tutelage, Monaco became a mecca for the arts. The Monte-Carlo Opera, under the direction of Raoul Gunsbourg, conducted performances sung by Caruso, Nelly Melba and Chaliapine. Premier performances of The Damnation of Faust, Don Quichote and L'Enfant et les Sortilèges were held in Monaco. Monte-Carlo landed a ballet corps with the best from the Russian Imperial School when Serge deDiaghilev moved to Monaco and installed his Ballet Russe.

Monaco was at its zenith and the small Principality enjoyed worldwide acclaim. However the Belle Époque came to an end with the outbreak of World War I. Monaco remained neutral, but difficulties remained with France and the Principality was obliged to negotiate its independence, sovereignty and territorial rights in 1918 under the treaty of Versailles.

Prince Albert's only son from his first marriage, Prince Louis II, succeeded him. He chose a French military career, and as a consequence spent little time in Monaco while growing up or while he reigned. He fathered a daughter, Charlotte, by his lover Marie Juliette Louvet, in Constantine. Prince Albert I opposed this union and Prince Louis did not marry Marie. However, with the Grimaldi succession in question, Prince Louis II's daughter Charlotte was legally recognized as the rightful heir. She married Count Pierre de Polignac, who was obliged to take the Grimaldi name and coat of arms. Prince Pierre was man of grace and charm, representing the Old World, in sharp contrast to Prince Louis II's military style. This union produced two children, Princesse Antoinette and Crown Prince Rainier III.

H.S.H. Prince Rainier III was born May 31, 1923 and was the first native-born Monégasque to rule since Honoré IV in 1758. He succeeded his grandfather in 1949. In 1956 he married American film star Grace Kelly, who died from injuries sustained in a tragic car accident in 1982. The union produced three children. Princess Caroline born in 1957, Prince Albert in 1958, and Princess Stephanie born in 1965.

The Grimaldi family celebrated 700 years of reign in 1997 and His Serene Highness Prince Rainier III marked 50 years of reign in 1999. The celebration of the Princes' 50th Jubilee has been a historic moment in Monégasque history, a history that has brought five decades of stability, prosperity and the strengthening of its city-state position on the international stage.

Prince Rainier's reign is characterized by his dynamic policy of urban renewal, renovation, modernization and expansion that has transformed his country. This transformation has allowed the economy to grow through diversification of business activity and job creation. His visionary commitment to the environment and its protection, both internationally and locally on land and sea. His desire to reach out to the international community though membership in the United Nations in 1993, and his request for membership in the Council of Europe. The Prince has maintained and continued to improve his relationships with France. He will go down in history as the builder Prince and the Prince who has made a strong commitment to the environment.

## 2000 AND THE FUTURE

Today, the Principality is adapting to the changing economic scene of the 21st century. It continues to spend money on public work programs, such as easy access tunnels, improved roads and the newly opened underground railway station, but it is also making plans for a broader future. The newest addition is The Grimaldi Forum, a new multi-plex convention and cultural center. The next projects underway are the extension of port facilities that will allow large cruise ships to dock (completion scheduled for 2002). Development of old railway track land; an addition to an underground tunnel that will allow cars on the way to Nice or Menton to by pass Monaco and renovation of the Princesse Grace

Hospital. On Monaco's drawing boards for the future are offices and homes to be built on pylons in the sea, creating floating islands.

Monaco is already a leader in encouraging of environmentally sound electric cars, trucks and motor scooters, it provides electric charging stations and offers economic incentives to companies who purchase electric vehicles.

Monaco still attracts high rollers to its casinos, but it is just as active in attracting investors in light, added-value industries and hosting business travelers and conventioneers. The Principality's growth rate continues to rise, and it has conserved enough cash to continue the public works programs for several years without borrowing a franc. It also plans to remain rich enough so that it doesn't need to levy income tax on its non-French residents.

This country may be small in size but not in its accomplishments in the international arena. Prince Albert headed the first-time delegation to the United Nations General Assembly. For decades Monaco has been a participant in: Interpol, the World Health Organization; the United Nation's Education, Scientific, and Cultural Organization; the World Intellectual Property Organization; the Universal Postal Property Organization; and the International Commission for the Scientific Organization of the Mediterranean Sea. The Principality is host to the International Hydrographic Bureau, whose duties include the standardization of marine maps. Also, as part of Monaco's strong commitment to the environment the International Atomic Energy Marine Environment Laboratory that analyzes water samples worldwide for pollutants and radioactivity is situated in Monaco. It was first in Europe to officially report the Chernobyl accident. The European Oceanographic Observatory, whose mission is to forecast possible oceanic ecological dangers and to study the biological regeneration of damaged environments, is part of the Oceanographic Museum.

Monaco is devoted to peace and the respect of law; to the preservation of nature, defense of the environment, humanitarian actions, the fight against crime and the protection of the arts and culture. Not many countries have had such ambitious plans or the success in realizing them. Little wonder that the Principality is one of the world's most desirable places to live and work or visit.